Maha-Hanaan Balala holds a DPhil in Law from The University of Oxford. She currently researches Islamic finance, law and women's rights.

INTERNATIONAL LIBRARY
OF ECONOMICS

Series ISBN: 978 1 84885 221 1

See www.ibtauris.com/ILE for a full list of titles

ISLAMIC FINANCE AND LAW

Theory and Practice in a Globalized World

MAHA-HANAAN BALALA

I.B. TAURIS

LONDON · NEW YORK

Published in 2011 by I.B.Tauris Co Ltd
6 Salem Road, London W2 4BU
175 Fifth Avenue, New York NY 10010
www.ibtauris.com

Distributed in the United States and Canada
Exclusively by Palgrave Macmillan
175 Fifth Avenue, New York NY 10010

International Library of Economics 5

ISBN 978 1 84885 076 7

A full CIP record for this book is available from the British Library
A full CIP record for this book is available from the Library of Congress

Library of Congress catalog card: available

Printed and bound in Great Britain by
CPI Antony Rowe, Chippenham, Wiltshire
Camera-ready copy edited and supplied by the author

FSC
www.fsc.org
MIX
Paper from
responsible sources
FSC® C013604

To the Almighty:
He who has sustained me every day of this
undertaking, and continues to do so.

CONTENTS

LIST OF CASES

ACKNOWLEDGEMENTS

I wish to thank my mother Waffya Mohammed, as well as my siblings, Suhailah, Jaber, Bushra and Sanad, for supporting me through the troughs and the triumphs of the past four years. I would also like to thank Hamid Hakimzadeh, who was instrumental in making the publication of this book possible. I am indebted especially to Professor Fidelis Oditah, QC without whom, and whose guidance, this book would not have been possible. Finally, I extend my thanks and appreciation to all who subliminally inspired my writing.

PREFACE

This book considers legal aspects of Islamic finance within the context of a securitisation transaction; and the viability of an Islamic finance securitisation within the context of global finance. The 'principle-centric' approach adopted emphasises enquiry into the principles that govern Islamic law of contract and finance and de-emphasise adherence to the current rules. It suggests that whilst the principles remain constant (the general framework), the rules may change and are not 'carved in stone'.

In recognition of the equitable and social aspect of the law – at the root of its legal and judicial aspect – this book undertakes more than just presenting a synthesis of literature on legal aspects of Islamic finance and their comparable equivalent under the common law. It stresses the need for fresh interpretation of the principles examined herein and their contextual application. It goes further to re-examine from fresh angles the textual sources on *gharar*, *riba* and *bay al dayn* (sale of debt/receivables) which are central to Islamic commercial and financial law. In this sense, the book is not merely descriptive, but also prescriptive as to how a certain rule or concept ought to be applied to serve social welfare and economic progress. Available literature and publications do not provide much detail on what Islamic finance really is beyond the hype, jargon and statistics. What makes it substantially different from conventional modes of finance? And what is currently missing, generally or in certain jurisdictions, the presence of which would ensure the sustainability of its development both in product array and market confidence? Therein lies the key to the development of Islamic finance structures and products and this book has suggested answers, albeit non-conclusive, to these questions.

1

ISLAMIC LAW AND THE ROLE OF INTERPRETATION

Few if any disciplines can be divorced from their social effects; a correlation that is more pronounced in law both as a discipline and as a body of rules. Laws, in any society, must apply and develop along lines that serve and facilitate individual and social existence and expansion, neither objective being secondary to the other. In Islamic law, this function is served by the principles of maslaha or istislah (facilitating ease/social welfare) being applied to fill any lacunae in the law, as well as to mitigate or remove any resulting hardship (raf' al haraj). Maslaha or istislah are juristically extrapolated principles drawn from the *Quran* and sunna (practices/traditions of Muhammad). They place emphasis on ease and social welfare as the basis of social rights and rules. They are applied to realise the objectives of the sharia (maqasid al-sharia')[1] and can be said to grease the cogs of the legal system so as to ensure the removal of hardship caused by any rigidity or inappropriate effect of the law.

The principles of *maslaha* and *istislah*, thus, moderate the overarching principle of permissibility in commercial transactions and serve the principle of contractual fairness,[2] as demonstrated by Muhammad's repeated concern toward, and repudiation of, contracts that flaunted (or threatened to flaunt) this principle of fairness: the intended outcome in every case being equity between the parties and social justice. The overarching principle of permissibility governing commercial affairs between individuals can be likened to the principle of freedom of contract and the general laissez-faire approach to commercial transactions under the common law.[3] *Maslaha* and *istislah* find parallels in the principles of equity that have long since applied to commercial transactions.

In recognition of the equitable and social aspect of the law – at the root of its legal and judicial aspect – this book undertakes more than just presenting

a synthesis of literature on legal aspects of Islamic finance and their comparable equivalent under the common law. It stresses the need for fresh interpretation of the principles examined herein and their contextual application.
It goes further to re-examine from fresh angles the textual sources on *gharar*,
riba and *bay al dayn* which are central to Islamic commercial and financial law. In this sense, the book is not merely descriptive, but also prescriptive as to how a certain rule or concept ought to be applied to serve social
welfare and economic progress. It is this equitable application of principles
and concepts in light of today's context that distinguishes the prescriptive
approach taken from what is currently applicable.

I refer mainly to the *Quran* and the *sunna* (traditions) or *hadith* (sayings)
of Muhammad in supporting my arguments on issues of Islamic law. The
Quran, like any other scripture is a living text, deriving life from the interpretation and extrapolation of the principles therein according to the current
needs and circumstances at any given stage of human civilisation. Without
this 'breath of life' through ongoing contemplation and tailored application,
the *Quran*, remains an amazing stream of parables and principles with no
grounded application today. Approached in this manner, the *Quran* serves
only one of its myriad purposes; that of being a liturgical recitation as one
form of exalting Allah, no more. Its other functions as a guiding text of
wisdom and profound truths, its nature as a penal, moral, economic, spiritual and social welfare code as well as a bastion of liberation and empower-
ment, literally become suspended because of a lack of grounding in current
existence. This is because whilst the *Quran* is a highly sophisticated code
embodying universal principles and truths, these are, in various instances,
couched in terms local to the very issue it was revealed to address at that
point in time. It is for this reason that the *Quran* also relays to us varied
stories of past peoples and prophets always stressing that they are *signs* or
indications for those who 'know' and 'understand', indicating the central
role of human intellect in extrapolating and localising universal principles
in a manner that befits the circumstances at hand.

Accordingly, our function is not to take the parables or stories in the
Quran or the sayings and traditions of Muhammad at face value but, rather,
it is incumbent upon us to unravel the wisdom and principles behind them
that we may then apply to whatever similar or disparate situations we face.
An apt illustration comes to mind: the *Quran* repeatedly mentions the fact
that Abraham was a Muslim (as was Adam and all the other prophets named
or unnamed therein) and it was he who coined the name 'Muslim' (meaning
one who yields to the will of God or the Creator)[4]. Yet, in his submission to
God, Abraham did not suspend reason; to the contrary, it is his heightened

introspective questioning of God's existence and logical challenge of the actions of his biological father and social community at large that led him to the altar of submission and to the will of God.[5] The *Quran* indicates great wisdom in Abraham's persona.[6] Further, given Abraham and all other 'men of God' before Muhammad are expressly acknowledged in the *Quran* as having yielded in faith to the Will of Allah[7] and having knowledge of and applying the same universal truths,[8] why is it that the *Quran* revealed local contextualised solutions to the social ailments and grievances at the time of Muhammad? If the currently endorsed mode of non-analytical application of the immutable and universal truths of the *Quran* (that the *Quran* stresses had all been previously revealed) is correct, why was Muhammad not simply satisfied with drawing from the books of the Christians and Jews (that the *Quran* stresses and Muhammad acknowledges as valid revelations of God) in addressing the spiritual, moral, economic and social needs that arose within his, and surrounding, communities? Indeed, Muhammad attempted to do so initially only to be left dissatisfied and disappointed with the solutions of the past,[9] causing him to turn to the Source within him in origination of fresh solutions to current social needs and circumstances. This Muhammad did through independent reasoning and proclamation of judgements, either in the form of revelation (the *Quran*) or recorded *hadiths*.[10]

The *sunna* (practices) of Muhammad are sometimes also taken by Muslims as a source of law since Muhammad is believed to have been guided and thus whatever he did was in alignment with that Higher law that guided him. Yet, as any biography or history of Muhammad will reveal to the reader, Muhammad was a revolutionist in his time, certainly not a conformist.[11] His clan and the people of Makkah plotted to kill him which eventually caused Muhammad to flee to Madina (along with hundreds of others) precisely because he was perceived to be blaspheming against the traditions of their 'forefathers' among whom were Abraham and Ishmael and Isaac, all of whom the *Quran* identifies and exalts as Muslims. We have mentioned above that the *Quran* states that Abraham coined the word 'Muslim' and, further, the *Quran* specifically states that Muhammad was inspired to follow the tradition of Abraham. How is it then that Muhammad was a Muslim, guided enough that the very words of the *Quran* were revealed through him, yet he abandoned specific ways and traditions of Abraham? Muhammad certainly did not pray or trade in the manner Abraham's community did, he did not dress the way they did, nor interact with and organise his community the way that of Abraham was, etc. How then was Muhammad following the way of Abraham? The answer is quite simple. The *Quran* urges not the conformity and copying of rules and practices of Abraham that were formulated and existed centuries (or more!) before Muhammad, but rather urges the emulation of the spirit of Abraham by being true to one's self and Allah, and in that, not fearing or 'bowing' to any human (or social) authority or associating the worship of Allah with that of mortals, creatures or inanimate objects.

The key point in the foregone explanation is that it is not sufficient simply to mirror past solutions and discoveries in present circumstances. For instance, the encouragement that parties to any future debt/commercial obligations record their dealings in writing and to be witnessed in the presence of two witnesses as stated in the *Quran* (*Baqara*: 282) was a commercial quantum leap in the context of seventh century AD indicating a progression in the laws to cater for the advancing commercial realities of Muhammad's time. It is clear, therefore, that in times of change and progress a return to principles and the original Source, both at a personal and collective level, must be undertaken so as to consider their intended purpose and how best they can be applied to changing contexts through fresh or existing rules and practices. This is the key role played by interpretation. As Kamali puts it:

> The sharia shows the way to justice and this way must be followed as far as possible. In the event however that the established rules of the sharia do not offer sufficient guidelines to administer justice, one may take any route, including those of natural rights and natural justice or the general rules of equity and fairness or that of a judicious policy (*siyasa shar'iyyah*) in order to secure justice and the result that is arrived at is a *fortiori* in accordance with the sharia and cannot be held to be contrary to it.[12]

Given the central role of interpretation, this chapter proceeds to consider the balance between form and substance in Islamic law.

1.1 Form versus substance in the *Quran*

Islam is full of prescribed forms and rituals governing all aspects of life and worship. Underpinning the structures and forms, however, is the substance that the *Quran*, at several instances, emphasises as taking precedence over form. *Al-Baqara*: 177, for instance, states that it matters not which direction one faces in prayer but rather what matters is faith and works of goodness. *Al-Hajj* 37 refers to the sacrifice made during the hajj pilgrimage and Allah states that neither the flesh nor the slaughter of the sacrifice matters but rather the God consciousness within one's self. In matters of commerce, *al-Baqara*: 175 is the quintessential reference stressing substance over form, as shall be discussed in greater detail in chapter 6. The retort exhorted from people upon the prohibition of *riba* was that 'sale/trade is like *riba*' and the response in the *Quran* was that Allah permitted trade and prohibited *riba*. This verse underscores the similarity of the forms of trade and *riba* but that in substance, one was prohibited whilst the other permitted. The point in drawing out these verses is to emphasise that Islam is not concerned with forms as long as the welfare of the people, individually and collectively, is served. Ultimately, what Allah is concerned with is the substance of any matter. Moreover, if substance takes precedence over form in matters of ritual/worship, what more of commerce in which Muslim societies throughout the ages have demonstrated fluidity and a willingness to evolve practices and structures to reflect the times and needs of the people?

1.1.1 *Form versus substance in Islamic finance transactions*
An enquiry into the purpose/s of the commercial forms of transactions employed by Islamic finance (a summary of all is provided in chapter 3) is not common. Most of these structures pre-date the Islamic civilisation. Others, like the *salam* contract (advance payment for future delivery of agricultural produce) and *istina'* contract (commission to manufacture), are innovations of society a few generations after Muhammad. Both the *Salam* and *Istina'* contracts were created as exceptions to the general rule of contract law because they involve the sale of not-yet-existent objects or what the common law terms 'potential property'.[13] The *salam* contract, for instance, was an invention of the agricultural people of the Hijaz/Iraq – a contract otherwise characterised as 'speculative' for purposes of *gharar*[14] and includes a price discount for time which is an element of *riba* as currently defined[15] – yet the contract was permitted due to the social need it fulfilled.[16] This, again, tallies with the common law position. Oditah explains that the permissibility of transferring 'potential property' as an exception to the general rule of transferring present property was confined almost exclusively to agricultural produce – mainly crops and livestock. That, '[t]he Common law courts never recognised that goods which a company may manufacture tomorrow or receivables expected from their sale, were things in potential'.[17] Today, however, Muslims have widely applied the *salam* concept to structured financial transactions for future delivery of goods that society demands, proving that Islamic law concepts can be applied dynamically and progressively in light of the underlying principle they serve.[18] Contrary to common perception, both the above named forms of transactions were neither revealed nor developed at the time of the prophet Muhammad; they simply comprise modes of transaction practiced by Muslim societies because

they did not oppose any fundamental principle of Islam. Muhammad did not need to sanction them personally, it is sufficient that he did not specifically prohibit them, as he did the *riba* sale or the *gharar* sale, to deem them permissible. Moreover, as we shall discuss in detail in chapters 4 and 5, in prohibiting the *gharar* or *riba* sales, Muhammad prohibited not the form, because these were often identical to perfectly permissible transactions, but the economic substance that the transactions in question effected.[19] The various forms (whether invented before the time of Muhammad or after) existed simply for purposes of serving a real and practical need within the society and commercial community.

Within this broad domain of 'social need', Islamic law of commerce plays a pivotal role of regulation by decreeing the twin principles of *riba* and *gharar* that seek to secure the twin objectives of equity between transacting parties and efficiency in transactions. The point this chapter stresses therefore is that Islamic contractual and financial structures must guard to serve above all else the principle of contractual fairness and social welfare. In this light, adherence to form must only be to serve the substance by effecting equity and social justice. For clarity, by substance it is here meant economic substance as opposed to legal or procedural substance – a key distinction between Islamic law and common law as we shall see in section 1.3 below.

El-Gamal suggests the achievement of such economic substance, today, through 'marking to market', that is, marking the terms of trade to market prices. He explains that, in the context of credit sales and lease to purchase financing, the substantive prohibition of *riba*, that is, aiming to ensure equity in exchange, dictates that credit in such transactions must be extended at the appropriate (market) interest rate. Thus, it is said, that conventional finance has played an important role for contemporary Islamic finance by determining the market interest rates for various borrowers and, further, that such benchmarking of the implicit interest rates (built into the Islamic finance structures) is quite appropriate for purposes of equity through efficiency.

Contrary to El-Gamal's allusion, the 'marking to market' concept is neither alien nor foreign to Islamic commercial practice.[20] Muhammad prescribed the 'marking to market' formula of efficiency in the sixth century ad, before common law commercial principles even came into existence, when he specifically asked Bilal to sell his inferior dates at market price and with the proceeds buy the superior dates he wanted instead of bartering two portions for one, respectively. Implicit in the disapproval of the barter transaction is the potential for inequity in bartering two portions of inferior dates for one portion of superior dates without an objective criterion to determine the appropriateness of the measures. This caused Muhammad to characterise the transaction as 'the very essence of *riba*'. Note, Muhammad did not say, 'ah, that is a *riba* transaction' because there was nothing wrong with the legal form of the transaction itself: instead, he said, 'the very *essence* of *riba*' meaning the economic effect of the transaction (inequity) was *riba*. One who is concerned with understanding the depth of this tradition will appreciate that through his direction to Bilal, Muhammad endorsed the use of market mechanisms, including 'marking to markets' as a cure for any inequity that may be (potentially or actually) effected through transactions, regardless of the legal form the transaction assumes. The same applies for securitisation transactions today. They are simply another form of transaction invented after the demise of Muhammad (as the *salam* transaction was) to serve a patent social need. As long as a securitisation is equitable in economic effect, there is nothing in the sharia that prohibits it (see chapters 7 and 8 for greater detail).

It is unsettling therefore that El-Gamal inadvertently proceeds to justify the emphasis on legal form in Islamic finance which insists on non-loan structures of finance simply to avoid charging interest yet effectively attain the same goal as a loan would and at the same financial margins/charges. Many of these so-called 'Islamic finance' transactions are also 'the very essence of *riba*' if one enquired into the economic substance of the forms employed. Further, El-Gamal's defence of the 'equity' of 'bundled' forms Islamic finance assumes in present-day practice, contradicts both his theory negating interest as riba and his acknowledgement of most Islamic finance structures as arbitrage – that is, structured finance transaction conjured to attain the same economic end as a counterpart conventional finance transaction.[21]

It is here proposed therefore that Islamic finance should redevelop its standards and criteria of 'compliance' to reflect the intended economic substance in light of modern commercial reality. It is the economic substance of any transaction, be it sale, lease or loan, which must be the focus of the industry and Islamic scholars if Islamic finance is to pride itself on being Islamic (ethical). Its products should be for purposes of creating access to finance for the general public/society much along the lines of the Tabung Haji scheme in Malaysia, the Egyptian Mit Ghamr scheme in the mid-twentieth century, and more recently the Grameen bank project in Bangladesh. The 'Islamic' nature of finance need have little to do with high profile, multi-billion dollar transactions of the kind emblazoned in our minds by the industry and media. Its focus should be 'local before global'. To go about it, as the industry is doing currently, is to put the cart before the horse, the consequence of which has been not only to alienate the majority of the Muslim population both in and outside Islamic banking jurisdictions, but also cause widespread disillusionment regarding the industry – a cost that has begun to weigh down heavily on the industry as precipitated by the potential default of Dubai World to its creditors and the failure to effectively communicate this to the market. This fact has been widely reported in the *Financial Times* in November and December of 2009.

1.2 The role of interpretation under the common law:

The English legal system, referred to as a 'common law' legal system, has its primary legal principles (mainly) made, and developed, progressively by judges (rather than the legislature) from case decisions in what is called a system of precedent, whereby the lower courts are bound to follow principles propounded by the higher courts in previous cases. The common law is as equally important as the law made by Parliament. For example, there is no Act of Parliament stating that murder is a crime; it is a common law crime that has been refined over the centuries by judges. Likewise, and especially, the principles and rules governing contracts and commercial transactions were almost exclusively developed by the courts. A distinctive feature of the common law is, therefore, that it represents the law of the courts as expressed in judicial decisions.[22]

In developing the law the judiciary plays an important role; that of statutory interpretation and contextual application in light of the facts before them. Whilst the meaning of law in a statute should be clear and explicit, this is not always so. Many cases come before the courts because there is a dispute over the meaning of a word in a statute. For instance, it is judicial interpretation that confirmed the independent existence of arbitration clauses in commercial contracts as demonstrated by the contrast between the decisions of the House of Lords *May and Butcher v Regis*[23] and *Fiona Trust & Holding Corporation and others v Privalov and others.*[24]

In *Fiona Trust* the relevant issue was whether the arbitration clause survived the rescission of the charter party agreements (Shelltime 4). This called for an interpretation of s. 7 of the Arbitration Act 1996, which provides:

> Unless otherwise agreed by the parties, an arbitration agreement which forms or was intended to form part of another agreement (whether or not in writing) shall not be regarded as invalid, non-existent or ineffective because that other agreement is invalid, or did not come into existence or has become ineffective, and it shall for that purpose be treated as a distinct agreement.

The House of Lords held that:

> On its proper construction, cl. 41 of the Shelltime 4 form contained nothing to exclude disputes about the validity of the contract, whether on the grounds that it was procured by fraud, bribery, misrepresentation or anything else. The principle of severability enacted in s. 7 of the Arbitration Act 1996 meant that the invalidity or rescission of the main contract did not necessarily entail the invalidity or rescission of the arbitration agreement. The arbitration agreement had to be treated as a 'distinct agreement' and could be void or voidable only on grounds which related directly to the arbitration agreement. There might be cases in which the grounds on which the main agreement was invalid were identical with the ground upon which the arbitration agreement was invalid ... Even if the allegation was that there was no concluded agreement, that was not necessarily an attack on the arbitration agreement. If the arbitration clause had been agreed, the parties would be presumed to have intended the question of whether there was a concluded main agreement to be decided by arbitration.

Lord Hoffman provided his reasons for the above judgement as follows:

> A proper approach to construction therefore requires the court to give effect, so far as the language used by the parties will permit, to the commercial purpose of the arbitration clause. But the same policy of giving effect to the commercial purpose also drives the approach of the courts (and the legislature) to the second question raised in this appeal, namely, whether there is any conceptual reason why parties who have agreed to submit the question of the validity of the contract to arbitration should not be allowed to do so.

There was for some time a view that arbitrators could never have jurisdiction to decide whether a contract was valid. If the contract was invalid, so was the arbitration clause. In *Overseas Insurance Ltd v AA Mutual International Insurance Co. Ltd* [1988] 2 Lloyd's Rep 63, 66, Evans J said that this rule 'owes as much to logic as it does to authority'. But the logic of the proposition was denied by the Court of Appeal in *Harbour Assurance Co. (UK) Ltd* v. *Kansa General International Insurance Co. Ltd* [1993] QB 701 and the question was put beyond doubt by section 7 of the Arbitration Act 1996.

Contrast the approach of Lord Hoffman in *Fiona Trust* with that of Lord Buckmuster of the House of Lords in the case of *May and Butcher v Regem*[25] where it was held, on the question of whether the arbitration clause survived the contract being rendered void:

> The next question is about the arbitration clause, and there I entirely agree with the majority of the Court of Appeal and also with Rowlatt J. The arbitration clause is to refer disputes 'with reference to or arising out of this agreement'. But, until the price has been fixed, the agreement is not there. The arbitration clause relates to the settlement of whatever may happen when once the agreement has been completed and the parties are regularly bound. There is nothing in the arbitration clause to enable a contract to be made which, in fact, the original bargain had left quite open.

In *May and Butcher*, the House of Lords, clearly adopted an interpretation that negated the seperability of an arbitration clause in a contract. Given this approach, it is no wonder that the legislature had to step in to remedy the unwillingness of the judiciary to give commercial effect to the intention of the parties expressed through the inclusion of an arbitration clause. This is now expressed in section 7 of the Arbitration Act 1996. The case of *May and Butcher* v. *Regem*[26] is discussed in greater detail in section 4.6.

Another illustration of the role of interpretation under the common law is gleaned from the interpretation of what constitutes a wagering contract. Under the common law, bets were enforceable and by a series of statute from 1710 to 1892, wagering contracts were rendered void[27] (these statutes now stand repealed by sections 334 and 356 of the Gambling Act 2005). A wagering contract was defined in *Carlill* v. *Carbolic Smoke Ball Co*,[28] which later received unqualified approval from the Court of appeal.[29]

However, the case of *Ellesmere* v. *Wallace* demonstrated that, though wagering contracts were prohibited by statute, what comprised a wagering contract and the consequent determination of whether the contract was void for illegality, was dependant on the interpretation of the court on the facts of the case. Thus, in *Ellesmere* v. *Wallace*, it was held that a bet placed with the Horse-racing totalisator was not a wagering contract within the meaning of the Gaming Act 1845, since the Board can neither win nor lose on the transaction. The Court of Appeal held that the money placed on the bet was recoverable.[30] Further, the Court observed that though an essential feature of a wagering contract is that the stake is the only interest which the parties have in the contract,[31] the question whether the parties are interested in something more than the mere winning or losing of the stake depends on the substance of the agreement, not upon its outward form. Thus, the Court in *Carlill v Carbolic* observed:

> In construing a contract with a view to determining whether it is a wagering one or not, the Court will receive evidence in order to arrive at the substance of it, and will not confine its attention to the mere words in which it is expressed, for a wagering contract may be sometimes concealed under the guise of language which on the face of it, if only the words were to be considered, might constitute a legally enforceable contract.[32]

Similarly, where there is a present price agreed, though the value of the article is unascertained at the time the contract for its sale is made, the transaction is not a wager.[33]

1.3 Form versus substance under the common law: the Exfinco scenario

A key feature of securitisation, as we shall see in chapter 7, is that the value of securities issued will be determined by the performance of the pool of segregated assets, and not by the continuing credit worthiness of the originator. The separation of the credit risk of the originator and the credit risk of the SPV in this way often enables the originator to obtain lower-cost financing through securitisation than it would otherwise be able to obtain. For example, before the advent of the credit downturn commencing September 2008, many originators with corporate credit ratings of BBB (the lowest investment grade rating at Standard & Poor) had securitised assets resulting in an issue of AAA-rated securities. Securitisation may also achieve other objectives; for example, it may allow a regulated entity to remove assets from its balance sheet for regulatory capital purposes, and thus do more business, by structuring a transaction as a sale rather than a loan. It is important to note therefore, in contrast to the emphasis this book has placed on economic substance in Islamic law, that in examining the question of whether a structured transaction is a sale or a loan, the courts enquire into the *legal* substance of the transaction and not the *economic* substance. (emphasis added) This is not to say that the common law does not concern itself with the economic substance of a transaction; it does so through equitable doctrines of unconscionable dealings and equitable principles generally. However, within the strict realm of financial transactions, the Court looks to the legal substance of the transaction for purposes of characterising the transaction as a (true sale) securitisation or loan. In other words, the Court pays no regard to whether the parties structure the transaction as a sale or a loan as long as, legally, the transaction is what they say it is and not a guise for something else. This is also the current approach of the Islamic finance industry, as this book argues, for a shift from, to a focus on, economic substance in line with the principles of Islam.

The Court of Appeal in *Welsh Development Agency* v. *Export Finance Co Ltd*[34] (aka *Exfinco*) considered the question of whether a transaction described by the parties as a sale of goods could be characterised as a secured loan. The court had regard to the manner in which the parties had described their transaction in the documents as evidence of what, in substance, the parties had agreed, and held that despite similarities to a mortgage or charge, the agreement was what it purported to be, that is, a sale transaction. However, the court indicated that its decision was not applicable where the transaction was a sham. The court examined the detailed terms of the documents and identified the legal substance of the matter, as set out in those terms, as being in accordance with the form – a sale and not a secured loan. Slaughton LJ pointed out that '*in such cases one was seeking to ascertain the legal nature of the transaction and not its economic effect*' (emphasis added). He identified two ways of examining the question: the external and internal route. The external route involved an allegation that the written document did not truly represent the agreement of the parties in that it was a sham or pretence. The internal route involved the examination of the written agreement in order to ascertain its legal nature from the terms contained in the document.

Under English law, for a transaction to be deemed a sham the parties must have intentionally executed documents that give the appearance of creating legal rights and obligations different from those which the parties intended to create.[35] Slaughton LJ observed[36] that 'the task of looking for the substance of the parties' agreement and disregarding the labels they have used' may arise in a case where their written agreement is a sham intended to mask their true agreement. The task of the courts there is to discover by extrinsic evidence what their true agreement was and to disregard, if inconsistent with the true agreement, the written words of the sham agreement. Slaughton LJ's analysis in the Exfinco case was applied by the Court of Appeal in *Lavin* v. *Johnson*[37] and found that the legal nature of one part of the document was in conformity with the form (a sale) whilst that of the other part of the document was not and thus represented a security transaction. In *Dutton* v. *Davis*,[38] the Court of Appeal again held that the legal nature of the transaction was in accordance with the form of the transaction and thus did not involve the grant of a security which could be redeemed.

Goode explains, with relevance to current Islamic finance practice, that an agreement that is in substance a loan may readily be disguised as a purchase to evade either the Money Lenders Act (now repealed) or, where the 'seller' is a company, the registration requirements embodied in section 395 of the Companies Act 1985 (now section 860 of the Companies Act 2006). Where an allegation of such disguise is made, the court must inquire into the facts of the case and, where necessary, look behind the labels given to the transaction by the parties.[39] He continues to say:

> The question to be decided is not whether the transaction would have the effect of avoiding the relevant statute – for parties are free to organise their affairs in any such way as to ensure they escape the legislation they consider burdensome – but what is its legal nature ...
>
> The external route is to show that the document does not record the real agreement between the parties – in other words, that the document is a sham and is designed to conceal the true nature of the transaction. ... But even where the document is a true record of the parties' agreement, the court may conclude from an examination of its terms that its legal character is that of a security, not a sale. This is the internal route. ... But in each case it is the legal *substance* to which the court has regard, not the economic *effect*.[40]

In the recent case of *Brighton & Hove City Council* v. *Audus*[41] Morgan J explains that, 'there are many ways of raising money besides borrowing. If the transaction is not in the form of a loan it is not to the point to say that its object was to raise money or that the parties could have produced the same result more conveniently by borrowing and lending money'.

This explanation is critical to understanding the distinct approaches taken by the common law courts and Islamic law regarding re-characterisation. This is because while it is also the case that under Islamic law the issue of re-characterisation does not turn on whether the *effect* of the transaction is to evade a prohibiting statute or law – Muhammad's advice to Bilal to sell his inferior dates so as to purchase superior from the proceeds of his sale had the effect of evading the prohibition of *riba* that was otherwise triggered by Bilal's barter – it does enquire into the economic effect of the transaction. Muhammad was not preferring a market transaction over a barter transaction other than in economic effect, which rendered a market sale transaction, on the facts, preferable (equitable) as opposed to a barter transaction.

Conclusion

Interpretation of the *Quran* and the sayings/practices of Muhammad play a central role in Islamic law generally. Interpretation is to be undertaken in line with the principles and spirit of the primary sources so as to uphold the principle of contractual fairness and bring about social justice. In this light, a consideration of form versus substance is undertaken both for comparative purposes as well as to stress the emphasis placed on the substance of Islamic commerce and contractual dealings. The spirit of equity and justice, as the centrepieces of an Islamic society, necessitates that adherence to the substance of any undertaking be paramount to the form it serves or mimics.

2

SCOPE, METHODOLOGY AND OBJECTIVE

This book considers legal aspects of Islamic finance within the context of a securitisation transaction – the process of converting illiquid assets into tradable securities so as to create liquidity and/or raise funds.[1] It considers the viability of securitisation as an Islamic finance structure within the context of global finance. In doing so, the book considers the following questions:

- What are the principles of Islamic contract law and commerce?
- What is the meaning and effect of *gharar* (i.e. whether conceptual or evidential uncertainty) in Islamic law?
- How is the prohibition against *riba*[2] to be interpreted and applied today?
- What is the meaning and legality of the 'sale of debt' in Islam?
- Is debt proprietary in nature? And if so, how does such proprietary nature affect current Islamic finance theory and practice?
- How can securitisations be structured so as to be compatible with both Islamic finance and conventional finance and what are the issues that arise in doing so?
- What function does the label 'Islamic' serve? And what is the way forward?

2.1 Scope

Of the several issues this book discusses within the analysis of greater viability of securitisation in Islamic finance, emphasis is placed on discussions of *gharar* (speculative risk), *riba* (increased returns on loans) and *bay al dayn* (the sale of debt obligations/receivables). This is because these three issues are of fundamental significance to the development and sustainability of an Islamic capital market: a feature that is necessary for the wider viability of securitisations. The great Andalusian philosopher and jurist Averroes or Ibn Rushd (d. 1198) is known to have said that there are four causes of invalidity intrinsic to the concept of sale: illicitness of the object (e.g. sale of pork or wine); *riba*; *gharar*; and 'those terms that conduce to one of the last two or some combination of them'.[3]

To illustrate briefly, the fundamental components of any true securitisation transaction comprise a contract (sale), a securitised asset/s and securities tradable on the secondary market. These raise three main issues under Islamic law: (i) any contract must guard against being tainted with excessive[4] *gharar* (uncertainty) lest it be vitiated, (ii) any asset that is to be securitised must be *halal* (permitted under Islamic law) thus triggering the issue of the proprietary nature of debt with regards both to the securitisation of debt/ receivables and the sale of the securities on the secondary market, and (iii) securities sold (bonds, shares, loan notes, etc.) must be asset backed lest they be considered invalid objects for violating the rule stipulating the non-proprietary nature of debt as well as violating the rule against *riba* (interest or increased return on debt/loan). Similarly, should the parties take loans to fund the securitisations, any increase charged or paid triggers the rule against *riba*, and if the securitisation is structured and transacted before the underlying asset comes into being, again, this triggers the issues of *gharar* and the validity of sale of debt obligations.

Consider, based on the above, that whilst the securitisation of debt is a popular mode of securitisation and the sale of debt or receivables a common feature of securitisation structures in conventional finance, it is prohibited in Islam by virtue of debt not being recognised as proprietary and therefore not qualifying as an asset for sale even in an asset backed securitisation.[5] The nullity of such a sale may in turn lead to the transaction being re-characterised as a loan and any increased return would be caught by the *riba* (interest) prohibition which renders the transaction void. Consider further that a securitisation structure may involve certain levels of uncertainty, risk and speculation and Islamic law theory, as it stands, prohibits contractual uncertainty and speculative risk (*gharar*). It is thus pertinent to clarify the status and effect of *gharar, riba* and the sale of receivable (debt) securities under Islamic law.

2.2 Methodology
The methodology used in conducting the research for this book is comparative. The comparison is conducted at two levels: A comparison of the current rules and practices of Islamic finance with the principles in the *Quran* and the traditions of Muhammad that the rules are ascribed to; and

a comparison of the position within Islamic law with that of the common law, to the extent possible.

Reference to the common law throughout implies English case law and the rules of Equity, which are the sources of contract and commercial law in England and to this day form the foundation for statutory law in this regard. The comparison is conducted on a concept by concept basis, where possible, by drawing similarities between the underlying principles of law in Islamic law and common law. However, where a distinction exists, attention is drawn to it and a contrast is made.

2.3 Objective

The objective of the comparison is to examine the practices and framework applied within the common law for potential compatibility and application to the development of Islamic law. Questions may be raised as to why a comparative study with the common law? Why not a comparison with the civil law given that the legal system in most Middle Eastern and North African (MENA) countries are deemed more aligned with civil law? This is done for four main reasons:

First, with the intention of appreciating the development of certain concepts and practices of the common law, thereby drawing lessons for the development of Islamic law of contract in an age where rapid growth and expansion of application and innovation is expected of Islamic law. This is done with the confidence that Muslims, throughout the ages, more so during the golden age of Islamic civilisation and at the time of the prophet Muhammad, have always been receptive and responsive to the ideas and cultures of other civilisations. The prophet Muhammad encouraged Muslims to pursue knowledge 'even in the land of China' (China being the farthest land one could then travel to) and incorporated many Christian, Jewish and pagan Arab practices within the daily practices of the Muslim community as long as the practices did not conflict with the principles outlined in the *Quran*. Wherever Muslims migrated to, during and after the time of Muhammad, they readily incorporated the commercial and customary practices of the land. Islamic law is inclusive, not exclusive, and the underlying message of the *Quran* requires that mankind strive to create a just and egalitarian society in which all people, especially the vulnerable, are treated justly.[6] Muslims today are free to emulate the same and shed their claims to exclusivity and/or superiority in consonance with the practice of the prophet and his companions. In fact, Muhammad (as all other men of God) was known for his practicality and forward-looking personality. He was quick to shed any encumbering custom if that would facilitate ease and egalitarianism among the people.

Second, a comparison with the common law is undertaken because it is the law most frequently used in drafting the legal and contractual documents in a securitisation transaction in Islamic finance (as is true for most global financial transactions). This is because the common law is generally more progressive and permissive than the civil law. Furthermore, though the MENA region may be civil law inclined, Islamic law finds many parallels with the common law, for instance, juristic reliance on precedent and legal reasoning based on analogy.[7] It, therefore, makes greater sense to compare the principles of Islamic law with the common law; a comparison which enables the examination of parallels that provide insight into potential trajectories for Islamic finance.

Third, the legal nature of Islamic jurisprudence on contract and commerce is similar to that of the common law. For instance, both are founded on the principle of laissez-faire whereby everything is permissible unless expressly prohibited. Similarity also extends to the methodology of legal inference based on reasoning by analogy and judicial judgements based on judicial precedent. Where the cannon is silent on a particular issue, Muslim jurists formulate law applicable to the specific situation in similar fashion to common law judges formulating the law for cases in which no precedent exists. This may explain the relative success of Islamic finance in countries that were historically ruled by the British (Bahrain) and more so in countries that retain the common law as their legal framework (Malaysia).[8] Likewise, contemporary developments in Islamic finance are owed more to juristic understandings of the primary texts and previous juristic decisions rather than to the text itself.

Fourth, and perhaps more importantly, drawing out commonalities between Islamic and common law principles allows for better regulation of Islamic finance products and markets by aligning them to conventional market standards and practices contrary to the exclusivity Islamic finance has inclined towards within the global financial fabric. By recognising that in essence the transactions in both spheres are the same, they can also be regulated alike. This should be welcomed news for Islamic finance jurisdictions because they would not have to worry about issues of double taxation or legal certainty in cases of dispute, as Islamic finance transaction would elicit similar legal treatment as conventional finance. Further, the commonality in essence also allows for uniformity in regulation of financial transactions within national frameworks. For instance, this would allow for uniformity in regulation of both conventional and Islamic finance investments by the Malaysian securities commission and other equivalent jurisdictional regulatory bodies. Such uniform regulation serves to instil public confidence in

Islamic finance products, especially in the current global financial climate, because of the greater legal and regulatory certainty it creates for Islamic finance products.[9]

2.4 Approach

The approach adopted here is one that focuses on principles rather than rules. This approach allows for the subsequent extrapolation of rules that are applicable to Islamic contract and finance contexts. In coining a term, this approach is called the 'principle-centric' approach in that it emphasises enquiry into the principles that govern Islamic law of contract and finance and de-emphasise adherence to the current rules. This approach suggests that principles are distinct from rules and argues that rules are derived from, and formulated to express, principles. Whilst the principles remain constant (the general framework), the rules may change and are not 'carved in stone'. This is particularly true in Islam and is emphasised by the very nature of the Faith that whilst governing every facet of Muslims' lives, provides mainly a framework of principles to be fleshed out according to the current need and context. In other words, the rules governing different areas of life are to be fleshed out according to the prevalent social needs whilst using the principles as a yard stick of keeping within the overall framework intended. Further, flexibility is provided for through the principle that new rules that fit new times and circumstances can be extrapolated from existing principles; this process is known as *qiyas* (analogical deduction).

Muhammad, in his lifetime, demonstrated the distinction between principles and rules repeatedly, mainly in the distinct judgements he passed in different situations regarding the same issue. For example, prayer is amongst the five pillars of Islam, yet different people throughout the ages have prayed in different manners whilst still being Muslims and acknowledged as such by the *Quran*. This is true of Adam, Abraham, Moses, Jesus and Muhammad – each of these messengers and their people prayed in a different manner according to their times, yet all were adhering to the same principle of prayer. Further, the *Quran* provides variations and concessions on prayer depending on different circumstances. For instance, one is excused from ritual prayer when ill and may choose to pray however one can best pray. Likewise, a traveller receives concession from prayer by being allowed to shorten as well as join two consecutive prayers. Thus, the principle of prayer endures in all circumstances but the form and format it takes changes according to the time and context of application. This flexibility is even greater outside the sphere of ritual, as in commercial transactions, where the operative principle is that everything is permissible that is not expressly prohibited by a clear text of the *Quran* or saying of the Prophet. The companions of the Prophet and early Muslim societies thereafter demonstrated this distinction through, for instance, *bay al-salam* (pre-paid contract of agricultural produce – long before harvest). *Salam* was permitted, despite its apparent uncertain and speculative (*gharar*) nature, because of both the presence of a pressing social need (i.e. to keep up with the rising levels of commercial development and growth in demand of agricultural products) and the acknowledged absence of a deceptive element in the transaction that the principle of contractual fairness guards against.[10]

I prefer the 'principle approach' because it brings balance back to commercial application. After the 'closing of the gates of Ijtihad'[11] increased emphasis was laid on rules (as opposed to the principles) of Islam with an insistence on the adhering of rules available at that time without the permission to partake in any thought process of analogy, deduction or extrapolation of other rules from underlying principles pertaining to the various (often novel) issues and aspects of life in Muslim societies. This led to a sharp decline in the intellectual vibrancy within the religion in the subsequent centuries, which contributed to the eventual decline of the Islamic civilisation. The point, therefore, is that rules need not remain the same; they may be modified, changed or done away with completely, as long as we remain within the principles and general framework of Islam. It acknowledges that achieving the objectives of Muslim societies today is part and parcel of the objectives of the sharia. Accordingly, this book also considers the argument that in attempting to replicate the substance of contemporary financial practice using pre-modern contract forms, Islamic finance fails to serve the objectives of the sharia both in terms of efficiency of contractual dealing and equity between the contracting parties.[12] The principle-centric approach proposes, wherever possible, that there should be minimal hesitation towards the adoption of contemporary financial practice for purposes of replicating the substance of Islamic finance. This 'return to principles' approach receives express sanction in the *Quran* where Allah says:

> O you who believe! Obey Allah, and obey the Messenger and those charged with authority among you. If you differ in anything among yourselves, refer it (back) to Allah and His Messenger, if you do believe in Allah and the Last Day: That is the best, and the most suitable course for final determination.[13]

Conclusion

In closing, I draw attention to the possible origins of the common law in Islamic law. This has been verified by credible studies in the recent past as well as the logical deduction drawn from the fact that the decline of the Islamic civilisation at the turn of the fourteenth century coincides with the rise of the Christian civilisation. This crossing in history is marked by the crusades that saw many a Muslim city and people destroyed. In doing so, many books and manuscripts were burnt or otherwise destroyed but many yet survived to be translated and studied by Christian missionaries and scholars, eventually becoming a basis of scientific and philosophical enquiry and the common law rooted in precedent and juristic analogy as we know it today.[14] One of the earliest studies in this area traced the British system of trusts to the Islamic institution of *waqf* (charitable trusts).[15] A more recent study by John Makdisi traced the origins of many innovations in British contract law to Islamic origins.[16] One can, thus, conclude that in drawing from the common law, Muslims today may in fact be drawing from their own origins. Part of the purpose of this book, therefore, is to reconcile aspects of Islamic finance with conventional finance. It acknowledges that the systematic emphasis of differences whilst ignoring similarities is unproductive.

3

ISLAMIC FINANCE

AN INTRODUCTION

Islamic finance is depicted as (and, in essence, ought to be) an ethical and equitable mode of financing that derives its principles from the sharia (Islamic law). Over a period of 45 odd years,[1] a variety of financial institutions have developed sophisticated methods to advance capital to both the private and public sector in a manner compatible with the sharia. However, it is only recently that tradable sharia compliant financial instruments have come to market in considerable amounts. In this respect, the development of an Islamic bond (*sukuk*) market has been the primary area of growth, providing an avenue for short and medium term placements of funds by investors.[2] The growth of this market has been fuelled not only by the desire of corporate and government entities to raise sharia compliant funds (as an alternative source of funding) but also by investor demands for sharia compliant products so much so that in 2004, for instance, a European federal institution with no Islamic constitutional links,[3] issued sharia compliant securities to attract Middle Eastern investors. Such investor appetite for alternative securities has inspired the creation of a sharia compatible securitisation market. As was reported, 'the Islamic financial industry's journey towards the mainstream has now reached a stage where several of the big investment banks think they miss out if they are unable to do the translation'.[4]

With the above backdrop, this chapter turns to examine the principles and the basis upon which Islamic finance operates, setting the ground for discussion in the ensuing chapters generally, and specifically chapter 8, on structuring securitisation deals to be compatible with both the sharia and conventional finance.

3.1 Principles governing contract and finance in Islam

Islamic Finance is governed by two main principles:

- *Contractual Fairness and Social Justice.* The *Quran* sets out principles of equity, justice, fairness, morality and social welfare, among others, as preferable underpinnings of any human society. We have called them 'Islamic' principles. The *Quran*[5] explains that Allah (God) creates and owns everything and human beings therefore hold wealth on *amanah* (Trust) for God to be spent and dealt with accordingly. The beneficiary of such wealth, held by any human being, is the collective community of humans whose interest must be served in spending or dealing with money. Contractual dealings, whilst governed primarily by the principle of permissibility and recognising the freedom of the individual to contract freely, was nonetheless to operate within the ambit of fairness as between the parties and social justice.

- *Permissibility.* The *Quran* grants substantial freedom in almost every aspect of life, including matters of commerce,[6] and property may be freely held or traded. In general, it is accepted that in all matters (*mu'amalaat*) other than faith (*'ibadaat*) the operating principle is that of permissibility (*ibaha*) unless there is a clear text in the primary sources to the contrary.[7] The principle of permissibility does not operate in a vacuum but rather goes back, and is linked, to the notion of human beings as trustees or stewards of God's wealth/creation on earth. Permissibility is therefore tempered by rules enunciated in the *Quran* which indicate, broadly, the extent to which contracting parties are free in deciding their terms and conditions.[8] Chief among these rules are that any given transaction should be devoid of *riba* or *gharar*,[9] both of which are defined briefly below and are dealt with in separate (ensuing) chapters of this book. It is a concern of Islamic law of contract and finance that no party suffers undue burden in any given transaction when it is possible, through care and proper investigation, to dispel risks of *riba* and *gharar*. Therefore, the principle of contractual fairness counterbalances the principle of permissibility with the objective of attaining social justice or equity between the parties. Within the principle of permissibility is the accommodation of divergent views and expanding perspectives. Thus, in order to declare an act or transaction valid or permissible, there is no requirement to establish affirmative textual evidence in support. All one needs is to ascertain that there is no clear text that prohibits it. Further, and importantly, the contracts and transactions endorsed by Islam (some existing before and others after the lifetime of Muhammad) are not exhaustive.

Novel transaction are permissible and valid as long as no clear text in the primary sources exists prohibiting it and even this may be waived if the social need for it (benefit) outweighs the perceived detriment (as was the case of *bay al-salam*). As Kamali explains, 'it is essentially incorrect to extend and apply a medieval juristic opinion to something that was not even known in those times'.[10]

These two principles provide a platform from which Islamic finance is to be applied in compliance with the objectives (*maqasid*) of the sharia.[11] Among the objectives of the sharia is the creation of ease (*maslaha*), both in this world and the hereafter (i.e. the material and spiritual spheres of existence), which is derived from the concept of *taysir* (making things easy) and relates closely to the concept of *raf' al haraj* (the removal of hardship).[12] These objectives of the sharia are meant to ensure that there is no hardship in the practice of the religion as the report by Tirmidhi about the prophet Muhammad that 'You [Muhammad] have been sent in order to make things easy, not as one who makes them difficult'.[13] An understanding of the *maqasid* therefore allows for practice in consonance with the principle of permissibility that governs contractual and commercial transactions in the context of Islam. As one author notes, Ibn Taymiyya wrote that 'Unless God and His Prophet have decreed them to be forbidden … they are permitted … But God, the most high, never prohibited a contract in which there is a benefit for the Muslims and does not inflict any harm upon them', there is no need therefore to search for affirmative evidence in the original sources to declare a transaction valid.[14]

3.2 Specific rules of the sharia governing contract and finance in Islam

The principles, in brief, whose parameters define the scope and nature of Islamic finance, are examined below through a discussion of the treatment pertaining to *riba*, gambling, *gharar*, hoarding, financial assets, predetermined profit, and prohibited transactions.

3.2.1 Riba

The *Quran* categorically prohibits the practice of *riba* as is evident in the following verses of the *Quran*:[15]

> …they say that trade is like *riba*, but God hath permitted trade and forbidden *riba*.[16]

O ye who believe! Fear Allah, and give up what remains of *riba*, if ye are indeed believers.[17]

What you give in *riba* to increase in people's wealth, does not gain anything with God. But if you give charitably, seeking God's pleasure, these are those who receive manifold reward.[18]

Riba has been, and remains, interpreted as any return on money that is predetermined in amount[19] and therefore includes present day forms of interest-based financing.[20] Since *Riba* is repeatedly discouraged in the primary sources,[21] any return on money employed is required to be linked to the profits of an enterprise or joint endeavour. Islamic finance therefore prefers deferred payment at a premium to spot price plus loan structures, be they sale or lease contracts, as the only viable (profitable) option to banks and financial institutions in the wake of the interest prohibition on financial transactions. Consequently, modern scholars encouraged asset-based financing where the return to the financier is linked either to the provision of an asset to the client or to the acquisition of an asset. Any higher returns earned are (supposed to be) linked, commensurately, to the assumption of risk – which emphasises the fact that Islam is not against higher returns on investments.

One of this book's premises, however, is that the concept of *riba* has little to do with the act of charging an increased return on finance extended and much to do with deceptive forms of transaction and a discouragement of the human obsession with monetary gains (in contrast to charitable spending in the cause of God that brings greater, albeit not immediate, returns). The *Quran*'s emphasis, wherever *riba* is addressed, pertains to equitable transactions and a general encouragement towards giving charitably, rather than focusing on making an increase of returns on an investment or money lent; this is the principle behind the prohibition.[22]

3.2.2 Gambling (maysir)

The caution against gambling (*maysir*) in the *Quran* is the basis upon which the sharia prohibits any form of speculation.[23] This has essentially deterred many Islamic financial institutions from participating in derivative transactions.[24] Speculative investments on the capital market in general are viewed suspiciously by sharia committees and avoided by financial institutions. Caution must, however, be taken not to confuse risk with speculation. Risk taking is inevitable in commercial and investment transactions (the basis for making a profit/increased returns). Speculation may on the other hand be viewed as excessive and/or avoidable risk taking. The prohibition of *gharar* derives from the prohibition against gambling and it is thus linked to speculative transactions.

3.2.3 Prohibited transactions/investments

Islam prohibits transactions involving prohibited elements such as pork, alcohol, armaments, activities involving speculation, gambling and any sort of immorality. By extension, Islamic institutions may have reservations about (and refrain from) investments involving businesses such as hotels and the entertainment industry (where alcohol and pork may be served and gambling may take place).

3.2.4 Predetermined profit

As a general rule, profit cannot be guaranteed or predetermined in amount and an Islamic financial institution must assume at least part of the risk of a given transaction.[25] There can be no guarantee of a fixed return and similarly, depositors/investors may not invest in Islamic financial institutions on the guarantee of a fixed return. Security may, however, be taken to guard against the eventuality of negligence, wilful wrongdoing, or breach of contract by contractual parties.[26]

3.2.5 Gharar

Gharar is often, and insufficiently, translated as uncertainty. It is much wider than uncertainty and encompasses speculation, excessive risk, ignorance and generally hints at consumer/investor protection. As a concept, it is predicated on the principles of equity and efficiency in transactions. The current position on gharar is that its existence in a contract is prohibited and may render the contract void. Hence, contracting parties must disclose all the terms and details of the contract. However, while scholars are at pains to stress that gharar is prohibited, there is little clarity on what gharar is.[27] Gharar is examined in greater detail in chapter 4.

3.2.6 Hoarding

Islam recognises that trade and enterprise generates wealth for society and is encouraged between people in any profit and loss sharing capacity. Hoarding, on the other hand, in whatever form, is strictly prohibited as it creates a sense of lack and erodes social welfare.

3.2.7 Financial assets

Money and financial assets in general are deemed merely media of exchange, not commodities that can be traded in (i.e. they are not deemed property).[28]

The sale of currency is therefore prohibited (both as a medium of exchange and/or a highly speculative investment) while the sale (through securitisation, restructuring or otherwise) of any debt remains largely doubtful in legality due to the scholastic consideration of debt as money. The legality of the sale of debt in Islam and issues involved in or surrounding financial assets are discussed in chapter 6.

3.3 Transactions in Islamic finance

Islamic finance is said to prefer equity financing over debt financing and that it is fundamentally asset-based because, according to the prevailing interpretations of Islamic law, profit and loss sharing (equity) contracts are not only consistent with Islamic beliefs, they are also superior to debt based financial instruments. Conventional debt financing (interest-based lending or conventional bonds) is deemed not to have a place in Islamic finance because it draws interest.[29] Accordingly, unlike conventional finance where the risk is reflected in the amount of interest paid by the borrower, Islamic finance requires sharing of both profit and loss and hence sharing the risk in general. The classical equity sharing transactions in Islamic law require partnership and profit sharing to which the contemporary structures of venture capitalism, investment management and project financing can be compared. Four of the sharia compliant financing and investment structures that have been developed are discussed here.

3.3.1 Musharaka

It may be defined as equity participation or profit sharing and simply means partnership. It is the umbrella financial structure of financing that encompasses other partnership arrangements like *mudharaba*. In the common form of *musharaka*, both parties provide capital and the contractual conditions are flexible enough to allow the creation and sale of participation notes to the investors or Islamic bank that provide the funding, which represents their share of their investment. The technique is therefore suitable for joint venture investments and can be used to package portfolios of assets whose returns, real property lease payments for example, are subsequently shared among the partners.

3.3.2 Mudharaba

Mudharaba or participation financing is a special form of partnership that has been developed and is now used by modern Islamic financial institutions to provide fund management services. It falls within and utilises the Islamic principles of profit and risk sharing and is characterised by one party (*rabb al mal*) entrusting his money to another party (*mudharib*) who is akin to a fund manager and whose contribution in the partnership is the provision of skill, managerial expertise or the necessary experience. The *mudharib* (fund manager) uses the capital in a mutually agreed fashion and subsequently returns the capital and profit (if any) to the *rabb al mal* (financier) and retains a predetermined share (as opposed to amount) of the profit for himself.

The operating principles of *mudharaba* are:

- The profits are divided on a predetermined proportional basis;[30]
- Any loss is borne by the *rabb al mal* only to the extent of the principle amount;
- The *mudharib* bears the loss of his time and effort in the enterprise.

A *mudharaba* transaction may be entered into for a single investment or on a continuing basis with the financial institution acting as a fiduciary. *Mudharaba* investments may also be made for a fixed term and arranged through negotiable instruments called investment deposit certificates or *mudharaba* certificates and in such situations, may have characteristics akin to shares. A number of Islamic banks have formed funds applying the rules of *mudharaba* to buy real estate assets.[31]

3.3.3 Murabaha

It may be defined as a sale at an agreed profit margin. It is one of the most common forms of Islamic financing, and although it is most applicable to trade financing transactions requiring short-term liquidity instruments, it can also be used for longer-term investments. In its modern day use, *murabaha* involves the purchase of a specific commodity by a financial institution upon the request of a client. The client then purchases the commodity from the financial institution on a deferred payment basis at an agreed mark-up that is structured to cover the cost of purchasing the commodity, the risk undertaken in financing the client and a profit margin.

This mark-up profit has been widely used as a substitute for the charging of interest by parties or institutions that wish to adapt interest-based banking to Islamic finance requirements. The calculation of the mark-up or profit may be in the form of a fixed lump sum or it may be calculated as a percentage (often not dissimilar to the market rate of interest at the time) of the financed amount. Nonetheless, this type of financing is deemed compliant with the sharia because the financial institutions initially takes title to the commodity (albeit briefly) at a risk to itself as well as to the buyer. The compliance with the sharia is thus deemed indisputable[32] on the basis that a *murabaha* transaction involves a sale and the passing of title on the basis of a literal reading of the *Quran* that: '…they [non-Muslims] say that trade is like *riba*, but God hath permitted trade and forbidden *riba*'.[33]

Some banks today prefer *murabaha* to *mudharaba* which they deem to be less risky. They argue that in a *murabaha*, there is no element of *riba* (as currently defined) because the element of assuming business risk in *murabaha* justifies the profit margin charged and distances the transaction even further from *riba*. The Accounting and Auditing Organisation of Islamic Financial Institutions (AAOIFI) allows the acquisition of assets that will be sold under *murabaha* contracts. Once sold, however, the certificates or *sukuk* may not be resold as the asset will then become ownership interests in debts (deemed similar in concept to money) and hence dealing in *riba*.[34]

3.3.4 Ijara

Ijara or leasing is very similar to and shares many characteristics with lease financing and/or hire purchase. A typical *ijara* structure involves a lessor (financial institution) purchasing an asset and renting it to a lessee for a specific time period at an agreed rental or receiving a share of the profits generated by the asset.

There are two main types of lease under the *ijara* structure. One involves a longer-term lease that usually ends with transfer of ownership in the property to the lessee (*ijara wa iqtina'*) which is similar to common law hire purchase contracts. The second type is short term and will normally end with the financial institution retaining ownership of the asset which is similar to an operating lease. In accordance with the sharia, the leased item should not be a prohibited item and must be used in ways permissible in the sharia (for example, the lease of a warehouse or premise for purposes of storing pork products or to operate a casino or bar is prohibited).

Apart from the above modes, Islamic finance also permits investing in certain stock and equity funds as long they conform to certain guidelines (that are similar in many respects to ethical or socially responsible investment). Generally, equity investments that discourage speculation and preclude short selling are deemed sharia compliant while conventional debt equities and derivatives are not. The reasons for this are based on the prohibition of *gharar*, *riba* and the legality of *bay al dayn* in Islamic law as will be discussed in detail in chapters 4, 5 and 6 respectively.

3.4 *Sukuk* (Islamic bonds) and the development of a *sukuk* market

Suk (or its plural *sukuk*) is a transferable instrument with bond-like qualities. It represents proportionate beneficial ownership in an underlying asset for a defined period with the risk and returns associated with the cash flows generated by the particular asset/s belonging to the investors (*sukuk* holders). Though sometimes referred to as Islamic bonds, they are better described as Islamic investment certificates.[35] This distinction is deemed crucial so as to avoid *sukuk* being regarded as substitute for conventional interest-based securities. Ideally, the aim of Islamic finance is not simply to engineer financial products that mimic fixed rate bills, bonds and floating rate notes as understood in conventional finance but rather to develop innovative types of assets backed securities that comply with the sharia.[36]

The *Fiqh* Academy of the Organisation of the Islamic Conference (OIC) first considered the question of Islamic investment certificates at their fourth annual plenary session[37] held in Jeddah in February 1988.[38] After noting that the sharia encourages the documentation of contracts[39] they went on to rule that:

> Subject to proper legal documentation … Any collection of assets can be represented in a written note or bond. This note or bond can be sold at a market price provided that the composition of the group of assets represented by the security, consists of a majority of physical assets and financial rights, with only a minority being cash and interpersonal debts.[40]

Fifteen years later, in May 2003, the sharia board of the Accounting and Auditing Organisation for Islamic Financial Institutions (AAOIFI) adopted sharia Standard No. 17 on Investment *Sukuk*.[41] Therein, investment *sukuk* is defined as: 'Certificates of equal value representing undivided shares in ownership of tangible assets, usufructs and services or (in the ownership of) the assets of particular projects or special investment activity'.

The standard makes it clear that *sukuk* must be asset backed and subject to a sharia compliant contract. It is worth stressing here that the key concepts are:

- transparency and clarity of rights and obligations;
- income from securities must be related to the purpose for which the funding is used, and simply not comprise interest; and
- securities should be backed by real underlying assets, rather than being paper derivatives and the assets must be *halal* (permissible) in nature and being utilised as part of a *halal* activity.[42]

The growth of the *sukuk* market may be attributed to the potential for liquidity management it provides, which has been identified as one of the key ingredients necessary for the further development of the Islamic banking and finance industry. Over the past seven years, *sukuk* have created new possibilities for the short- and medium-term placement of funds. The market is, however, very young compared to other bond sectors; and though sovereign and quasi-sovereign entities such as banks and state agencies have fuelled early growth in the asset class, maintenance of the upward trend depends on whether the other sectors, particularly the private sector, jump on the *sukuk* band wagon. It is likely, however, that the market's growing appetite will persist with the continuing need for financing coming out of the Middle East and issuers both globally and locally increasingly turning to *sukuk* to raise funds. However, the growing awareness and understanding, among both Muslim and non-Muslims, of the details of Islamic finance transactions is causing disillusionment towards the industry. To sustain long-term growth Islamic finance, therefore, may be forced to turn inward and focus on providing the substance its title alludes to instead of modified versions of conventional transactions at a surcharge.[43]

3.5 Distinguishing *sukuk* from conventional bonds

The obvious benefit of *sukuk* is the provision of a sharia compatible alternative to conventional bonds that earn interest which is perceived to be prohibited by the sharia. Furthermore, conventional bonds may be financing activities and industries considered *haram* (prohibited) either directly (e.g. through the production and sale of alcohol, gambling, etc.) or indirectly (through the securitisation of assets used in the production of prohibited goods or financed from the proceeds of sales of prohibited activities). Similarly, companies that are highly leveraged with bank debts may seek refinancing through bond issues (i.e. the sale and securitisation of debts) but as will be discussed in chapter 6 pertaining to 'the sale of debt', such companies are not regarded as suitable for Islamic investments.

The aim of bond trading is usually to make capital gains from the rise in price of the fixed interest bond when variable market interest rates fall. Bond trading may therefore be considered to be largely about exploiting interest rate developments and trading in paper that is usually unrelated to the real value or existence of any underlying asset. The major risk for holders of conventional bonds is of payment default, but this risk is usually assessed solely based on credit ratings by the rating agencies rather than the bond purchasers estimating the actual risk involved. Hence, the bonds are often regarded as pieces of paper with third parties estimating the risk and the purchaser at best only making a risk return calculation without any reference to the business being financed. The recent economic downturn evidenced this when otherwise AAA rated institutions were downgraded (ABN AMRO) or went bankrupt (Lehman Bros). Further, unlike *sukuk* investors, those who invest in conventional bonds are seldom interested in what is being financed through the bond issue which is generally unacceptable in Islam.

A number of sharia scholars, most notably Muhammad Taqi Usmani, stress that what distinguishes Islamic bonds from their conventional counterpart is that Islamic bonds must involve the funding of trade in or the production of real assets.[44] Accordingly, merely funding the purchase of securities would involve second order financing akin to lending for derivatives, the subsequent gearing being speculative and increasing uncertainty (*gharar*).[45] Alternatively, Islamic bonds structured through *Murabaha,* for instance, involve commodities purchased on behalf of the client and sold to the client, the ownership (though temporary) is taken to justify the financier's mark up. Similarly, *ijara* bonds (i.e. *sukuk ijara*) involve the leasing of real assets, with the use of the assets justifying the payment of rental to the owner. The one thing all these contracts are deemed to have in common is the fact that they have underlying assets for which the financing is sought or advanced. *Sukuk* are even distinguished from their conventional asset-backed securities (ABS) counterparts in that conventional ABS may have as their underlying assets different types of loans,[46] all of which are interest bearing and, therefore, may make the product fundamentally different from *sukuk,*[47] and given that debts are not deemed proprietary under the sharia, they are not legally permissible securities.[48] The key distinction, therefore, between Islamic finance and conventional finance is *not* whether the finance is asset backed or not but rather that Islamic finance does not yet recognise debt rights (receivables) as proprietary whilst conventional finance does. This distinction is discussed in detail in chapter 6.

3.6 The four *madhahibs* (schools) of Islamic jurisprudence
In chapters on *gharar, riba and bay al dayn*, where relevant, I refer to views of the four schools of Sunni Islamic jurisprudence: Hanafi, Shafie, Maliki and Hanbali. This is done to present the current positions pertaining the validity (or invalidity) of the issue in discussion. It is important, therefore, that a brief explanation of the background of the four schools is given.

Before that, however, it is important to note the distinction between the primary sources of the sharia (Divine law) and *Fiqh* (man-made jurisprudence). The sharia comprises the *Quran* and the *sunna* while *Fiqh* derives from the secondary sources: *Ijma* (consensus) of the Muslim community on an issue, *Qiyas* (analogical deduction), *Ijtihad* (independent reasoning),

Urf (customs and practices of the people) *Maslaha/Istislah* (social welfare and equity). The jurisprudence of the four schools fall under the category of derived man-made law and hence is not divine law or immutable in nature. Only the primary sources of the sharia – *Quran* and *sunna* – are immutable and accordingly will be given the most focus and weight in this book. Where I refer to the *Fiqh*/scholastic opinions and differences, I do so mainly to highlight the current position on the issue and practice under discussion as well as to provide a platform to bounce off in offering an alternative theory of application today that is in line with the spirit of the sharia. This methodology is, in fact, in line with that of Abu Hanifa himself whose school and followers were dubbed *Ahl al Rai* (people of independent opinion) whilst the other three schools were dubbed *Ahl al Sunna* (people of the tradition). The Abu Hanifa school is the oldest of the four schools and often the most progressive and facilitative of social welfare, as we shall see.

These four main schools (and many others existed then as do now) were born partly out of lack of agreement on the application of the teachings of the *Quran* and the recorded Hadith to the issues and circumstances of daily life. Not everyone felt capable of extrapolating for themselves from the primary sources on how to address the issues and circumstances they faced in daily life and, therefore, gradually, people gave their allegiance to courageous insightful individuals who were willing to put themselves to the task. Historically, the adherence to the four main (and other) schools were attributable to a dynastic order that sought to quell disagreement, and the consequent unrest it could give rise to, by creating uniformity and conformity in matters of faith that would be controlled by the state to the best possible extent (the degree of extent has differed across the ages). This happened during the period of the Mongol rulers (1220–1500) who were powerful enough to put constraints on the *ulama* (scholars) and civilian population on matters of faith – who had previously enjoyed much freedom in matters of faith in daily life.

Consequently, the *ulama* could no longer use their own independent judgement (*ijtihad*) in creative legislation and it was said that 'the gates of ijtihad were shut'. Henceforth, Muslims were obliged to conform to the rulings of past authorities. The sharia, in principle, had become a system of established rules, which could not jeopardise the more dynamic dynastic law of the ruling house. The Mongol irruption into Muslim life had been traumatic[49].

Today it is said that adherence to these schools preserves the unity of Muslims by preventing too many scattered and weak opinions, or impostors from claiming to be *mujtahids* (qualified persons to engage in independent reasoning). Yet it is acknowledged that the differences of opinion between these schools exist for purposes of plurality and is in line with the general principle of permissibility. There is no 'right' or 'wrong' answer to many of the issues and each of the four schools is accepted as equally valid. One, there-fore, may adhere to the opinion/s of any school on any matter and, other-wise, may even choose to exercise one's own reasoning, based on the *Quran* and *sunna*, on which course of action to follow. The four Sunni schools do, however, represent the generally accepted Sunni authority for Islamic (man-made) jurisprudence. They differ mainly in their methodology of extrapo-lating laws from the sharia sources. The Hanafi school is most distinguished among the four schools in that Abu Hanifa, founder of the Hanafi Schools resorted more to independent reasoning (*Qiyas*) after referring to the *Quran* and *sunna* than any other of the other sources of *Fiqh*.

Conclusion

This chapter set out, in brief, the principles of Islamic finance in an effort to inform the structure and ensuing paragraphs of this book. Chapters 4, 5 and 6 all flow from the concepts outlined above and chapter 8 looks at the structuring of a securitisation to be compatible with both the sharia and conventional finance. In doing so, the chapter will identify the diffi-culties that are faced and issues that arise, offering alternative applications and suggestions for reform with the intention of facilitating the take-off of securitisation transactions in Islamic finance. The emphasis, however, in every chapter that follows, is in compliance with the principles and spirit of the *Quran* and *sunna*, not the current views or practices of the Islamic finance industry.

4

GHARAR IN ISLAMIC LAW

It is normal for transactions, especially commercial transactions,[1] to possess
a level of uncertainty or risk, of which, securitisations (the focus of this
book) is no exception. Islamic law of transactions states, however, that
gharar (loosely translated as uncertainty or speculative risk) is prohibited in
commercial transactions. Of course, given the prohibition of *gharar* is not
a decree of the *Quran* but a product of human ratiocination, disputes arise
as to the precise meaning, application and effect of *gharar*. This chapter,
therefore, considers the following issues: (i) what is *gharar*, (ii) what is its
raison d'être or purpose, (iii) what effect does it have on Islamic contracts
and structured finance, (iv) is *gharar* evidential or conceptual in nature, and
(v) how does the contextual formulation of the rules on *gharar* affect application of the principle today?

These issues concern securitisation structures directly because the lack of
contractual certainty or knowledge threatens the validity of a securitisation
depending on the approach taken towards, and application of, *gharar*.

A comparison with the common law is undertaken for purposes of drawing
lessons or useful points of reference from the concept of certainty of terms
as a fundamental element of contract formation. For want of a single word
that succinctly describes *gharar*, I retain usage of the Arabic term.

4.1 Origins of the prohibition

The prohibition of *gharar* in Islamic contracts is derived from the *Quran* and
the *Quran* (sayings) of Muhammad. The *Quran* does not expressly prohibit
gharar but speaks instead of the ills of gambling to which *gharar* contracts
are deemed akin.[2] This is a significant clue in determining the nature of
gharar since we know that *gharar* is that which is so uncertain or speculative
as to render the contract akin to gambling. By determining the nature of a
gambling contract, one may thus, gain insight into the nature of *gharar*.

The verse of the *Quran* from which the prohibition of *gharar* is derived is *Al- Maidah:* 90. It states: 'O ye who believe! Intoxicants and gambling, stones and arrows, are an abomination of Satan's handwork: eschew such that ye may prosper'. Muhammad is reported to have issued categorical statements expressly prohibiting transactions tainted by *gharar*.[3] The most commonly cited of these statements are:

The Prophet forbade the pebble sale (sale of an object selected by throwing of a pebble) and the *gharar* sale.[4]

Whoever *buys* foodstuffs let him not *sell* them until he has possession of them.[5] (emphasis added)

He who sells food shall not sell it until he weighs it.[6]

The Prophet forbade the sale of grapes until they become black and the sale of grain until it is strong[7].

The Prophet forbade the sale of a runaway slave or animal, the sale of a bird in the air or fish in the sea, the sale of what the vendor is not able to deliver, or the unborn when the mother is not part of the transaction and milk in the udder.

The last statement above has been has been given considerable weight by sharia scholars and is interpreted as having three juristic consequences[8]: (i) a *gharar* sale is prohibited, (ii) such prohibition is total and extends to all transactions that qualify as a *'gharar* sale', and (iii) the effect of the prohibition is that a *gharar* sale is void.

Careful consideration of the above statements indicates caution extended to the seller for purposes of adhering to the principle of contractual fairness that we set out in chapter one as the underlying principle of contract and commerce. In contrast to the *caveat emptor* principle under the common law, Muhammad seems to shift the burden onto the seller to act fairly (perhaps in light of the seller's stronger bargaining power and control over the transaction in sixth- to seventh-century AD context). The statements also indicate that *gharar* sales involve a certain type of risk or uncertainty that is not readily dispelled by evidence or inspection on the part of the buyer either because the seller is in sole possession of the information required to create certainty or because of the future nature of the subject matter of the sale which renders it out of reasonable control of both parties therefore making the transaction speculative.

Given the categorical prohibition of *gharar* that has been interpreted as nullifying a *'gharar* sale',[9] yet acknowledging the fact that Islam makes allowance for both risk and/or uncertainty in a contract, it is vital that the definition of both *gharar* and *'gharar* sale' be clarified.

4.2 Defining *gharar* and the '*gharar* sale'

Gharar literally means risk or hazard and is derived from the root concept *gha-rra* meaning deception.[10] *Taghreer*, the verbal noun of *gharar*, means to *unknowingly* expose one's property to jeopardy.[11] Accordingly, *Fiqh* (Islamic jurisprudence) scholars have also defined *gharar* as ignorance[12] or the lack of knowledge pertaining to the material attributes of the terms, the subject matter of a sale, as well as the availability and existence thereof.[13] Ibn Rushd, on the other hand, defines *gharar* as the inequality in bargaining power that arises from ignorance (*jahl*) or lack of knowledge pertaining to an aspect, quality, subject matter or feature of the contract.[14] Thus, to Ibn Rushd, *gharar* is the *effect* of inequality of bargaining power rather than a condition of lack of knowledge. More recently, El-Gamal suggests that *gharar* generally encompasses some forms of incomplete information and/or deception, as well as risk and uncertainty *intrinsic* to the objects of contract[15] (emphasis added). He adds that, '*gharar* incorporates uncertainty regarding future events and qualities of goods, and it may be the result of a one-sided or two-sided and intentional or unintentional incomplete information'[16].

Indeed, few scholars have felt the need to define *gharar* or outline its ambit precisely. Whilst this suggests that *gharar* is a concept that does not attach to any defined circumstance or transaction, the lack of precise ambit or definition contributes to the controversy over the effect it has on present-day transactions in Islamic finance.

Consequently, Muslim scholars have described the '*gharar* sale' in the following ways, by derivation from the above cited sayings of Muhammad:[17]

1 *Pure speculation.* These are transactions akin to gambling and are exemplified by the 'pebble sale', that is, where one agrees to purchase whatever item hit by throwing a pebble at several items.
2 *Uncertain outcome.* These are transactions where the counter value is of not only uncertain value and/or specification but may not be realised at all, for instance, the sale of the fish in the sea, the bird in the air or the runaway slave. It is opined that the sale of goods not yet in one's possession falls into this category[18]. Risk seems greater in this category but it is less essential to the transaction and may be cured by making the sale conditional on the elimination of the relevant risk, for example, the fish being caught.[19] Among those who define *gharar* as uncertainty of subject matter is Ibn Abidin.[20]
3 *Unknown future benefit.* In such transactions, though beneficial to the purchaser, materialisation of the object of sale in the future remains

unknown. Such transactions could be deemed tainted by the characteristics of gambling especially if, for instance, the buyer optimistically paid
what later materialises to be an excessive price for a harvest, catch of fish,
etc. Such transactions are deemed void unless the contract is, or becomes,
customary and occurs between informed parties therefore becoming
innocuous and perhaps indispensable to society. This curability through
customs (*urf*) and need (*hajat*) indicates the curable nature of *gharar* as
well as it being a consumer protection means to an end of social welfare
(*maslaha*). Among those who describe *gharar* as the unknown future
consequence of a contract is Sarakhsi.[21]

4 *In-exactitude.* These transactions possess the least element of gambling
(exemplified by the warning not to sell until the item/s have been
weighed). Such sales may involve the deliberate blinding of one's self
to risks in transactions like selling by the pound or the exchange of one
heap of goods for another without measuring either.

5 *Non-existent subject matter.* In such transactions, the vendor is not in a
position to hand over to the buyer the subject matter because it does
not exist. Some scholars like Ibn al Qayyim[22] have given non-existence a
restrictive meaning, that is, the inability to hand over the subject to the
buyer whether it exists or not and regardless of whether it will come into
existence in the future. However, the validation of the pre-paid contract
of agriculture (*salam*) and manufacture (*istisna*) as a consequence of
social evolution and need is an indication that contractual ambit and
permissibility evolves with time and that social need may facilitate an
otherwise invalid contract becoming valid.

6 *Ignorance as to material terms.* Al-Sanhuri defines *gharar* sale as a contract
lacking in information of its material terms. Accordingly, a *gharar* sale
would take place in circumstances of:[23]

- doubt as to the existence of the subject matter;
- if the subject matter does exists, doubt as to the seller's ability to
  hand it over;
- where a lack of knowledge affects the identification of the genus or
  species of subject matter;
- where the quantity or identity of the subject matter (or the necessary
  conditions) of the contract are affected;
- in contracts of future performance.[24]

Note that, unlike Ibn Rushd who considers *gharar* as the inequality that
arises from a contracting party's lack of knowledge, Al-Sanhuri implies that
the lack of knowledge itself is *gharar*. Al-Sanhuri's view is supported by Ibn

Juzzay who lists ten cases of 'lack of knowledge' which in his view constitute the 'forbidden *gharar*' which in turn implies that *gharar* is of the 'forbidden' and 'permissible' type.[25] This distinction between permissible and prohibited *gharar* points to the fact that only *gharar* of the 'forbidden' kind is of vitiating effect. Thus, Al-Baji Al-Andalusi[26] noted that:

> the prohibition of *gharar* sales render such sales defective. The meaning of '*gharar* sale' … is any sale in which *gharar* is the major component. This is the type of sale justifiably characterised as a *gharar* sale and it is unanimously forbidden. However, minor *gharar* would not render a sales contract defective, since no contract can be entirely free of *gharar*.

From the distinction that Al-Baji draws between the effect of 'major' *gharar* on a transaction (forbidden) and 'minor' *gharar* (ineffective) it is clear that the effect of *gharar* on a transaction justifiably characterised as a '*gharar* sale' is to render it void. However, a *gharar* sale is only that which is majorly tainted by *gharar*. This makes allowance for contracts to be tainted by a degree of *gharar* without having a vitiating effect unless such *gharar* is a major component thereof. Mansuri expresses the same view in different words by classifying *gharar* transactions as 'irregular' (*fasid*) instead of valid (*sahih*) or void (*batil*). He describes an irregular transaction as one whose elements (offer and acceptance) are complete and all the essential conditions are complete but an external attribute attached to the contract has been prohibited.[27] Mansuri's approach designates all *gharar* tainted contracts as irregular until they are confirmed as void or valid which indicates an evidential, as opposed to a conceptual, nature of *gharar*.[28]

How then does one determine whether *gharar* forms a 'major component' of a contract so as to render it forbidden? Al-Dhareer lays down four criteria as comprising, what he describes as, excessive *gharar*:[29]

- It should be excessive.
- The contract is a one of exchange/commercial (non-gratuitous).
- The object of the contract is the principle item afflicted by *gharar*.
- There is no *need* compelling the conclusion of the contract.

If *any* of the above four criteria is missing then *gharar* has no vitiating effect on the contract and the contract retains validity.

It is pertinent to note the distinction between *gharar*, which renders a contract defective, and the *gharar* sale, which renders the contract void.

Until the *gharar* in a contract is deemed major enough to designate the transaction as '*gharar* sale', the contract is merely voidable pending determination of whether the transaction is tainted to the extent as to render it void.[30] To this, Professor Mustafa Al-Zarqa provides further assistance in clarifying the deciphering criteria through his definition of the (forbidden) '*gharar* sale' as that 'of probable items whose existence or characteristics are not certain, the risky nature of which makes the transaction akin to gambling'.[31] The gold in Zarqa's definition is that it ties down the risky/speculative/uncertain elements of the forbidden *gharar* sale to gambling. It follows therefore that an uncertain, speculative or future transaction not akin to gambling does not fall within the ambit of the forbidden *gharar* sale and retains validity. The definition also gives implied recognition to the fact that complete contract language is impossible and some measure of risk and uncertainty is inevitable in contractual dealings.

The pertinent points to note from the above definitions and explanations are:

- *Gharar* is of degree, the prohibited type being 'major' or that akin to gambling.
- Only *Gharar* major enough to designate a transaction as '*gharar* sale' renders the contract void.
- The vitiating effect of 'major' *gharar* can nonetheless be cured by removing the conditions causing it.

Most important of all, however, even after reviewing the varied definitions and descriptions of *gharar* and the *gharar* sale, is recognising the fact that *gharar* is neither a type of transaction nor does the prohibition pertain particularly to risk or knowledge or the requirement of contractual certainty, etc. Rather, the prohibition of *gharar* pertains to the ensuing *effect* of a transaction that characterises it as a *gharar* sale on the basis of being 'akin to gambling'. The effect is inequity between the parties yet the available literature focuses on the rules and not what the rules set out to attain or the mischief they seek to address. Muhammad sought simply to foster contractual equity between trading parties through the prohibition of *gharar*.

4.3 The principle behind the prohibition of *gharar*

In the previous section we considered that the concept of *gharar* contracts derives from the Quranic prohibition of gambling[32] and that, read in this light, Muhammad's statements indicate an aversion to (potential or actual) inequitable bargains, whether caused by the vendor's inability to deliver, the non-existence or the unknown characteristics of the subject matter, the unknown date or future performance of the contract, etc., all of which (may) render the transaction detrimental or deceptive in nature.[33] We noted also that the outright prohibition derived from Muhammad's statements pertains to partaking in what is described as 'gharar sale' which scholars have defined as a sale comprising an excessive element of gharar and all such sales are void. What follows, therefore, is an inquiry into the principle behind the prohibition.

Nabil Saleh[34] proposed that the raison d'être behind the prohibition against gharar is the prevention of detriment to the parties involved in the transaction.[35] 'Detriment' can be read as inequity effected as he goes on to explain that Muhammad prohibited gharar because he recognised the inequality in bargaining power of the traders over the buyers, plus their superiority of knowledge (of products and markets) and experience, and, therefore, sought to protect the weaker parties from deception. Over time, he notes, scholastic reasoning was oversimplified to the extent that non-existence of the subject matter was improperly considered a sufficient and even sole reason for nullifying the transaction without further inquiry into whether it was deceptive.[36] The renowned scholar, Ibn al-Qayyim al Jawziyyah,[37] long since denounced this confusion in his treatises[38] that

> there is no mention in the book of Allah or in the Sunna or in the Tradition of the companions that the sale of what is non-existent is prohibited ... the motive[39] behind the prohibition is not the existence or non-existence, but ... the sale producing gharar and what the vendor is not in a position to deliver, whether or not it exists. (emphasis added)

In light of the primary sources and juristic opinions considered above, this book proffers that the concept of gharar has likewise been unjustifiably been reduced to 'uncertainty', just as it was once reduced to 'non-existence' of the subject matter, while ignoring the fact that the prohibition pertains to the much broader principle: that of contractual fairness in aim of attaining equity (maslaha) in commercial transactions and preventing detriment (sad al dhira'a) to contracting parties.[40] There seems to be no literature expressly describing gharar as a prohibition against striking inequitable bargains but my study and understanding of the Quranic text and the sayings of Muhammad has lead me to this conclusion. El-Gamal indirectly supports this conclusion by noting that the factor common to all the categories of gharar expounded by Muslim scholars is, 'the possibility of unanticipated loss to at least one party may be a form of gambling or may lead to ex-post disputation between contracting parties'. He says, therefore, that 'The prohibition of *bay al gharar* (the *gharar* sale) may thus be seen as a prohibition of unbundled and unnecessary sale of risk'.

4.4 The effect of *gharar* and the differing opinions within Islamic jurisprudence

Although the general categorisations of *gharar* (minor and major) and the effect on a transaction imputed by *gharar* have been discussed here, further categorisation and consequent effect of *gharar* in current Islamic finance circles is still based, variably, on the differing opinions of each (of the four) school of Islamic jurisprudence regarding contractual certainty and knowledge.[41]

According to al-Dhareer, whose seminal work is the most referred to in all current literature on *gharar*, jurisprudents divide the effect of *gharar* on contracts into two: *gharar* in the essence of the contract and *gharar* in the subject matter.[42] In a nutshell, *gharar* in the essence of [a] contract renders the contract void whereas *gharar* pertaining to the subject matter renders the contract voidable. However, whether pertaining to the essence or the subject matter, the premise remains that it is only excessive or major *gharar* that is of effect; minor *gharar* is inconsequential.

Thus, whereas a *gharar* sale affecting the essence of a contract is void, difference of opinion arises only as to whether the primary source of the sharia (i.e. the statement/s of Muhammad) actually prohibits a particular type of transaction or not. For instance, the *Arbun*[43] (advance-payment) sale is reported to have been prohibited by one statement of Muhammad and permitted by another statement of Muhammad. Those who accept the prohibitory statement deem all *arbun* sales void *ab initio* while those who accept the statement permitting the *arbun* sale deem it valid.[44] Alternatively, a *mu'allaq* (conditional) sale upon the occurrence of an uncertain event, for example, 'I sell you this house of mine if X sells me his' is deemed void *ab initio* by a majority of the jurists.[45] Ibn Taymiyya and Ibn al-Qayyim, both prominent Hanbali jurists allow the above type of conditional sale on the basis that there is no *gharar* in it. Note, the dissenting jurists allow the *mu'allaq* sale because they do not deem it a *gharar* sale; distinct from deeming *gharar* imputed in the transaction yet validating the transaction anyway. Presumably, had they, too, deemed *gharar* present in the contract, the conclusion would have been the same – that the transaction is void *ab initio* given that the prohibited degree of *gharar* taints the essence of the contract.

On the other hand, where *gharar* is imputed in the subject matter, the disagreement between scholars pertains not to whether the transaction is prohibited but as to whether such *gharar* is curable or not. For instance, want of knowledge or ignorance regarding the genus is said to be the most exorbitant kind of *gharar* afflicting the subject matter because it includes ignorance of the entity, type and attributes of the object.[46] Most Muslim jurisprudents are thus of the opinion that knowledge of the genus of the subject matter being sold is a condition precedent to the validity of the contract and a contract without the requisite knowledge of the subject matter is prohibited.[47] However, a view within the Maliki[48] school of jurisprudence permits the sale of an object of unknown genus on the condition that the buyer reserves the option of inspection (khiyar-al-ru'ya) through a stipulation in the contract.[49] According to this view, an option of inspection cures the potentially deceptive character that the contract otherwise assumes and which serves the objective behind the prohibition of *gharar* – equity. Similarly, the Hanafi school of jurisprudence permits the sale of a yet unknown subject matter on the basis that the buyer (in their view) always has the right to repudiate the sale once he is in a position to inspect the object without having to stipulate this right in the contract (akin to an implied term that the subject matter will match the agreed description and/or be fit for purpose). Therefore, the Hanafi school validates the contract of sale in which the genus of the object is unknown regardless of whether or not the contract makes explicit reference to the option of inspection because the guaranteed right to repudiate the contract serves to protect the buyer from deception (hence curing *gharar*).[50] The Maliki and Hanafi approach are both pragmatic and aligned to current contractual contexts.

4.5 *Gharar*: conceptual or evidential?

The 'conceptual' and 'evidential' distinction derives from common law considerations of sufficiency of certainty in cases relating to the law of trusts. The leading case in this regard is *McPhail v Doulton*[51] which concerned the validity of a trust created 'by deed dated 17 July 1941 and through which a fund was established for the benefit of officers and employees, etc. of a company'. The House of Lords held that:

> [T]he test to be applied to ascertain the validity of the trust ought to be similar to that accepted in *Re Gulbenkian's Settlement Trusts*.'

In *Re Gulbenkian's Settlement Trusts*, a case concerning a determination of certainty of object of a trust fund, the House of Lords, per Lord Upjohn, observed that:

Suppose the donor directs that a fund be divided equally between 'my old friends', then unless there is some admissible evidence that the donor has given some special 'dictionary' meaning to that phrase which enables the trustees to identify the class with sufficient certainty, it is plainly bad as being too uncertain.

The principle is, in my opinion, that the donor must make his intention sufficiently plain as to the objects of his trust and the court cannot give effect to it by misinterpreting his intentions by dividing the fund merely among those present. Secondly, and perhaps it is the most hallowed principle, the Court of Chancery, which acts in default of trustees, must know with sufficient certainty the objects of the beneficence of the donor so as to execute the trust ... So if the class is insufficiently defined the donor's intentions must in such cases fail for uncertainty.[52]

The implication of *McPhail* and *Re Gulbenkian's* is that unless the uncertainty in question is capable of ascertainment by admissible evidence, the underlying trust or contract must fail for uncertainty. If ascertainable, then the trust or contract is valid and the fact that it is capable of admitting admissible evidence makes it evidential in nature and, thus, curable. If unascertainable by admissible evidence, the uncertainty in question is conceptual and the trust or contract is void *ab initio*. Stated otherwise, conceptual uncertainty is that which, by its very nature, is incapable of ascertainment and thus no amount of evidence rendered is of any use for purposes of creating certainty. For example, if the very concept of life is uncertain, no amount of evidence can possibly help ascertain whether abortion, at any or all stages, is murder. Once the concept of life is clear, then evidence as to which trimester it took place in, whether intentional or not, whether defences such as danger to the mother's life or necessity are applicable, etc., all become admissible to ascertain the question of murder. The same is the case in contract law; as long as the concept of certainty itself remains unclear, no amount of evidence can ascertain the existence of 'sufficient certainty' for purposes of determining whether a valid contract was created. Alternatively, if the concept of intention to create legal relations is unclear, no amount of evidence could ascertain 'meeting of the minds' because it is uncertain what intending to create legal relations 'looks like'. In any case, for the minds to have 'met' thus forming a contract, the concepts underpinning a contract must be clear which probably explains why conceptual uncertainty results in the contract been deemed never to have been formed.

By analogy, if the very concept of *gharar* is uncertain then the uncertainty in question is conceptual and no amount of evidence as to the terms or aspects of the contract will provide sufficient certainty. The question, therefore, is whether the propounded rules of *gharar* in Islamic contracts and commercial transactions pertain to conceptual or evidential uncertainty.

Gharar, as a concept, is conceptual in nature. By this it is meant that if the very concept of *gharar* is uncertain, then no amount of admissible evidence can be adduced to ascertain the uncertainty in the contract. Once the concept of *gharar* is clear, then *gharar* imputed in the contract is ascertainable by admissible evidence and is, thus, evidential in nature. We also know, from the delineation and discussion in section 4.4 that the '*gharar* sale' is of two types: (i) g*harar* imputed in the essence of a contract rendering it void (such *gharar* can be said to be conceptual since it is by nature incurable by admissible evidence); and (ii) *gharar* imputed to the subject matter of the contract rendering it voidable (and curable). G*harar* imputed in the subject matter is thus evidential.

The significance of identifying and establishing the distinction between the evidential and conceptual aspect of *gharar* is, thus, of great magnitude. It clarifies the effect *gharar* has on contracts and it indicates that the prohibition against *gharar* in contracts is, partially, merely a means of preventing inequitable transactions akin to gambling as originally expressed in the *Quran*. As far as evidential *gharar* is concerned, it shifts the focus from vitiation of transactions imputed with excessive *gharar* to developing definitive processes and criteria of determining what amounts to excessive *gharar* and how best, if possible, to cure transactions of its effect. Accordingly, the *raison d'être* behind *gharar* – encouraging equitable transactions – can be interpreted to permit a necessary measure of uncertainty in contracts regardless of whether it pertains to non-existence or precise knowledge of the subject matter for purposes of commercial expedience and facilitating progress. This affects the future and development of Islamic finance in the global context by creating room for both flexibility and creativity in structuring securitisation and other financial transactions. The tendency of treating *gharar* as outright conceptual has to date only brought us to a position of rigidity and arbitrage in a financial context demanding rapid development.

4.6 Certainty under English common law: conceptual or evidential?

Certainty of terms is a fundamental element of the valid formation of a contract under English common law and, thus, a central aspect thereof. Insufficient certainty of terms could render a contract unenforceable[53] and the courts have experienced considerable difficulty in determining whether a contract has been expressed in *sufficiently*[54] certain terms to be enforced.[55] Emphasis is added to the word sufficiently because the concept of certainty is not an absolute one, as illustrated by the cases discussing it.[56] A contract is only deemed invalid or unenforceable if its term/s is/are so vague or uncertain as to deem an agreement between the parties to be impossible.[57]

A parallel can be drawn between the requirement that *gharar* be excessive or 'major' so as to render a transaction void and a contract being so vague as to fail to give rise to a contract.[58] Further, as shall be discussed below, the nature of the transaction (whether commercial or social) is pivotal in determining the legal nature and enforceability of the transaction as well as the approach courts take towards interpreting a contract. Often, a non-commercial transaction will not trigger the issue of legal certainty as the very nature of the transaction negates an intention to be legally bound.[59]

The issue of whether a general principle of good faith exists is a good example of conceptual uncertainty since unless the parties explicitly stipulate its application with sufficient certainty as to what that duty entails, a contract to be negotiated in 'good faith' would fail because the court cannot be certain what 'good faith' is or amounts to and no amount of admissible evidence could cure that uncertainty. A discussion of the 'principle of good faith' is beyond the bounds of this chapter but suffice it to say that the denial of the English courts of its existence is based primarily on the lack of sufficient certainty upon which to determine the discharge of 'good faith' obligations.[60]

I shall not delve into what amounts to sufficient, and what does not, under the common law but rather turn to consider the almost century long debate on whether a lack of sufficient certainty renders the transaction void *ab initio* (unenforceable) or merely voidable (remediable and enforceable).[61] In doing so, I also examine whether the concept of certainty of terms under English common law is conceptual or evidential in nature.

In theory, the enquiry into whether sufficient certainty exists commences from the premise that it is for the parties to make their agreement and ensure that the terms are sufficiently certain to be enforced.[62] Therefore, whilst the courts are hesitant to appear to be making contracts for the parties, they are nonetheless reluctant to deny legal effect of agreements.[63] In practice, therefore, the courts are slow to vitiate contracts and will instead seek to balance the need for contractual certainty with the general principle that it is for the parties to make their agreement, avoiding a situation where contracting parties use allegations of uncertainty to escape bad bargains, especially where the allegedly uncertain agreement has been (partially or fully) performed. Based on the facts of the case, the courts may, therefore, rescue the agreement if some objective evidence is available to fill the gaps.[64] Such cases indicate the evidential nature of the certainty of terms requirement because, as explained in section 4.5 and as indicated in both *McPhail v Doulton* and *Re Gulbenkian Trust*, if the uncertainty in question is incapable of admitting (admissible) evidence for purposes of ascertaining the uncertainty in question, then, by definition, the uncertainty is conceptual and the trust (or contract in the context of securitisation) must fail for uncertainty.

Cursorily, a similarity may be drawn between Islamic law's delineation between *gharar* imputed in the essence and the subject matter of the contract, on the one hand, and the common law delineation between incomplete and uncertain agreements.[65] The Islamic law position is discussed in section 4.4. Under the common law, incomplete agreements are, in some fundamental way, contingent upon a further occurrence and do not, as a general rule, form valid agreements. They may take the form of an agreement to agree aka 'a contract to make a contract'[66] or one upon which terms its operation depend are yet to be determined at the time of making the agreement.[67] Uncertain agreements, on the other hand, are apparently complete agreements but lack sufficient certainty of terms (e.g. determination of price or subject matter) that may or may not render the agreement invalid, depending on whether sufficient certainty is established.[68]

English cases pertaining to the determination of certainty of terms, traditionally, fall into two categories: those that decided that the contract was too vague or uncertain to be enforceable and those that deemed the contract valid and enforceable despite the contractual uncertainty alleged. No discerning explanation or criteria has, to date, been deciphered as to how the courts reach either of the two conclusions or how the judges determine which of the two competing views to adopt so as to fall within either of the two categories.[69] My contribution in this regard, after due consideration of the main common law cases on certainty of terms, is to offer the 'conceptual' and 'evidential' distinctions as discerning approaches the courts seem to have latently adopted in deciding the cases before them.

The first case to consider is the House of Lords case of *May & Butcher v King* [70] which is the leading, though not the first to be decided, case on certainty of terms and falls in the traditional category of 'contracts deemed too uncertain to be enforced'. The brief facts are that May & Butcher Ltd, the suppliants[71] (referred to in the judgement as appellants), alleged that they had concluded a contract with the Controller of Disposals Board under which they agreed to buy the whole tentage which might become available in the United Kingdom for disposal up to 31 March 1923. On 29 June 1921, the controller wrote to the suppliants to 'confirm the sale to you of

the whole of the old tentage which may become available ... up to and
including December 31, 1921' and proceeded to set out the terms of the
agreement. The contractual clause in contention stated that:

> (3) The price to be paid, and the date or dates on which payment is
> to be made by the purchasers to the Commission for such old tentage
> shall be agreed upon from time to time between the Commission and
> the purchasers as the quantities of the said old tentage become available
> for disposal, and are offered to the purchasers by the Commission.

In a second letter, dated 7 January 1922, the Controller of Disposals
confirmed the sale to the suppliants of the old tentage that might become
available for disposal up to 31 March 1923. This letter, which varied the
earlier terms in certain respects, stated with regard to the above quoted
clause that 'the prices to be agreed upon between the Commission and the
purchasers in accordance with the terms of clause (iii) of the said earlier
contract shall include delivery free on rail ... nearest to the depots at which
the said tentage'.[72]
On August 1922, after the suppliants had made proposals to purchase
tentage that were not acceptable to the Controller, the Disposals Board
wrote to the suppliants and stated that they considered themselves no longer
bound by the agreement. The suppliants then filed their petition of right
which was dismissed by the House of Lords.[73]
The central issue in the case, per Lord Buckmuster, was whether or not
the terms of the contract were sufficiently defined to constitute a legally
binding contract. The Crown alleged that the price was never agreed and the
appellants alleged that if the price was not agreed then it would be a reasonable price and, moreover, the arbitration clause in the contract was intended
to cover this very question of price. In reaching the decision that a contract
was never concluded between the parties and, therefore, the alleged contract
was unenforceable, Lord Buckmuster remarked:[74]

> [T]he only points that arise for determination are these: Whether or
> not the terms of the contract were sufficiently defined to constitute a
> legal binding bargain between the parties in one of three respects. The
> Crown says, in the first place, that the price was never agreed. The
> appellants say that, if it was not agreed, then, according to the proper
> law applicable, it would be a reasonable price; and secondly they say
> that, even if the price was not agreed and it is not fair to assume that,
> therefore, a reasonable price was intended, the arbitration clause in the

contract was intended to cover this very question of price, and that, consequently, the reasonableness of the price was referred to arbitration under the contract ...

Those being the contentions, it is obvious that the whole matter depends on regarding the actual words of the bargain itself. In the first place, the contract is contained in the form of a letter.

What resulted was this: It was impossible to agree the prices, and, unless the appellants are in a position to establish either that this failure to agree resulted in a definite agreement to buy at a reasonable price, or that the price had become subject to arbitration, it is plain on the first two points which have been mentioned that this appeal must fail.

In my opinion, there never was a concluded contract between the parties in this case at all. It has been a well-recognised principle of contract law for many years that an agreement between two parties to enter into an agreement by which some critical part of the contract matter is left to be determined is no contract at all. It is, of course, perfectly possible for two people to contract that they will sign a document which contains all the relevant terms, but it is not open to people to agree that they will in the future agree on a matter which, vital to the arrangement between them, has not yet been determined.[75]

Several points may be noted from the case of *May & Butcher* that prove helpful in the discussion. First, the contract is presumably commercial in nature as it was couched in commercial verbiage and it contained an arbitration clause which, in the early twentieth century, was a feature almost exclusively of commercial contracts. Second, the facts of the case reveal no trading history between the two parties. Third, though the parties did provide a mechanism (arbitration) to resolve any disagreement as to the price (term in contention), the arbitration clause was *part of* the contract, and given the Courts conclusion that no contract was formed to begin with, such arbitration clauses could not kick in to resolve the dispute. Apparently, therefore, the House of Lords adopted a conceptual approach to the issue of certainty (as per the description in section 4.5) and, accordingly, sought to establish certainty of the price term solely from what the parties had already made provision for in the contractual term since no recourse to any external evidence or machinery could, according to the House of Lords, resolve the uncertainty alleged. These factors become more relevant as we consider the other cases.

The conceptual uncertainty in *May & Butcher* pertains to the concept of an 'agreement to agree' and no amount of admissible evidence could cure the contract of its uncertainty as the price was determinable by the parties' agreement in the future. Conceptually, that was impossible to ascertain in the present and the contract had to fail. Lord Ackner in *Walford v Miles*[76] expressed it succinctly as follows:

> The reason why an agreement to negotiate, like an agreement to agree, is unenforceable is simply because it lacks the necessary certainty. The same does not apply to an agreement to use best endeavours. This uncertainty is demonstrated in the instant case by the provision which it is said has to be implied in the agreement for the determination of the negotiations. How can a court be expected to decide whether, subjectively, a proper reason existed for the termination of negotiations? The answer suggested depends upon whether the negotiations have been determined 'in good faith'. However, the concept of a duty to carry on negotiations in good faith is inherently repugnant to the adversarial position of the parties when involved in negotiations. Each party to the negotiations is entitled to pursue his (or her) own interest, so long as he avoids making misrepresentations.
>
> Thus, given the very concept of negotiating in good faith, like the concept of an agreement to agree, is uncertain, any contract to negotiate in good faith or to agree, *must fail for conceptual uncertainty*. (emphasis added)

The second case to discuss is a House of Lords case that arrived at a conclusion in line with *May & Butcher*, that is, that no agreement was formed due to a lack of sufficient certainty. The case is that of *Scammell & Nephew v Ouston*[77] where it was held that an agreement to acquire goods on hire purchase was too vague since there were many kinds of hire-purchase agreements in widely different terms, so that it was impossible to specify the terms on which the parties had agreed.

The facts are, briefly, that D wrote to P and offered to sell them a Commer van for £268, allowing for £100 out of the £268 to be paid by taking P's Bedford van in part exchange. The next day D wrote to P asking them to place an official order for the van, which P did 'on the understanding that the balance of the purchase price can be had on hire-purchase terms over a period of 2 years'. The relationship thereafter deteriorated principally due to a disagreement over the condition of the Bedford van that resulted in D refusing to take it in part exchange, as earlier agreed. P claimed that the refusal amounted to a breach of contract and brought a claim for damages. D denied liability on the basis that no contract had in fact been concluded.

The question before the court was whether the terms of the contract (specifically pertaining to contractual price and manner of payment) were sufficiently certain to have concluded a contract between the parties. If yes, then the part exchange could be enforced against D. If not, then the part exchange could not be enforceable and no damages would lie against D. The House of Lords held it was impossible to conclude that a binding agreement had been established and thus the contract was unenforceable. On the simple basis of the court's finding against a binding agreement, *Scammell* is categorised with *May & Butcher*. However, a nuance in the facts of the two cases indicates a further similarity that may have led to the same outcome in the two cases.

Viscount Maugham, delivering his judgement in *Scammell*, points out the nuance by drawing a distinction between *Scammell* and *Hillas v Arcos*. [78] He explains that *Scammell* turned on the question as to whether informal letters or like documents (non-commercial or non-legal documents) resulted in a binding agreement. Therefore, in *Scammell* unlike *Hillas v Arcos*, the facts indicated that, 'laymen unassisted by persons with legal training are not always accustomed to use words or phrases with a precise or definite meaning'.[79]

He explains that, generally:

> In order to constitute a valid contract the parties must so express themselves that their meaning can be determined with a *reasonable degree of certainty*. It is plain that unless this can be done it is impossible to hold that the contracting parties had the same intention. (emphasis is mine) ...
>
> This general rule, however, applies somewhat differently in different cases. In commercial documents connected with dealings in trade, with which the parties are perfectly familiar, the court is very willing, if satisfied that the parties thought that there may be a binding contract, to imply terms and in particular terms as to the method of carrying out the contract which it would be impossible to supply in other kinds of contract.

An analysis of the facts and judgement in *Scammell* indicated that the uncertainty pertained to the concept of 'intention to form legal relations' in a contract between lay parties. Because the concept was unclear, and there was no trading history on the facts or commercial customs that could be drawn from to clarify the concept, no amount of external evidence could ascertain whether a contract had been formed or, in other words, whether the contracting parties' minds had met. Of crucial importance was the fact that the contract was described as a sale on hire purchase – a fact that Viscount Maugham deemed a contradiction in terms. He observed that 'hire purchase offers a *mere option to purchase at completion of payment of instalments while sale passes title*' (emphasis added). Further, that the term 'hire purchase' was amenable to many forms and nuances and thus the very concept of hire purchase, on the facts of the case, was uncertainty. Consequently, the contract failed for uncertainty. Viscount Maugham observed:

> Bearing these facts in mind, what do the words 'hire-purchase terms' mean in the present case? They may indicate that the hire-purchase agreement was to be granted by the appellants, or, on the other hand, by some finance company acting in collaboration with the appellants. They may contemplate that the appellants were to receive by instalments a sum of £168 spread over a period of 2 years upon delivering the new van and receiving the old car, or, on the other hand, that the appellants were to receive from a third party a lump sum of £168, and that the third party, presumably a finance company, was to receive from the respondents a larger sum than £168, to include interest and profit spread over a period of 2 years. Moreover, nothing is said (except as to the 2-years' period) as to the terms of the hire-purchase agreement – for instance, as to the interest payable, and as to the rights of the letter, whoever he may be, in the event of default by the respondents in payment of the instalments at the due dates. As regards the last matters, there was no evidence to suggest that there are any well-known 'usual terms' in such a contract, and I think that it is common knowledge that in fact many letters, though by no means all of them, insist on terms which the legislature regards as so unfair and unconscionable that it was recently found necessary to deal with the matter in the Hire-Purchase Act 1938. These, my Lords, are very serious difficulties.

Given the conceptual difficulties faced and the lay nature of the parties, it is not difficult to understand how the court reached its decision.

The third case to look at is *Hillas v Arcos* which is in contrast to the above two cases and is the leading case in the category of cases in which the courts have held the agreement to be a valid and binding contract despite the alleged uncertainty of terms.[81] The brief facts are that A agreed to buy from R, by an agreement dated 21 May 1930, '22,000 standards of soft-wood goods of fair specification over the season 1930'. The contract was also subject to certain conditions among which was that A had the option of entering into a contract with R for the purchase of 100,000 standards of delivery during 1931 – such an option to be declared before the 1st of January 1931. A purported to exercise the option on 22 December 1930 but R had already agreed to sell the whole of the output of the 1931 season to a third party. A sued for damage for breach of contract but were met by the defence that the document of May 1931 did not constitute an enforceable agreement because it did not sufficiently describe the goods to be sold to enable their identification and, also, that it contemplated in the future some further agreement upon essential terms. The House of Lords rejected the defence and held that, the option having being exercised; the agreement was complete and binding in itself and was not dependant on any future agreement for its validity.[82]

Lord Tomlin's judgement crystallises the factual distinction between *Hillas* and *Scammell* that led to the conclusion arrived at in *Hillas*. He points out that, in *Hillas*, the parties were both intimately acquainted with the course of business in the Russian softwood timber trade, and had, without difficulty, carried out the sale and purchase of 22,000 standards under the first part of the document of 21 May 1930. Second, he pointed out that the validity of the contract in contention hinged mainly on the meaning of the phrase 'of fair specification'. This implied that if the court was able to determine, and thus resolve the meaning of such a phrase, a valid contract would have been formed. Thirdly, clause 11 of the May 1930 document demonstrated the parties' intention to be bound.

In determining the meaning of the phrase 'of fair specification', Lord Tomlin held that the document of 21 May 1930 was to be read as a whole and had regard to the admissible evidence as to the course of trade. In his opinion, the true construction of the phrase was used in connection with the 22,000 standards and meant that the 22,000 standards are to be satisfied in goods distributed over kinds, qualities and sizes in the fair proportions having regard to the output of the season 1930. That is something which, if the parties fail to agree, can be ascertained just as much as the fair value of property.[83]

The purpose of setting out the above facts and judgements is to point out the role that the context (facts) of the case plays in determining the approach the court towards the issue of sufficient certainty. In *Hillas*, the context was clearly commercial, the parties were intimately acquainted with the trade and there were previous dealings from which inferences could be drawn to establish contractual certainty. On this basis, the court was amenable to admitting external and surrounding evidence so as to establish contractual certainty and, thus, the uncertainty in question was deemed evidential in nature.

In contrast, in both *Scammell* and *May & Butcher* the parties were not 'intimately acquainted' with the trade in case. Moreover, *Scammell* was a case of laymen purporting to enter into a contractual agreement and, therefore, the court was not amenable to external evidence being adduced because of the non-commercial nature of the contract and instead focused only on the written terms of the contract. Simply stated, in commercial contexts with established customs or trading histories between the parties, there is far less likelihood that conceptual uncertainty would afflict a contract because ample means and methods are available to create the requisite level of certainty (as we shall see in section 4.6.1). The same is not true in non-commercial contexts and/or where no previous relationship existed between the parties.

Primarily, therefore, that the distinction between the decisions in *May & Butcher* and *Scammell* on the one hand and *Hillas v Arcos* on the other is not so much whether the court took a restrictive or permissive approach, respectively, to the question of certainty of terms but rather whether the court deemed the uncertainty in the particular case to be conceptual or evidential. In *May & Butcher* and *Scammell* the Court deemed the uncertainty to pertain to the concept in question (agreement to agree and hire-purchase sale/intention to create legal relations respectively) and, thus, no evidence could be adduced to cure this. In *Hillas*, on the other hand, the uncertainty pertained to the determination of price under a contract that had already been concluded in all other respects. As such, the uncertain aspect of the contract could be ascertained by admissible evidence.

Considered from the point of view that the discerning criterion is whether the court deemed the uncertainty in question to be conceptual or evidential, the decision of the House of Lords in *May & Butcher* ceases to be a legal enigma and can be safely laid to rest while the courts adopt a coherent approach in reaching decisions in the future regarding contractual certainty of terms.[84]

This coherent approach is simply that if the question of sufficient certainty pertains to conceptual uncertainty then the contract must fail unless the uncertainty can be ascertained from the agreement of the parties. This was the case in *May & Butcher* and in *Scammell*. However, if the uncertainty pertains to an aspect of an otherwise concluded contract, then the uncertainty is evidential and the contract may be cured by admissible evidence.

In final demonstration of the application of, and consequent clarity that arises from adopting, the contextual/evidential distinction, let us consider the case of *Foley v Classique Coaches Ltd*.[85] In *Foley* the contract between the parties provided that:

> The vendor shall sell to the company and the company shall purchase from the vendor all petrol which shall be required by the company for the running of their said business at a price to be agreed by the parties in writing and from time to time.

At face value, the above term indicates a lack of certainty of terms of not only the contractual price, which is to be agreed from time to time, but also the quantity of petrol to be purchased/sold. A dispute arose between the parties and among the issues in contention was whether a valid agreement existed despite the parties' failure to reach an agreement on the price at which the petrol was to be sold. The purchasers argued that the agreement was not binding based on the lack of certainty as to the (price) term. The vendors argued that it was binding, relying on the fact that the agreement in question had been relied on for three years and that the agreement contained an arbitration clause which covered the failure to agree the price of sale of petrol. The Court of Appeal decided in favour of the vendors, that is, that a valid contract had been formed despite the apparent uncertainty as to the price at which the petrol was to be sold.[86]

The contrast between the outcomes in *Foley v Classique* and *May & Butcher* could not be starker. It will be recalled that the contract in *May & Butcher* was also a commercial agreement containing an arbitration clause that was to resolve any failure to agree the contractual price yet the House of Lords deemed the arbitration clause inoperable since no contract was deemed formed to begin with. How, then, can the contrast between *May & Butcher* and *Foley* be explained? An apparent explanation seems to be that the factor influencing the Court of Appeal's approach towards the issue of certainty of terms in *Foley* (despite having two at par yet conflicting cases previously decided by the House of Lords to follow (*May & Butcher* and *Hillas*, respectively) was that the agreement in *Foley* was not only commercial but had been relied on for the past three years. There was a trading history and an established relationship between the trading parties in *Foley* that was referred to so as to impute certainty in an otherwise uncertain term. By virtue of the established trading history between the parties and, by implication, given all the concepts engaged in the contract were sufficiently certain, any uncertainty could easily be ascertained by external admissible evidence.

Finally, *Foley v Classique Coaches* crystallises the fact, as stated by Scrutton LJ, that the principles of certainty, even as enunciated by the

HOL, are not 'universal' but rather are case/context specific. It follows, therefore, that the concept of certainty under English law is neither exclusively conceptual nor evidential but rather, either conceptual or evidential depending on the context and facts of each case. The determination of whether the uncertainty pertains to an underlying concept or merely an aspect of the contract depends on the context of the contractual agreement, the nature of contractual term/s in question and the parties' trading relationship.[87]

The contrast between the two approaches, conceptual or evidential, is perhaps best expressed by the statement of Blanchard J[88] in his commentary on *May & Butcher Ltd v King*.[89] He expresses the approach taken by the House of Lords in *May & Butcher* as follows:

> *prima facie*, if something essential is left to be agreed upon by the parties at a later time, there is no binding agreement.[90]

Later in his opinion, he disagrees with the above approach and observes that:

> No longer should it be said, on the basis of that case, that prima facie, if something essential is left to be agreed upon by the parties at a later time, there is no binding agreement. The intention of the parties, as discerned by the court, to be bound or not to be bound should be paramount.

From Blanchard J's statement we can discern that the intention to be bound is the underlying concept directing the determination of certainty. Therefore, as long as the concept of contractual intention is clear, any uncertainty as to the terms is ascertainable by adducing evidence as to the parties' intention in the particular case.

4.6.1 *Curing contracts of uncertainty under the common law*
We have seen that certainty of terms of an agreement affects the enforceability of the contract as a whole and effectively determines whether the contract is valid or not. Therefore, a brief consideration of a sample of means that the common law courts of England employ to cure contracts of uncertainty would be useful. It should be noted, as discussed above, that the mechanisms outlined below would apply in cases where the question of certainty of terms takes an evidential character as opposed to a conceptual character.

The general position regarding certainty of terms, we have noted, is that:

the parties must have agreed on the essential terms or have provided the method by which these are to be determined, and these must be reasonably certain otherwise there is no contract, merely an agreement to agree or an agreement to negotiate neither of which is considered to have legal force. But if the essential terms have been agreed, the fact that the parties have agreed to negotiate as to the remaining terms does not preclude the establishment of a contract; indeed, the court may also be willing to infer an agreement to negotiate in good faith to settle the remaining terms.[91]

From the above quotation we infer that the first measure the court may adopt in creating certainty where it appears to lack is, therefore, to examine the contractual language in light of its context. By this it is meant, look at what has been said and done, the context in which the words or acts were said and done, and the relative importance of the unsettled matter in the entire scheme of the agreement.[92] The language of the contract is the principle tool used by the court in determining what the parties have agreed.[93] Generally, the contract will be interpreted in accordance with any rules of interpretation provided by the contract itself. Technical terms will be accorded their technical meaning, and any language accorded special meaning according to custom or usage will be accorded such meaning if the contract is entered into in the light of such custom or usage.[94] Extrinsic evidence is, as a rule, admissible to resolve any ambiguity, whether latent or patent,[95] thus indicating a general evidential approach to the issue of certainty of terms.

Secondly, the court also pays heed to whether the parties have themselves stipulated machinery for settling the uncertainty (also indicating the eviden-tial/curable nature of contractual uncertainty) and the mode of cure the parties have contemplated or provided for.[96] In addition, the courts consider the following factors:

- Commercial practice and previous performance: illustrated by the case of *Hillas v Arcos*[97] (considered at length in section 4.6 above) where the contract provided for the sale of Russian timber of 'fair specification', but that did not provide for the kind, size or quality of the timber nor the mode of shipment to be used. These omissions were ascertained from previous transactions between the same parties and the custom of the particular trade. The court held that there was an intention to be bound from the previous transactions and the uncertain terms could be ascertained by reference to previous dealings and the original contract.

- Standards of reasonableness: could alternatively be used to settle uncertain terms including standards such as 'market value'[98] or 'open market value'.[99] In the case of price of goods or services, the matter is governed by statute – The Sale of Goods Act 1979 provides in section 8 (2) that where the price is not determined in section 8 (1), the buyer must then pay a reasonable price. Section 8 (2) however applies only where the contract is silent as to the price and not where the parties agree to subsequently determine the price.[100]

- Machinery for ascertainment: a contract will not be void for uncertainty if the contract stipulates a mechanism for ascertaining the uncertain. The provided mechanism could be an arbitration clause[101], an agreement to appoint a valuer to determine the price or any other method agreeable to the parties. In the recent case of *Bruce v Carpenter and others*, the court observed that in determining contractual certainty the court must also determine whether the machinery set out by the parties was essential to the ascertainment of the term in question (in this case ascertainment of contractual price through a named expert's valuation) or whether certainty could be established by applying objective standards, for instance, by reference to a fair price.[102] The approach taken in *Bruce* reflects the evidential approach to certainty of terms whereas where the court chooses to adopt a conceptual approach to certainty of terms, as in *May & Butcher*[103] for instance, then a provision of any such machinery in the contract is of no value should the court determine that no agreement was formed due to lack of certainty.[104]

- Severability of term: if the uncertain clause or term is meaningless or can be done without, the court can order it to be severed from the rest of the contract leaving the rest of the contract valid.[105]

- Other Implied terms: the court will be willing to read into a contract terms not expressly spelt out between the parties on several other grounds depending on whether such terms are either implied in fact or in law.

Terms implied in fact are those that are implicit in express terms such as those deemed too obvious to need stating;[106] or are necessary to give business efficacy to the contract[107]but the term sought to be implied must be such that without it the contract would be commercially non-viable;[108]

Terms implied in law are either terms implied as rules of the common law or statute law. We are here concerned more with terms implied under the common law, for instance, fitness and merchantable quality implied in contracts of sale of goods in the nineteenth century prior to the enactment of the Sales of Goods Act.[109] Where such terms are not already implied as a matter of law by the courts, they will do so as a matter of policy where the term is one which the law should imply as a necessary incident of a defined contractual relationship.[110] For instance, in a contract for labour and materials, that the materials will be of proper quality and fit for purpose[111] and in a contract for supply of services, that they will be performed with such care and skill as is reasonable (having regard to the degree of experience the provider holds out as possessing).[112]

All of these curing mechanisms are open to be employed by Islamic law to cure contracts lacking sufficient certainty of terms, as per the *gharar* principle, where applicable.

4.7 Historical context and the rules of *gharar*

Appreciating the context within which the Quranic verses were revealed and Muhammad's statements were made is an essential (and universally accepted) component of interpreting the rules of Islamic law that were created to express the principles behind them.[113] It is vital, therefore, for an appropriate application of *gharar*, to look at the context within which the prohibition was extrapolated by Muhammad from the Quranic verses on gambling. Muhammad's sayings cited as prohibiting *gharar* depict transactions involving items of daily use or even basic necessities such as food, livestock or currency metals, used directly or indirectly for sustenance. The context of the prohibition is 6th–7th-century desert Arabia afflicted by harsh weather, scarce water and limited food sources making it common for tribes to experience food shortages or for traders to try and deceive consumers so as to maximise gains by exploiting people's need. Even as better times fell on the Arabs and food was better available among the people of Quraysh, through combining mercantile trading with livestock breeding, money was still coveted and loved dearly by the Arabs, as mentioned in several verses of the *Quran*.[114] Sharp market practices in hope of making quick gains proliferated amongst traders[115] and the emergence of Islam amongst the Arabs of Makkah found an atmosphere of cut-throat capitalism and high finance at a time when merchants were beginning to wrest some of the power which had once been solely in the hands of the kings and the aristocrats[116]. This new prosperity drew Muhammad's attention to the disparity between rich and poor and made him deeply concerned with problems of social justice. Muhammad's uncle, Abu-Lahab imposed a two-year food ban on Muslims from 617–619 AD in hope of subduing them back to the tradition of their forefathers. Finding this treatment unbearable, and having lost his beloved wife Khadija that year,[117] Muhammad fled Makkah to Madina along with several hundred followers.[118] In those conditions, the migrants left whatever possessions they had behind and were completely at the mercy of their hosts (*Ansaar*) in Madina. In founding a new community of Muslims in Madina, Muhammad stressed the principles of justice and equity in all human affairs, let alone contractual dealings; a policy measure to protect the weak from the potentially harmful clout of the strong and wealthy and as a means of emphasising that everyone was entitled to what was lawfully theirs regardless of race, tribe, class or gender. Justice and equality are the two fundamental themes underlying the message of Islam as the foundation of the Muslim community and in the sphere of transactions these principles are expressed through the rules of *gharar* (and *riba*).

4.8 Present context application of Islamic law of transaction

Chapter 5 refers to the Quranic distinction between commercial and non-commercial transactions for the purposes of applying rules of *riba*.[119] *Gharar*, on the other hand, concerns only commercial transactions much like the concept of certainty of terms concerns commercial transactions. Social and family arrangements are not subject to the rules of *gharar* as the parties are taken either to have an understanding of the transactional terms or not to have intended to be bound. This demarcation is evidenced by the fact that any discussion on *gharar* (be it in books or fora) pertain to commercial transactions. Islam is not alone or unique in stressing the paramount need to protect contracting parties in commercial or non-commercial transactions. Under the common law a demarcation has always been drawn between commercial and non-commercial contracts with a more cautious approach being adopted towards the latter as discussed in section 4.6 above. In fact, these principles and laws have been in place, used and refined, for several decades in England while Muslims are still grappling with the definition of *gharar* and making necessary distinctions between its application in different contexts and contracts.

In today's context, sophisticated legal and regulatory frameworks are either available or may be put in place to facilitate equity in commercial or financial transactions. It is open to parties to opt to enter into the transactions only after consideration of their circumstances and consequences of the transaction coupled with legal and financial advice. Moreover, market mechanisms may be invoked as an objective standard of ensuring equity.[120] In most developed financial jurisdictions, for instance, securitisation transactions (as all other financial transactions) are subject to regulatory standards that by implication guard against financial transactions falling foul of *gharar* (uncertainty/speculation). The more pertinent inquiry is whether these regulatory standards also guard against inequity?[121] We have stressed that the principle behind *gharar* indicates that preventing uncertainty and speculation is not a goal but rather a means to facilitating contractual equity between the parties. Viability of the application of current financial regulatory (or other) standards to Islamic finance securitisations so as to satisfy the principle behind *gharar* can today be facilitated by the sharia boards present in all Islamic finance institutions. These sharia boards ought to be, and are increasingly becoming, internal regulatory bodies within banks and financial institutions that enforce accountability and transparency (over and above ensuring an adherence to the requisite form of nominal contracts) and thereby safeguarding the best interest of the investors by eliminating excessive risk or speculation. In fact, the scope and role of sharia boards has the potential of evolving into a unified regulatory body that monitors and regulates sharia compliant transactions. It is envisioned that through such an enhanced role, the balance between form and substance will be better attained and, if accomplished, it will spur more sustainable growth within Islamic finance. A detailed discussion of sharia boards and their roles is, however, beyond the scope of this book.

Conclusion

Appreciating the rules of *gharar* in the context of their formulation and adopting an evidential approach to *gharar*, as some schools of Islamic jurisprudence have, is of great consequence for securitisation as it no longer threatens to automatically vitiate the structure but merely puts the parties on guard against insufficient certainty of contractual terms that would call the transaction's validity into question. It also implies that securitisation transaction involving physical assets not a yet in existence or not yet actually owned would not be rendered automatically void and such validity would be determined on a case-to-case basis guided by the yardstick of whether the transaction is, in effect, akin to gambling.

In this spirit, Islamic finance should utilise the principle of *gharar* to ensure contractual equity without hindering the practice and evolution of commercial and financial transactions. The balance between the two is fine but one that Muslim societies must consider striking. Consideration may also be given to the role of sharia boards and their capacity to contribute constructively to the growth and development of Islamic Finance through their embodiment as a corporate governing body as opposed to their current 'certifying' role.

5

RIBA

MEANING, SCOPE AND APPLICATION

A cardinal principle of Islamic law of contract is the prohibition of *riba*. Any study or consideration of an Islamic finance-related subject is, therefore, incomplete without a discussion of the meaning of *riba*, the principle underpinning it and its application in commercial transactions today. *Riba* has been translated, and applied, as a prohibition of interest charged on loans. To say so, however, is to not only oversimplify the matter but to misconstrue it all together because the concept of *riba* applies to more than just loans; it applies equally to all transactions be they loan or sale or lease.[1]

Riba, as a concept within Islamic law of contract,[2] is a vitiating factor that aims at attaining transactional equity by requiring exchanges to be bargains by way of mutual consent as a basis for eliciting consideration.[3] The principle of *riba* is, therefore, one that regulates the elicitation of consideration: only commercial[4] exchanges may elicit consideration.[5] Non-commercial exchanges (family and social arrangements or otherwise unenforceable agreements) may not elicit consideration. Evidence of the established validity of this demarcation in Islam is furnished by a universally accepted contract – the wedding contract (*Aqd al-nikah*). The *Quran* and the teachings of Muhammad establish the contractual nature of a marriage. Both primary sources emphasise the necessity of dowry (*mahr*) as a gift to the lady upon marriage (*nikah*). Muhammad repeatedly advised that dowry must be extended and a wedding feast (*walima*) prepared. Neither the dowry nor the feast need be extravagant or lavish – every man is to prepare and present what his capacity can afford. This corresponds with the fact that in a contract, consideration need not to be adequate; it need only be sufficient, as per English common law.[6] The description of *mahr* as a 'gift'[7] as opposed to contractual consideration is interesting to note because it is in consonance with the distinction between social contracts that cannot elicit consideration *as of right* and commercial contracts that can. The same distinction exists under the common law.[8]

In direct reference to *riba*, the *Quran* expressly distinguishes between commercial and non-commercial transactions for purposes of application of the *riba* principle.[9] Commercial transactions are *prima facie* deemed to be bargains of mutual consent between the parties with an intention to be bound and thus contracts eligible to claim consideration/gain *because* of this presumed equitable nature. Non-commercial transactions, on the other hand, are *prima facie* ineligible to stipulate consideration (though consideration may gratuitously be extended by the promisee) not because they are inequitable but because of their potential to result in inequity given the transaction is either not conducted at arm's length or is lacking in mutual consent as a result of a social need. Any claim for or receipt of consideration/gain in a non-commercial transaction renders it potentially inequitable and thus voidable. Thus, it is the claim for consideration/gain in non-commercial transactions that the *Quran* describes as *riba*[10] and all such *riba*-tainted transaction are rendered 'defective'[11] (not void) and may be cured of the vitiating effect by altering its nature to 'commercial'.[12]

Evidently, the understanding expressed above is in contrast to the current understanding of *riba* as interest or any increased returns on loans/credit extended. Islamic commercial banking and finance demonstrates, in practice, the non-viability of defining *riba* as interest and of prohibiting the charge of an increased return for financial and debt transactions especially given the acknowledged cost of finance and the risks undertaken by the lender.[13] This reality is manifested in the prevailing practices of the Islamic finance industry which, whilst compelled not to charge interest explicitly, elicit 'profit margins' and 'fees' of various kinds and amounts under the guise of 'profit-sharing', 'service fees' or 'rent'.

In recognition of the apparent contradiction between the theory, as currently interpreted, and commercial practice, El-Diwany[14] (broadly) advocates for the return to the gold and silver standard of money (these being the original media of exchange and only true measures of value) so as to guard against the proliferation of *riba* transactions. He presents a proposal for an Islamic banking and financial system based on no interest to be conducted solely via contracts of exchange and investment. Thus, according to El-Diwany, riba *is* interest. He justifies the equation of *riba* to interest on the basis that Islam discourages the mere transfer of wealth[15] (i.e. loans) for a gain and encourages instead the creation of wealth[16] through trade and exchange (e.g. the investment or use of £50 to create £51 and more). His position is not peculiar and is predicated on the traditional and seldom questioned definition and scope of the term *riba* as any increased return on money lent whatever the loan's nature or purpose, which in turn implies a theoretical preference of equity over debt finance. Suffice it to say now that El-Diwany's characterisation of money lending as involving the mere transfer of wealth is inaccurate because whilst Islam may discourage the mere transfer of wealth at an increase (i.e. consideration *demanded* for no bargain), money lending is not purely a transfer of wealth process. Loans create value through the provision of credit and financing commercial endeavours, both being vital to the functioning of any robust economy, including Muslim economies. Loans also involve undertaking a risk of default, inflation, devaluation, loss of liquidity, incurring the costs of capital adequacy and the opportunity cost of lending it to debtors toward which Islam is not inequitable as to deny the lender due compensation[17]. Given money lending took place in both the pre- and post-Islam Arabia, the prohibition of *riba* could not have intended to discourage money lending, for reports have it that prominent companions[18] of the Prophet were well-known moneylenders. If indeed money lending was similar to the mere transfer of wealth, and Islam discourages such transfer of wealth, it follows that Islam would have discouraged money lending. Islam does not. The *Quran* merely prohibited the practice of *riba* – which, as this chapter will show, is neither defined nor limited to the *form* a transaction takes (money lending) or to increased returns (charging interest or receiving gains from loans). *Riba*, as is discussed in this chapter, is any illicitly or inequitably elicited gain – the fundamental distinction between a valid and invalid contract.

Further, it is a well-accepted fact that it takes money to create money, therefore, just as one would invest in a business so as to earn profit, so may one borrow money to trade, invest, or otherwise employ the money borrowed towards earning a profit. Money lending for commercial purposes is part and parcel of the wealth creation process as is any business or commercial investment undertaking. El-Diwany's 'transfer v creation of wealth' theory, therefore, cannot be the operational factor behind the prohibition of *riba*.

It is in light of the above backdrop that this chapter undertakes an analysis of the concept of *riba* with the aim of reconciling the apparent conflict between the principle of *riba* and the rule prohibiting interest so as to clarify the effect of *riba* in structuring sharia compliant securitisations.[19] In summary, an analysis beyond the literal interpretation of the textual wording prohibiting *riba* reveals the following possibilities:

- That *riba* is not so much a matter of interest on loans (*dayn*) than it is a matter of distinguishing unlawful gain[20] from legitimate gain especially because the *Quran* does not use *riba* in reference to loans but in reference to the unjustified (illegitimately or illicitly) taking of others' wealth, generally.[21]
- The *Quran's* distinction between *bay'* and *riba* implies a distinction between a legitimate and non-legitimate transactions for purposes of drawing consideration or profit making. *Riba*, generally, pertains to the prohibition against eliciting illegitimate gains in any transaction,[22] whether they be debt, sale, lease or a combination thereof in nature. Such transactions lack the element of mutuality or that of being a bargain.[23]
- The no-gain rule of *riba* is only one limb of the *riba* principle. This limb of the rule discourages the *elicitation or receipt* of increased returns in non-commercial transactions and encourages, instead, being charitable and generous in one's dealings with others in the non-commercial context.
- The zero-gain principle does not apply to commercial transactions; in commercial transaction it is universal fact that consideration may be drawn/profit made. Instead, the *riba* principle applies to commercial transactions indirectly through the rule that, all transactions must be equitable/bargains. This is the second limb of the *riba* principle.
- Commercial transactions encompass commercial credit, which include loan, sale and lease finance.[24]
- Loans, being commercial transactions, are eligible to draw a benefit from the transaction just as any other commercial transaction but subject to application of the second limb of *riba*.[25] This means increased returns may be charged on commercial loans as consideration as long as the transaction is equitable.

The rest of this chapter considers and substantiates the above set out premise.

5.1 *Riba* redefined

The Quranic verses on *riba* are categorical in their discouragement of the practice of *riba* and in their admonition of those who engage in *riba* practices (both the giver and recipient). The primary sources, however, do not define what *riba* is. The commentary number 324 to verse Al-Baqara: 275 of the *Quran*, by Abdullah Yusuf Ali reveals as much:

> *Riba* is condemned and prohibited in the strongest possible terms. There can be no question about the prohibition. When we come to the

definition of *riba* there is room for difference of opinion. 'Umar Ibn Khattab,[26] according to Ibn Kathir, felt some difficulty in the matter, as the Apostle left this world before the details of the question were settled. This was one of the three questions on which he wished he had more light from the Prophet.

The definitions that exist in Islamic scholarship are merely a matter of deduction and independent reasoning by individual scholars. It is this *what* of *riba* that is examined and redefined here. In doing so I refer to the primary sources of the *riba* principle and am inspired by the observation made by Ibn al-Qayyim, 'There is nothing prohibited except that which God prohibits … To declare something permitted prohibited is like declaring something prohibited permitted'.[27]

The most oft-quoted verse in the *Quran* on *riba* states, in Baqara: 275, that:

> Those who eat *riba* shall rise up before Allah like men whom Satan has demented by his touch, for they claim that *bay'* (sale) is like *riba*; and Allah has permitted sale and prohibited *riba*.

The verse implies a pertinent distinction exists between *bay'* and *riba*. The obvious question, therefore, is: what *is* the difference between *bay'* and *riba*? The Arabic term *al-bay'* literally means 'the sale'[28] denoting the contract of sale. Technically, *al-bay'* denotes the concept of trade or commerce (producing profit for one party and contractual benefit for the other). *Riba*, on the other hand, literally means increase or multiplication and has come to be interpreted, narrowly, as stipulated increase on loans. Narrowly is used here because there is nothing in the Quranic or in Muhammad's usage that limits the term *riba* to 'increase in loan repayments'. In fact, the above meanings of both *al-bay'* and *riba* prove inadequate by the very standards of the *Quran*.

Bay', as used in the *Quran*, does not simply mean sale or even trade in the limited sense of buying and selling or commerce, rather it denotes any 'trade of life', that is, any lawful profession or commercial endeavour. This meaning is explicit in the *Quran*, in *al-Jum'a*: 9–10, which says:

> O you who believe! When the call is proclaimed for the prayer on the day of *Jumaa'* (Friday) come to the remembrance of Allah and leave off trade (*bay*). That is preferable for you if you did but know! Then when the prayer is finished, you may disperse through the land, and

seek the Bounty of Allah, and remember Allah much that you may be
successful.

If *bay'* simply meant sale, or trade in the literal sense of buying and selling
or business, the only people addressed by this verse to set aside 'business'
and attend Friday prayer would be trade and businesspeople (literally). Yet,
it is accepted fact that Friday congregational prayer has been decreed, in
this verse, for all men whatever their profession, occupation or status. In
this sense, bay is extended not only to business trading but, generically, to
cover all and any lawful engagement or commercial endeavour within which
banking and finance validly falls. The *Quran* in *al-Jum'a*:10 confirms this
conclusion by asking the very same people it addresses to leave their *bay'* and
come to prayer, to thereafter disperse and 'seek of the bounty of Allah'. If
bay' strictly meant trade for profit then the latter verse would have asked the
people it had earlier asked to leave their 'trade' to return, specifically, to their
bay' in the limited 'trade' sense. The word the *Quran* uses to signify trade
(in the strict buying and selling sense) is *tijara*.[29] For instance: 'O ye who
believe! Eat not up your property among yourselves in vanity: But let there
be amongst you trade (*tijara*) by mutual consent: Nor destroy yourselves: for
verily Allah hath been to you, Merciful!'[30]

The meaning of *riba* is also best understood by referring directly to its use
in the *Quran*. Its designated literal meaning – increase or multiplication – is
demonstrated in *al-Rum*: 39, is the first verse to be revealed on *riba* and it
states:

> That which ye lay out for increase (*riba*) through the property of (other)
> people, has no increase (*riba*) with Allah, but that which ye lay out for
> charity (*zakat*), seeking the Countenance of Allah, it is these who will
> get a recompense multiplied.

In essence, this verse on *riba* discourages the seeking of worldly gains
from others (through one's property) and encourages instead the seeking of
spiritual gains from Allah though the extension of charity to others.

Consequently, several questions arise from the above verses.

1 If Islam is not against growth, increase or multiplication of wealth and
   riba literally means growth or increase, what does *riba* pertain to that it
   should be so vehemently prohibited?
2 What does the *Quran* imply by contrasting *riba* to charity, on the one
   hand, and by distinguishing *riba* from *al-bay'* (commerce), on the other?

Given that there are many more precise words denoting charging or stipulating an increase on loans, why does Allah use the words akl[31] (consume/devour) or akhdh[32] (taking) in relation to riba? Is it merely coincidental that both words, akl and akhdh denote non-consensual taking/devouring of others' property and have no commercial or contractual connotation?

3 If Allah intended riba to mean, specifically, interest charged on loans why is that not clearly stated or any mention of loans made in any of the verses pertaining to riba?

4 Does commercial lending and finance fall within the concept of al-bay' and is, therefore, according to the Quran, distinct from riba?

5 What distinguishes commercial from non-commercial transactions for purposes of legitimising any gain made or consideration drawn?

These questions are answered in what follows.

5.1.1 Riba *according to the* Quran

A careful and contextualised read of the Quranic verses mentioning riba indicates that the word (riba) is used repeatedly to encourage people to cease their obsession with increase sought in material wealth (of others) and seek, instead, to spend in the cause of God (through charity). This is, as we considered above, demonstrated clearly in the first verse revealed on riba in Quran, al-Rum: 39 which states:

That which ye lay out for increase (riba) through the property of (other) people, has no increase (riba) with Allah, but that which ye lay out for charity (zakat), seeking the Countenance of Allah, it is these who will get a recompense multiplied.

Evidently, the verse contrasts riba with charity; one seeking monetary returns, the other seeking not monetary returns but recompense through the pleasure of Allah. No indication is made of loans and increased returns on loans and therefore an objective contextualised reading of the verse (in light of the context of society before and during Muhammad's time) defies the association or restriction of riba to increased returns on loans.

The second verse that was revealed on riba was al-Nisa: 161, which recalls the inequitable practices of Bani Israel (the people of Israel):

And their taking of riba though they were forbidden it and their devouring people's property wrongfully. And we prepared for those among them who deny (the Truth) a grievous punishment.

This verse is claimed by some Muslims to infer that *riba* means an increased return on loans as was the practice among Jews. There is nothing, however, both in the text of the *Quran* and in the explanations of Muhammad (or his trusted companions) that substantiates this claim. Indeed, if the inference was correct, Umar, a very close companion of Muhammad and the second caliph, a mere three years after Muhammad's demise, would not have been so distraught and confused as to the meaning and application of *riba*, as pointed out in section 5.1.

The third verse on *riba*, *al-Imran*: 130, states:

O you who Believe! Do not consume *riba*, double and multiplied, and be conscious of God that you may prosper.

Again, this verse, by the use of 'double and multiplied' has been taken to imply the custom prevalent among Jews and Arab moneylenders to charge compounding interest at (often) exorbitant rates. Nonetheless, we have emphasised that the verses are themselves not specific about the form of practice *riba* embodies. The verse(s) simply set out the principle against unjust taking ('consuming') of people's wealth or property in a non-commercial, non-consensual manner.

This brings us to the most oft-quoted set of verses revealed on *riba*. The profound sense one gets from a study of these verses is that the prohibition is a spiritual admonition pertaining to the taking, eating or devouring of another's/others' wealth without mutual consent. To this, the protesting retort was, such *Riba* (increase/gain) taken is like that acquired through *bay'* (trade)! In response, the *Quran* in *al-Baqara*: 275 provided, 'Those who consume riba will not stand except as one whom Satan has, by his touch, driven to madness. That is because they say: "*bay'* (trade) is like *riba*" but Allah hath permitted *bay* and forbidden *riba*'.

The *Quran*, therefore, clarifies that the spiritual admonition to relent on seeking material gains and the encouragement to seek spending freely in the cause of Allah, is qualified by allowing (indeed encouraging) the acquisition of gain/profit through (consensual) commercial engagement and exchanges. For completeness of the contrast the verses provide, I quote below all the relevant verses pertaining to the concept of *riba* in the *al-Baqara* chapter (272–281). Notice, in particular, the contrast between verses 274 and 275.

272. It is not you (O Messenger), to set them on the right path, but Allah sets on the right path whom He pleases. Whatever of good ye give benefits your own souls, and ye do not spend except seeking the

'Face' of Allah. Whatever good ye give, shall be rendered back to you, and ye shall not be dealt with unjustly.

273. (Charity is) for those in need, who, in Allah's cause are restricted (from travel), and cannot move about in the land, seeking (For trade or work): the ignorant man thinks, because of their modesty, that they are free from want. Thou shalt know them by their (Unfailing) mark: They beg not importunately from all and sundry. And whatever of good ye give, be assured Allah knoweth it well.

274. Those who (in charity) spend of their goods by night and by day, in secret and in public, have their reward with their Lord: on them shall be no fear, nor shall they grieve.

275. Those who eat *riba* will not stand except as stand one whom the Evil one by his touch hath driven to madness. That is because they say: '*bay*' is like *riba*', but Allah hath permitted trade and forbidden *riba*. Those who, after receiving direction from their Lord, desist, shall be pardoned for the past; their case is for Allah (to judge); but those who persist are companions of the Fire: They will abide therein (for ever).

276. Allah will deprive *riba* of all blessing, but will give increase for deeds of charity: For He loveth not creatures ungrateful and wicked.

277. Those who believe, and do deeds of righteousness, and establish regular prayers and regular charity, will have their reward with their Lord: on them shall be no fear, nor shall they grieve.

278. O ye who believe! Fear Allah, and give up what remains of your demand for *riba*, if ye are indeed believers.

279. If ye do it not, take notice of war from Allah and His Messenger. But if ye turn back, ye shall have your capital sums: Deal not unjustly, and ye shall not be dealt with unjustly.

280. If one is in difficulty (financially), grant him time till it is easy for him to repay. But if ye remit it by way of charity, that is best for you if ye only knew.

281. And fear the Day when ye shall be brought back to Allah. Then shall every soul be paid what it earned, and none shall be dealt with unjustly.

The next verse[33] deals in great detail with future credit obligations (*dayn*) and simply encourages that they be written and witnessed in a manner resembling a common law deed (that dispenses with the need for consideration). It explains in great detail the manner and evidential procedure such contracts for future obligations should comply with so as to prevent *riba* in the transaction.

We have already noted that, collectively, the Quranic verses on *riba* draw a distinction between commerce and *riba* on the one hand, and between charity (or *zakat*) and *riba*, on the other. In answer to question (2), therefore, this implies a similarity between charity and commerce. Charity implies giving and is the opposite of *riba* which is expressly described as 'taking others' wealth/substance'. Extended, in like fashion, to the contrast between commercial sale (*bay*) and *riba*, *bay'* involves the exchange or giving of mutual benefit between contracting parties while *Riba* involves the taking or deriving of benefit from another without mutual consent.

Why, then, does the *Quran* use the term 'taking' in regard to *riba* practices in contrast to giving on the one hand and in contrast to trade (*bay*) on the other? Taking indicates lack of consent or compulsion in acquiring something from another. Taking (*akhdh*), as used in the *Quran*, implies indirect thieving. Giving, on the other hand, indicates consent or a willingness of the giver and the exercise of choice in acceptance on the part of the recipient. Consent and choice are an integral part of contractual transactions, the two elements that legitimise the making of profit/gain. The lack of consent or compulsion thus deems any gain made illegitimate, be it under Islamic law or the English common law. One appreciates, therefore, that the *riba* prohibition pertains to the non-consensual or compelled taking from another/others.

Consistent with this line of thought is also the understanding that the sayings of the Prophet describe transactions that, then, were deemed the practice of *riba*. *Riba* is not today limited to those transactions depicted in the traditions of Muhammad; it is a much broader concept that was simply exemplified (then) by those *forms* of (inequitable/inefficient) transactions. *Riba* transactions today may validly take different forms from those of the barter transactions of seventh-century Arabia.

As for question (3), that is, if the intention was simply to prohibit any stipulated increase on loans, as many claim today, why is it that the *Quran* simply mentions *riba* with reference to future/credit obligations generally and even then, the risk of *riba* arising in such credit transactions is obviated by the direction to reduce the transaction to writing and take two witnesses thereto. Similarly, the sayings of Muhammad, which were always intended to clarify and explain the text of the *Quran*, indicate that *riba* has nothing particular to do with the act of lending because all explanations of *riba*'s application in Muhammad's sayings pertain to commercial-like exchanges with no reference to loans. Given the tone and intensity of the verses on *riba*, the *Quran* and the prophetic sayings would certainly have been clearer and more precise had the prohibition been one intended to pertain strictly to an *increase* charged on *loans*.[34] No such indication exists.

5.1.2 Riba *according to Muhammad*

Riba in the sayings of Muhammad fall under two categories: *riba al fadl* and *riba al nasia*.

The first category, *Riba al fadl*, has been translated by many as *riba* of increase, but given *riba* literally means increase, it does not make much sense. I prefer to use *riba* of excess.[35] It is derived from the saying (I) of Muhammad:

> Gold is to be paid for by gold, silver by silver, wheat by wheat, barley by barley, dates by dates, and salt by salt – like for like, equal for equal, payment being made on the spot. If the species differ, sell as you wish provided payment is made on the spot.[36]

Traditionally, this saying has been interpreted and applied as not only requiring equanimity in all homogenous exchanges but also prohibiting any increase arising from an exchange of money based on gold and silver being equated to money. The likening of gold and silver to money is dealt with in chapter 6 so suffice it to say here that money at Muhammad's time was in the currency form of dirhams and dinars, not in gold and silver as distinct and freely tradable commodities in their own right. Any tradition of that time speaks of money in terms of these two currencies, not in terms of gold and silver yet the saying (I) speaks specifically of gold and silver not of the currency forms.

A critical reading of the saying indicates that Muhammad was simply stipulating the requirement of equanimity in homogenous exchanges as underscored by the proviso, 'If the species differ, *sell* as you wish provided *payment* is made on the spot' (emphasis added). It is easy to appreciate that the uniformity required in the subject matter being exchanged (weight, measure and quality) and execution on spot basis,[37] was necessary to ensure (in that context) that equity was upheld between the exchanging parties and perhaps to encourage a money market economy given there would be no commercial advantage to be gained out of such exchanges. This is not surprising given the entire social fabric of Islam as a religion and way of life is woven upon the notion of justice and social welfare. One was, therefore, exempt from the above stipulated requirements if an item was exchanged for money which is then used to buy any other item, at a price agreed to between the parties, as explained in the following saying (II) of Muhammad:[38]

> Abu Said Al-Kudriy narrated that Bilal brought to the prophet some high quality dates and when the prophet asked him how the dates had

been obtained, Bilal replied, 'I had some inferior dates so I sold two *sas* for one *sa*'.[39] On this the prophet said, 'Ah, the very essence of *riba*, the very essence of *riba*. Do not do so, but if you wish to buy, sell your dates in a separate transaction, then buy with the proceeds.'

Is the 'essence' Muhammad speaks of the barter (form) or the potential for inequity that arises from it? It cannot be the barter form of exchange because Muhammad does not prohibit bartering. Muhammad simply requires equanimity in the bartering of items. Bilal was free to buy and sell dates as he wished if he did so for cash. Saying (II), thus, affirms the fact that *riba* has little to do with form or loans particularly because whilst the transaction itself is one describable as 'trade' and (otherwise) lawful, Muhammad describes it as 'the very essence of *riba*'. It also indicates that Muhammad endorsed and encouraged the use of a market economy as far back as sixth century ad. Market transactions are deemed equitable in result as a consequence of the market forces of supply and demand coupled by the free consent of the parties that makes the transaction a bargain entitled to elicit consideration.[40]

It is apparent therefore that *riba al fadl* has little to do with everyday commercial loans and much to do with the encouragement towards engaging in equitable and efficient commercial transaction which the saying (I) of Muhammad exemplifies through an exchange of like for like, equal for equal or (alternatively) selling the commodity for cash at the best market price and thereafter buying (with the cash) any other commodity at market price. Note also that the sayings do not stipulate a 'fair' price or specific price at which the buying and selling ought to take place, and leaves such price to be determined by the parties in implied recognition of the inherent equity in mutual consent and the market forces of supply and demand/competition.

The meaning and implication of sayings (I) and (II) above may be better understood in light of their context: a barter economy. Oditah notes that, '[i]n a barter economy there may be no need for credit since goods, services, and facilities will be exchanged immediately for the bargained consideration. Such an economy necessarily assumes that performance and counter performance of contractual obligations will be simultaneous'.[41] A barter transaction is thus universally acknowledged not to involve credit and Muhammad's saying (I) merely states the obvious regarding the requirement of spot payment. It is the emphasis on 'like for like, equal for equal' that strikes at the heart of ensuring equitable exchanges in light of possible unequal bargaining power or lack of objective means of determining fairness of bartered items and measures. The saying was not intended to prohibit credit transactions or increased returns in credit transactions – both of which Islam expressly permits, as we shall see below.

Riba al nasia, is the second category of *riba* and literally means *riba* of delay.[42] Technically, it has been interpreted as an increased charge that is elicited as a consequence of time extension for the repayment of a loan. Muslim scholars stress, therefore, that the prohibition of *riba* is not to be limited[43] to usury practiced in the pre-Muhammad societies (*Riba al jahiliyya*[44]) as illustrated in the *Quran, Ali-Imran*: 130: 'O you who believe, do not devour *riba*, double and redoubled, that you may prosper'. Rather, that *riba* pertains to all money lending transactions. Accordingly, *riba* entails a prohibition of usury, compound interest as well as any increased returns on money lent.

The prohibition against *riba al nasia* is also derived from the same saying (I) referred to above, that is, 'gold is to be paid for by gold ... like for like, equal for equal, payment being made on the spot'. However, greater credence is given to another saying of Muhammad (III) that is frequently referred to: 'Every loan that attracts a benefit is *riba*'.[45] Though the authenticity of this saying is much in doubt, the ruling it implies is referred to by scholars as deriving from the saying (I) which they deem to be sufficient basis to grant them reliance on it. Consequently, Muslim scholars in the past have used this saying to justify the prohibition of any interest or increase charged on loans.

5.2 The principle behind *riba* and its implications for Islamic finance
Ibn Rushd's central economic analysis of Muhammad's saying (I) pertaining to barter exchanges of the six specified commodities (which Ibn Rushd extended to all fungible commodities) hints at the principle behind *riba*. He says:

> It is thus apparent from the law that what is targeted by the prohibition of *riba* is the excessive inequity it entails. In this regard, equity in certain transactions is achieved through equality ... thus, equity may be ensured through proportionality of value for goods that are not measured by weight and volume ... As for fungible goods measured by volume or weight, equity requires equality, since they are relatively homogeneous and have similar benefits ... justice in this case is achieved by equating volume or weight, since the benefits are very similar.[46]

Therefore, defined in light of the context in which the ruling was revealed,[47] the saying of Muhammad on *riba al fadl* (excess) points to an underlying principle of equity and efficiency requiring a bargain made by mutual consent – the most efficient means of ensuring which is to sell one's item/s for money at market price. The principle of *riba* thus applies at two distinct levels:

1 Distinguishing market (commercial) transactions from non-market transactions, permitting the derivation of gain from the former and prohibiting gain from the latter;
2 In non-market transactions to prevent inequity in transactions by requiring that all contracts of homogenous exchange be conducted on like for like basis and, otherwise, for equal return at no benefit or consideration as of right.

It is crucial to note that in his saying (I), Muhammad did not disapprove of the gain made in the exchange of dates, but merely of the fact that superior dates were exchanged for inferior dates without (impliedly) an objective yardstick or regulating mechanism in place to ensure an equitable exchange. Muhammad expressed a preference for a sale of the dates at the best possible market price followed by the procuring of superior dates with the monetary proceeds thereof, this being the most equitable and efficient means to attain the (same) intended outcome.

The measurability of the items exchanged, which have no inherent or objective market value, and the absence of market forces regulation (demand and supply) seems to be the concern at the root of what Muhammad describes as 'the very essence of *riba*' in the specific context Muhammad was faced with.

The ensuing implications of this conclusion for Islamic finance are impressive on several levels. First, it negates the general theory that Islam prohibits interest on loans – money lending is a commercial transaction entailing an exchange in counter values and for which due consideration must be extended to the financier. Second, equity and efficiency in debt markets are satisfied through market competition and market regulation mechanisms. This is directly derived from Muhammad's saying (II) on dates.

Along the same vein, El-Gamal concludes that the twin objectives of equity and efficiency thus necessitate a marking-to-market approach in establishing trading ratios.[48] Accordingly, he points out that conventional finance plays a very important role for Islamic finance by determining the market interest rates for various borrowers based on credit worthiness and security provisions; that benchmarking the implicit interest rates in Islamic credit sales and lease-to-purchase transactions to conventional interest rates are, thus, quite appropriate.[49]

It has even been suggested that Islamic banks are well advised to abandon characterising their mark up in credit sales as 'profit' and list them as interest.[50] Why? Because the extent of 'profit' is potentially limitless whilst interest is capped by various contemporary anti-usury laws (in the US) and credit regulatory framework (in the UK) that protect those in need of credit against predatory lenders or otherwise illegitimate stipulations of gains on transactions. These conclusions negate any distinction between Islamic finance and conventional finance that the industry has strived to establish for arbitrage purposes.

5.2.1 Riba: *the what or the how?*

The form *riba* takes was never meant to be defined or carved in stone because, as an understanding of the primary sources' text on *riba* reveals (see 5.1.1 and 5.1.2), *riba* is a public policy rule that presumes the legitimacy of gain making in commercial transactions and the inverse in non-commercial cases. The effect of such a presumption is that *riba* can render an otherwise valid commercial contract, deriving gain, invalid if such a transaction is inequitable. This is verified through Muhammad's saying (II). Unfortunately, as far back as recorded Islamic history takes us, Muslims have strived, out of their misunderstanding of the concept and principle behind *riba*, to define and confine it to certain forms and practices. The purpose of this was, of course, to make life and commerce easier for the merchant since what was once a broad-based public policy principle was pinned down to certain practices and eventually to *one* specific practice (lending money) that relieved people of the moral obligation to conduct themselves equitably in all commercial and personal interactions with others. *Riba* eventually became the *what* not the *how* and, with time, so narrow was the principle's ambit reduced and so devoid in substance that the very purpose it was intended to serve was neglected if not violated. This is the reality of the current definition and application of *riba*.

It is noted, however, that a clear understanding of the relevant text in the primary sources indicates that the distinction drawn between trade and *riba* (despite claims of their apparent similarity) distinguishes *riba* as inequitable practices or transactions *resembling* commercial transactions in *form* yet lacking the *substance* of an equitable commercial transaction. The illegitimate (*riba*) transaction is distinguishable from the legitimate (trade/commerce) through the *effect*, that is, to question if the transaction is equitable.[51] This deduction follows directly from the fact that the *Quran* does not say Allah permits *profit* and prohibits *riba* – it says Allah permits *trade* and prohibits *riba*. The contrasting of *trade* with *riba* (a negation of the comparison of *trade* to *riba*) is a clear indication that *riba* is any transaction much like trade in *form* but, in fact, different in *substance* and *effect*.

We, therefore, can deduce that, in the context of the *Quran*, *riba* is to commercial transactions what extramarital sex is to marital sex. The operational factor distinguishing the prohibited from the permitted lies not in form but rather in the context and substance of the action engaged in. *Riba* is any inequitable transaction – or one that is prone to inequity – in contrast to equitable transactions described as 'trade'. The benefit from *riba* transactions, in contrast to the benefit arising from commercial transactions, is thus akin to an illegitimate child born out of wedlock, in contrast to a child born from marriage. The prohibition against extramarital sex (*zina*) is certainly not a prohibition against sexual intercourse or procreation in exactly the same fashion that the prohibition against *riba* is a not prohibition against deriving benefit or gain. This is the distinction the text of the *Quran* in *al-Baqara*: 275 alludes to. Further, *al-Baqara*: 276 states that Allah extinguishes *riba* and nurtures (causes to increase) acts of charity. If *riba* was interest, the translated text of the verse would read, 'Allah extinguishes interest' which makes little sense. *Al-Baqara*: 276 is better read as 'Allah extinguishes illegitimate gains and nurtures acts of charity'.

The significance of this distinction cannot be overstated, for just as profit/gain is the result of legitimate commercial engagements, devouring others wealth unjustly was the result of *riba* engagements. The mislaid equation of interest to *riba* arises from not paying attention to the above drawn distinction and, seen in this fresh light, the distinction has grave implication for the sharia arbitrage practices of Islamic finance today that resemble sale and lease transactions but are really guises for debt financing that consequently escape the more stringent debt regulatory compliance requirements and are effectively less equitable (and less economically efficient) compared to conventional finance transactions. In any case, though still prevalent, sharia arbitrage transactions that mimic conventional finance with few synthetic changes to ensure 'sharia compliance', like the *Murabaha*[52] (or *tawarruq*[53]) transactions, are gradually being denounced by Muslims.[54]

5.2.2 *Principles of Islamic law on matters of commerce vis-à-vis rituals*

It is useful to remember that earlier Muslim scholars and jurists sought equity and efficiency in commercial and social matters by adopting Roman or other legal forms much like Muhammad did by adopting the practices of the Jewish and Christian communities around him. It is only several centuries after the demise of Muhammad that jurists began feeling obliged to work under the heavy burden of 'sacred' history and the unreasonable admiration of the presumed timeless 'wisdom' of their predecessors.[55] It is this book's proposal that, as Al-Misri suggests, all distinctions pertaining to whether stipulated increases are termed 'fee' or interest and whether finance transactions are structured as loans or 'sale and buy back' be secondary to the primary concern of whether the transaction is equitable and efficient. The works of El-Gamal,[56] Dr Saleem,[57] and Abdul Ghafoor[58] all point toward this conclusion but stop short of its explicit expression. El-Gamal, apologetically concedes after rigorous analysis that adherence to religion has, historically, been ensured through adherence to forms, equally in the area of ritual and transaction. However, Islam is much more than a religion with set rules to follow. Islam is a way of life (*din*). This way of life has several spheres, ritual worship being only one sphere because, in essence, all of life is worship and thus all of life must be lived embodying the spirit of Islam. The domain of ritual worship in Islam has always required a degree of adherence to set forms that ensure a measure of continuity of practice through time. Outside the domain of ritual worship, human action was, and remains, entirely free of set forms and is governed by our free will and individual accountability yet regulated by customary practices and legal principles very similar to the (democratic ideal of) individual liberties counterbalanced by political governance and social justice. The principles governing the two distinct domains are best summarised by the prominent Maliki jurist, Ibn Taymiyya:[59]

> The acts and deeds of individuals are of two types: *ibadat* (devotional acts) whereby their religiousness is improved and *'adat* (transactions) which they need in their worldly matters. An inductive survey of sources of the sharia establishes that devotional acts are sanctioned by express injunctions of the sharia. Thus what is not commanded cannot be made obligatory. As for transactions, the principles governing them would be permissibility and absence of prohibition. So nothing can be prohibited unless it is proscribed by Allah and His messenger.

Therefore, adherence in the domain of commercial/non-ritual matters is more a matter of upholding the spirit and essence of Islam (justice and social welfare) because neither the *Quran* nor the Prophet laid down set forms or detailed laws (of transactions or actions). The primary sources hint at the intended socio-economic outcome to be attained, but do not mention the prescribed form to be adhered to. We have chained, out of our own doing, ourselves to the forms we created and insist on adhering to them. Religious canon has no part in such insistence. Indeed, for a spirituality founded on the very basis of forbidding an attachment to forms (to prevent the mischief of idolatry) it is only natural that Islam would require the same (detachment to form) in every other facet of life. The Islamic finance industry and jurisdictions will not hear of this because it pulls the rug from under their feet and denies them the sharia arbitrage opportunities derived from the distinctions they have established between 'Islamic' and conventional finance. Ultimately, however, the charade must end sometime and it is herein shown using the *Quran*, prophetic traditions, scholastic reasoning and Islamic economic writings of recent past and present times that it is not interest that Islam prohibits, rather it is inequity and inefficiency that is the target of the prohibition. We see that interest and marking to market can, in fact, be means of ensuring equity and efficiency in the financial market much like the Prophet's advice to sell at the highest price possible and buy at the lowest price possible was at his time. From this vantage point, the future for Islamic finance is as wide and as indeterminable as we choose to create it. By implication, the complexity of structures that have inhibited the take-off of any genuine sharia compliant securitisation to date, or any other financial structure for that matter, need no longer persist to be so. If the question then posed is on how are we, now, to ensure equity and efficiency, the answer is replete in the established market and customary practices prevalent today. It will be recalled that the Prophet freely adopted the practices of the Christians and the Jews of his time to fill in any lacunae that the *Quran* was silent on or not in direct conflict with. Likewise, it is open to us today, as it was open to the jurists who adopted from the Roman and other more advanced civilisations of their time, to adopt practices, institutions and laws that serve the spirit of Islam.

It will be remembered that the *Quran* is a text of guidance not only to a given people, but to the entirety of Humanity – it does not distinguish a people from another and speaks readily to all those who believe regardless of their religion or creed. In fact, there is nothing like 'Islamic' finance. There is only *one* finance because the contractual principles indicated in the *Quran* and the authentic sayings of Muhammad, are the very same that underpin the common law contractual and commercial framework. This is demonstrated herein by establishing that every concept discussed under Islamic finance throughout the ages exists today in a more complex, advanced and refined form under the common law. The rationale behind such principles of Islamic finance, thus, can be served better and more comprehensively under the common law. Likewise, in matters of debt finance, we need not bother with any demarcation between 'Islamic' and conventional for the twin objectives of equity and efficiency are nowhere better served and catered for today than under the common law. The objection may be raised that the common law is not perfect; it has its flaws. The response to that is, certainly, no human system is or can be perfect. The beauty of the common law, as Islamic law, however, is that it possesses an efficient and balanced mechanism dedicated to the constant review and improvement of its laws, regulations and processes, a discussion of which is beyond the scope of this book. The point being that if something is wrong with the system, why not fix it instead of trying to build an entirely new system just for purposes of distinction, yet remaining effectively more inefficient and inequitable. That is akin to setting out to reinvent the wheel just because one does not deem it 'Islamic'. The wiser option is to perfect the existing wheel in accordance with the universal principles of Islam hence attaining one's goal faster. In the latter option, one finds equity and efficiency of outcome and in the former, unnecessary hardship and inefficiency afflicted.

5.3 Social justice and implications of the redefinition for Islamic finance

The argument often put forward against interest in commercial lending is that the prohibition of *riba* pertains to the making of money out of money without effort or counter value in exchange. Others argue that making money out of money is prohibited regardless of the value it brings or adds. This indicates a misunderstanding of both *riba* and commercial banking on two levels:

- Commercial endeavour of banks and financial institutions is evidenced in the setting up and rendering services of credit provision to those who choose to borrow complete with premises, professional advisors, managers, machinery and secure safekeeping for money kept available for additional borrowing. What difference, if at all, is there between a bank offering money lending services and a realtor offering properties for rent? Or a car dealer offering a fleet of cars for hire? Is the effort not mainly in the start-up costs with a diminishing portion (over time) going toward the maintenance of the items to be lent, rented or hired? This is especially so in light of the discredited notion of loan-credit being likened to money and the acknowledgement of credit rights being proprietary, as is discussed in chapter 6.

• It is agreed that any contract (for goods or services) must be a mutually consented to bargain. This is a principle derived from the saying of Muhammad (II) pertaining to the barter of dates. In this regard, a money lending contract for an increased return is a mutually consented to bargain whereby the borrower gains credit to use for his own purposes (often) for profitable gain or an increased return whilst the lender gains the increased return on his money in compensation for the loss of liquidity and the risk of losing his principle (in case of default) in addition to suffering the twin effects of inflation and devaluation over time.

Nonetheless, the proposal that interest is not prohibited in commercial loans is still countered with the concern that the creditors will charge 'excessive' rates of returns that is prohibited by the *Quran* in *Ali-Imran*: 130 ' ... devour not *riba* double and redoubled'. This concern is however allayed once one appreciates the counter intuitive notion that the characterisation of interest as 'excessive' makes little economic sense since the definition of excessive is subjective and is unlikely to materialise in the regulated financial context we exist in today.[60] Reality establishes that 'excessive' rates of interest are not the norm in commercial lending practice. If interest rates of a certain bank are excessive, one has the choice not to borrow money from that bank at such 'excessive' rates just as one has the choice not to choose to eat in an expensive restaurant. One cannot say that the charging of exorbitant prices for a cup of coffee and toast in a five star restaurant means that such a transaction is unlawful and the coffee and toast must be given to the customer for free. That is ludicrous. The transaction is like any other commercial transaction and one may choose to participate in it or not depending on his needs or means. The same goes for commercial loan transactions. The concern of 'excessive' interest rates, thus, is best dealt with through the very same element required in any transaction, that is, a mutually consented decision between the parties involved to strike a bargain. The parties are free to negotiate a rate that compensates the lender for the opportunity, cost of lending, inflation, devaluation and the risk of default as well as a reasonable gain for the bargain struck, and interest rate guidelines or benchmarks may be developed at a national or international level. Moreover, in line with Muhammad's recommendation, market forces of supply (of money) and demand (for credit) already acts as a natural regulatory mechanism that prevents the charging of exorbitant interest rates.

It is, in fact, the potential of unregulated Islamic banks that structure loans and finance in the form of sale and leases or buy-backs that is of greater concern. Their potential to charge excessive rates of interest guised as 'fee' or 'gratuity' or 'profit sharing' and the inequity that results there from (being 'the very essence of *riba*' Muhammad spoke of) has led practicing academics like El-Gamal to emphasise the appropriateness of Islamic banks' 'marking to market'.[61] This emphasis acknowledges that in a regulated financial market, interest is capped whereas profit making being unregulated, gives Islamic banks a blank cheque to charge uncapped fees on their financial products in the name of 'profit' that may in effect be unjustifiably high and inequitable.

In other words, it is not excessive interest we should be concerned about, but the excessive 'profit' presently being made by the Islamic finance industry. Adopting the definition and scope of application of *riba* preferred in this book, the principle of *riba* could be used to regulate commercial loans in such a way that whilst inequity is prevented, interest may be legitimately charged. This would be in line with the verse of the *Quran* that prohibits the taking of *riba* 'double and multiplied' as well as the sayings of Muhammad whilst at the same time allowing for bargains by mutual consent expressly permitted in *al-Nisa*: 29.

The soundness of the permissibility of charging interest in commercial lending transactions is strengthened by a consideration of the inverse scenario, that is, a prohibition on all interest bearing loans whatever the purpose. This would lead to great social inequity and inadvertent failure in Islam's objective of social justice resulting from a compulsion to lend money charitably (in the cause of God). How could it be decreed by God that the debtor may borrow at the loss of the creditor (through inflation, devaluation and illiquidity) so as to enable the debtor to profit? Hardly anyone would want to lend his money to another and suffer loss merely for the increase in other's wealth; it defies human nature. This is expressly acknowledged in the *Quran*, *al-Baqara*: 279, when it says pertaining to *riba*, 'you render not injustice nor shall you be rendered injustice', that is, the principle cuts both ways.

The wealthy would prefer to use their money in their own business, keep it for themselves (i.e. the opportunity cost of extending credit) or otherwise continue to give of it to charity as they please whilst desisting in extending loans commercially for the fear of *riba*. Needless to say, in both social and economic terms, this would be vastly detrimental to society because it would hinder availability of credit and, in turn, the circulation and redistribution of wealth.[62] In this sense, the *riba* prohibition dictates that whilst encouraging the giving of charity through interest free interpersonal loans, trade credit can be extended for an appropriate fee.

On this note, I refer to El-Gamal's explanation that, generally, one lends in Islam not to seek repayment at an increase but for purposes of giving charitably the time value of money (a sufficient counter value in any loan transaction) or usufruct lent whilst affording the poor debtor the retention of his dignity by allowing him or her to repay the amount borrowed as opposed to an outright donation made. Indeed, other writers on social justice and the current economic state of nations have openly acknowledged the humiliating character of charity to those who receive it owing to its top-down nature.[63] However, El-Gamal's explanation is inapplicable to commercial transactions (which include loans) because commercial loans are horizontal, taking place between individuals with freedom of choice and intending contractual legal relations at arm's length hence the dignity of both parties remains intact regardless of their economic status. Increased returns may be charged on commercial loans for why should one not in need be allowed the 'dignity of borrowing' if he does not need charity? Recall that the categories of those entitled to charity are expressly laid out in the *Quran* at *al-Tauba*: 60. Therefore, outside the eight categories, why is a debtor to be exempt from paying a counter value for the credit extended to him?

5.4 *Riba* and the common law doctrine of consideration

We have, so far, established that *riba* as expressed in the *Quran* and explained by Muhammad is a general principle requiring equity in all transactions. To ensure transactional equity, the *riba* principle applies through two respective rules depending on the nature of the transaction: (i) no consideration or gain may be drawn or elicited in non-commercial contexts, that non-commercial transactions are equitable as long as they do not draw a profit, gain or consideration; and (ii) commercial transactions may freely elicit gain or consideration but the bargain struck must be equitable in effect as demonstrated by Muhammad's saying (II) regarding the barter of dates. Therefore, while commercial transactions are unaffected by the first rule and may elicit consideration or make a profit, only consideration *effecting* an equitable bargain is legitimate otherwise the transaction is vitiated by the *riba* principle.[64]

Ultimately, however, it is the bargain that must be equitable, not the consideration. Consideration, whatever form or value it takes, is valid as long as the parties are mutually agreed and the bargain effected is equitable. What, then, is meant by a bargain being *equitable*? This is explained in subsection 5.4.1.

Riba can thus be said to pertain to the doctrine of consideration – but is not the Islamic law counterpart to the doctrine of consideration. Instead, while *riba* affects whether consideration may be elicited, it is in essence a vitiating factor that *determines* whether the transaction is, in effect, equitable or not. Therefore, if the drawing of consideration effects an equitable bargain, the contract is valid at law. Otherwise, the *riba* principle kicks in to vitiate the transaction and the consideration elicited would automatically be nullified.

Under the common law, consideration has been described as follows: 'A valuable consideration, in the sense of the law, may consist either in some right, interest, profit, or benefit accruing to one party, or some forbearance, detriment, loss or responsibility, given, suffered or undertaken by the other'.[65] The doctrine of consideration provides that a promisee cannot enforce a promise unless he has given or promised to give something in exchange for the promise. Winn LJ in *D & C Builders v Rees*,[66] observed that an agreement is only binding if either made under seal or supported by consideration. To be a valid and enforceable contract, therefore, there must be a bargain between the parties not a promise to give gratuitously,[67] and consideration, whatever form it takes, is a strong indicator of the presence of a bargain.[68] In *Williams v Roffey*[69] the court explained that if:

> as a result of giving his promise, B obtains in practice a benefit, or obviates a disbenefit; and (v) B's promise is not given as a result of economic duress or fraud on the part of A; then (vi) the benefit to B is capable of being consideration for B's promise, so that the promise will be legally binding.

As McKendrick explains, as long as considerations is sufficient, albeit nominal,[70] the transaction becomes enforceable *unless* a further element of duress or fraud or other vitiating factor is present. Therefore, despite requiring only 'sufficient, not adequate consideration' a transaction, nonetheless, could be vitiated if it was concluded in an illicit manner indicating that the bargain is not equitable. So, comparable to the position under Islamic law, while consideration need not to be adequate under the common law, the transaction, nonetheless, must be equitable because, otherwise, it is caught by the appropriate vitiating factor that may render it unenforceable. This distinction is of further significance as we shall return to see in subsection 5.4.1.

The intention, in what follows, is to compare the two rules that give expression to the *riba* principle with their corresponding aspects under the doctrine of consideration under English common law. It is not intended to provide an overview of the doctrine of consideration, either under Islamic law or under common law, since any good contract law text on either legal system provides that already. My contribution lies in the enquiry into *riba*'s relationship with consideration and in particular as to *riba*'s requirement of transactional equity vis-à-vis the common law and whether transactional equity is the basis of *eliciting* or *enforcing* consideration.

5.4.1 Equitable transaction versus adequate consideration

At first blush, the requirement that transactions must be equitable under Islamic law appears to be in sharp contrast with the requirement of adequate consideration under common law. A deeper consideration of the apparent, however, reveals that the two doctrines say the same thing in different terms. To reach this conclusion, let us commence with considering the apparent distinction that arises indirectly from the fact that *consideration under the common law pertains to the promise made*, not the contract sought to be enforced. As Professor Treitel explains, 'consideration being the *reciprocal benefit or forbearance on the part of each party in consideration for the other's promise*, is unconcerned with whether the seller (or the buyer for that matter) has made a *good* bargain'[71] (emphasis added). The common law position on consideration is, thus, that consideration need only be sufficient (something of value); it need not be adequate nor is it concerned with whether a good bargain is made.[72] Therefore, a £1 consideration for the sale of a business was deemed sufficient[73] as were three chocolate wrappers for gramophone records in the case of *Chappel & Co Ltd v The Nestle Co Ltd*.[74] The principle of *riba*, however, also requires that bargains be equitable and, therefore, that the *effect* of eliciting consideration as one element of contract formation must also be equitable. Yet, if one recalls the excerpt from *Williams v Roffey*,[75] above, the position under the common law is the same and was recently affirmed in the case of *Forde v Birmingham City Council*.[76]

Two issues immediately arise from the above distinctions, respectively: what does an equitable bargain entail; and, does 'equitable bargain' equate to 'adequate' consideration or 'good' bargain? The word bargain implies an agreement attained between two parties (often after negotiation of some sort). The Oxford Dictionary defines bargain as 'an agreement made between people saying what each will do for the other'. Bargains, therefore, are simply mutually agreed to transactions. Why then does a bargain have to be equitable if it is consented to? Simply because the equitable nature of the transaction acts as the litmus test of veracity of the consent given by the parties. Islamic law and common law possess principles towards this end. The principle of *riba* requires equitable transactions as indicated by Muhammad's sayings on *riba* and the application of common law vitiating factors (duress, undue influence, unconscionability and inequality of bargaining power or other policy consideration) also indicate the requirement of equitable transaction, even if the requirement of 'sufficient' consideration has been satisfied. In *Antons Trawling v Smith*,[77] Baragwanath J held that:

> Where there is no element of duress or other policy factor suggesting that an agreement duly performed should not attract the consequences that each party must reasonably be taken to have expected. The importance of consideration is as a valuable signal that the parties intend to be bound by their agreement, rather than an end in itself. Where the parties who have already made such intention clear by entering legal relations have acted upon agreement to a variation, in the absence of policy reasons to the contrary, they should be bound by their agreement.

The 'equitable bargain' requirement simply underscores the concern, in all cases where vitiating factors apply to issues of consideration, that one party will exploit the vulnerability of the other. Consideration is, thus, one element of a valid contract and the existence of valid consideration does not guarantee the existence of a valid contract. To be a valid and enforceable contract, the transaction as a whole must be equitable, which is to say, must not be vitiated by any policy considerations or vitiating factors of the likes of duress or unconscionability.

As to whether 'equitable bargain' equates to requiring 'adequate' consideration or 'good' bargain, the Oxford Dictionary defines the word adequate as 'satisfactory or acceptable' and provides that the origin of the term is the Latin word *adaequare* which means to 'make equal to'.[78] English common law contract texts describe 'adequate' consideration as that which brings about a fair or good bargain.[79] A transaction need not comprise adequate consideration to be an equitable bargain: the equitable nature of a bargain is otherwise secured by operation of the vitiating factors (fraud, deceit, coercion, etc.) or by ensuring that the consideration is not, itself, unlawful, for example, stolen property. In a nutshell, therefore, equitable bargain does not equate to a 'good' bargain in terms of requiring 'adequate' consideration.

It is important to reiterate the fact that *riba* requires equitable *bargains* does not translate to a requirement that the consideration itself must be commensurate or adequate. Even where complete equanimity is required (in barter transactions) as in saying (I) of Muhammad, the target is preventing inequitable transactions, not requiring adequate consideration. Therefore, in the words of Professor Treitel, it is equally irrelevant under

Islamic law 'that the seller has made a good bargain'.[80] The focus of *riba* is that the transaction as a whole is of equitable effect to both parties and not whether the consideration was adequate or not. In all exchanges for cash or otherwise in non-barter transactions, as long as something of value has passed between the parties by their mutual agreement in equitable manner, then the law honours the agreement of the parties. This position is illustrated by Muhammad's saying (I) and (II). In saying (I) he concludes, 'if the species differ, sell as you wish provided payment is made on the spot'. Muhammad gives no direction as to the appropriate consideration or price but rather leaves it entirely to the parties. He requires only 'payment on the spot' which, in the context of sixth/seventh century ad, was necessary to prevent inequity being rendered through delay or absconding payment for the exchange. Similarly, in saying (II) Muhammad vitiates an otherwise perfectly valid barter transaction not because the consideration is not adequate, but due to the latent inequity of exchanging two portions of inferior quality dates for one portion of superior quality dates. This is confirmed by the fact that Muhammad then directs Bilal to sell his (low quality) dates at the highest market price and buy the (high quality) dates he wants at the lowest possible market price indicating there is no 'adequate' consideration requirement, only that the bargain be equitable which is satisfied by buying and selling through the market mechanism. Islamic law and common law, therefore, are aligned on the issues of consideration and equitable bargains.[81]

Moreover, the common law also distinguishes between cases where the consideration takes the form of a money payment for a service or product and cases where the consideration takes the form of non-monetary benefit. McKendrick explains that, 'where the promise is one to pay money for a service or a product (here used to encompass both goods and land) the law generally does not encounter any difficulty'. This is in direct agreement with Muhammad's saying (II) where he advises Bilal to sell his dates at market price instead of bartering them for high quality dates. McKendrick continues explaining that:

> the issue is more difficult where the alleged consideration takes a form other than a promise to pay a sum of money. Here we encounter the question whether it is for the courts or the parties to determine what constitutes sufficient consideration … The courts have generally adopted a liberal approach to the identification of consideration and cases can be found in which trifling or apparently insignificant acts have been held to constitute consideration.[82]

However, the conventional definition of consideration, adopted by Lush J in *Currie v Misa*,[83] as 'a valuable consideration, *in the sense of the law*', (emphasis added) implies that it is the court to determine what amounts to valuable consideration in a case, not the parties.

5.4.2 Raison d'être *behind* riba *and the doctrine of consideration*

Both Islamic law and the common law have protected contracting parties from inequity as a basis of determining enforceability of transactions. Under Islamic law, this is the function of *riba* as a vitiating factor with regard to consideration. Under the common law, this is the function of the various applicable vitiating factors.

Riba is currently *presumed* to be limited to the protection of *consumers* or *debtors* from the powerful merchants who occupied a dominant position in the (then) capitalist society. I say *presumed* because neither the *Quran* nor Muhammad mentions this; a deduction has been made from the context of revelation of the verses pertaining to *riba*, Muhammad's sayings and the capitalist reality of Makkah in the sixth/seventh century. However, even assuming this deduction is plausible, we also know that the *Quran* not once alludes to *riba* being a one-sided 'protection' principle and in Muhammad's saying (II), *riba* is experienced as a vitiating factor applicable regardless of the form of the transaction or the party on which it is imputed. It is the inequity of the transaction that *riba* catches and consequently vitiates the transaction unless the inequitable element is removed or remedied.

Lord Denning's judgement in *D & C Builders*, commonly used in illustration of consideration serving a protective purpose, indicates that the aim of the law is to protect both parties from *inequity*. It is equity in the case at hand that the court is really striving to attain, not the protection of either party. Denning explains, invoking the broad principle stated by Lord Cairns in *Hughes v Metropolitan Railway Co.*[84] that, 'parties who have entered into definite and distinct terms involving certain legal results ... who otherwise might have enforced those rights will not be allowed to enforce them when it would be *inequitable* having regard to the dealing which have taken place within and between the parties' (emphasis added).

The equitable principle of estoppels is thus a general principle of the common law that is applied to different cases, and in protection (a shield) of either party, as appropriate. Lord Denning explains:

> This principle has been applied to cases where a creditor agrees to accept a lesser sum in discharge of a greater. So much so that we can now say

that, when a debtor and a creditor enter into a course of negotiation, which leads the debtor to suppose that on the payment of a lesser sum the creditor will not enforce payment of the balance, and on the faith thereof the debtor pays the lesser sum and the creditor accepts it as satisfaction: then the creditor will not be allowed to enforce payment of the balance when it would be inequitable to do so ... see *Central London Property Trust Ltd v High Trees House* [1947] 1 KB 130.

In applying this principle, however, we must note the qualification: The creditor is only barred from his legal right when it would be inequitable for him to insist upon them. When there has been true accord, under which the creditor voluntarily agrees to accept a lesser sum, and the debtor acts upon that accord by paying the lesser sum and the creditor accepts it, then it is inequitable for the creditor afterwards to insist on the balance.

In *D & C Builders*, equity between the parties just so happened to yield to judgement being pronounced in favour of the creditor, as Lord Denning explains:

on the facts ... it seems to me that there was no true accord. The debtor's wife held the creditor to ransom. The creditor was in need of money for his own commitments, and she knew it ... She was making a threat to break the contract (by paying nothing) and she was doing it so as to compel the creditor to do what he was unwilling to do (to accept £300 in settlement of the £480 due to him): and she succeeded. In these circumstances there is no true accord so as to found a defence of accord and satisfaction: There is also no equity in the defendant to warrant any departure from the due course of law.

Lord Denning stresses the *equity* of the transaction as being the foundation upon which a contract becomes enforceable, including, for purposes of (accepting or foregoing) consideration.

Although the above referred to cases are on estoppel and not strictly relating to consideration, the value in their reference lies in that they illustrate the principle of estoppels in relation to contractual price or credit obligations in direct parallel with the principle behind *riba*. The principle is that any inequity in dealing between the parties will prevent or estop the inequitable party from exercising or enforcing their right/s in question (including eliciting consideration).

The principle behind *riba* and the doctrine of consideration are thus agreed on the fact that an equitable bargain is the *basis* for eliciting or enforcing consideration because it is the equitable nature of a dealing that signifies attainment of 'true accord' per Lord Denning's dicta.

5.4.3 Riba *as a vitiating factor versus consideration as a distinct element of contract formation*

A possible distinction between *riba* and consideration is the effect of each on a contract. Consideration, unlike *riba*, is a distinct element of contract formation. Lack of, or insufficient, consideration is thus not strictly speaking a vitiating factor in that without sufficient consideration no contract would have been formed to be vitiated in the first place. *Riba*, on the other hand, is a vitiating factor that determines whether a bargain is equitable and thus whether consideration was legitimately elicited. Therefore, regardless of whether consideration exists and the consideration is deemed sufficient by the parties themselves (as was the case in Bilal's barter of dates) the transaction can still be vitiated by *riba* if inequitable. We noted in section 5.4.1 that the same position is true under the common law in reference to the role of vitiating factors.

5.5 *Riba*, consideration and intention to create legal relations

This chapter has defined *riba* as a vitiating factor pertaining to consideration that is based on the underlying principle requiring transactional equity. It has emphasised that a cornerstone of *riba's* principle is that it draws a distinction between commercial and non-commercial transactions for purposes of application of the two rules giving expression to it, respectively. A commercial transaction is one characterised as a mutually consented to bargain or 'trade' and this characterisation *legitimises* the drawing of consideration.[85] In principle, it is the *intention* to 'trade' behind the transaction (regardless of form) that designates it as commercial or non-commercial. The commercial nature of a transaction, in turn, raises a rebuttable presumption that the transaction is equitable in effect and forms the basis of eliciting consideration. This answers question (5) that was posed at the end of section 5.1, that is, *what distinguishes a commercial agreement from a non-commercial agreement that deems a commercial agreement eligible to elicit consideration?*

However, being latent, the intention to 'trade' is generally inferred from the context and surrounding circumstances of the transaction that reveal whether the transaction was a mutual bargain. In the case of Bilal's barter of dates, for instance, Muhammad advised Bilal to sell his (low quality) dates at market price and buy the other (high quality) dates from the proceeds so as to obviate the vitiating effect of *riba* on the barter transaction. The resort to market mechanism or market forces of demand and supply is a circumstantial factor that implies the *intention* to trade (as opposed to being a social exchange) and evidences the mutuality of the bargain which, in turn, legitimises the gain derived from another. The barter transaction, on the other hand, was described as being 'the very essence of *riba*' (as opposed to trade) even though it was carried out by the same parties with the same outcome. This can be rationalised as being the consequence of the lack of an objective determinant of the mutuality of the bargain that coloured the transaction as '*riba*'.

This relationship between consideration and the intention to 'trade' under the principle of *riba* prompts us to compare it with the common law relationship between consideration and the intention to create legal relations.

The general rule, under the English common law, is that a promise is not binding as a contract unless it is either made by deed or supported by some 'consideration'.[86] The common law also distinguishes between domestic or social agreements on the one hand and commercial contracts on the other for purposes of contractual force.[87] In domestic[88] and social[89] agreements, the courts presume against the parties having had an intention to create legal relations, whilst in commercial[90] agreements the courts presume that the parties did have an intention to create legal relations. The presumption is, in both contexts, rebuttable albeit not an easy one to rebut. The '*rationale behind the presumption under the common law derives mainly from public policy, rather than the parties' actual intention*', as explained by Lord Atkin in *Balfour v Balfour*[91] to avoid the 'floodgates' of cases that would otherwise be brought to court if social and domestic arrangements were held to result in legal relations (emphasis added). To put it bluntly, the presumption is a convenient criterion through which transactions are recognised as enforceable contracts or not, while limiting the number of cases brought to the courts for such determination. This is not to say, however, that the presumptions based on the nature of the transaction renders the actual intentions of the parties irrelevant; the parties' intentions are relevant for the purposes of rebutting the presumption the nature of the transaction raises. For instance, a husband can be his wife's tenant[92] and where a man, before marriage, promised his future wife to leave her a house if she married him, was able to enforce the promise though it was made informally and in affectionate terms.[93]

Consideration and the intention to create legal relations are, however, doctrinally distinct under the common law and, as explained by lord Atkin in *Balfour v Balfour* that, for instance, even if Mrs Balfour had succeeded in proving that she provided consideration for her husband's promise to pay her £30 a month, she would still have had to prove that she and her husband intended to create legal relations. Similarly, Duke LJ in *Balfour v Balfour* explained that while a link between the doctrines of consideration and the intention to create legal relations exists, they remain two distinct doctrines both of which must be proved in establishing that a contract was formed between the parties. Therefore, a transaction formed with, or presumed to have, an intention to create legal relations is, nonetheless, unenforceable unless consideration is given in return of the promise. Alternatively, even though consideration passing from the promisee to the promisor is, generally, a strong indicator of an intention to create legal relations under the common law[94] it does not itself establish such an intention.[95] Both elements must exist for a transaction to be a contract enforceable at law.

The two doctrines, nonetheless, do overlap and it is sometimes difficult to discern whether the court's decision is one based on the absence of consideration or that of an intention to create legal intent as in *White v Bluet*. In this case, the court's language was one of absence of consideration having rendered the agreement unenforceable yet the court implied that the absence of consideration was a cause for unenforceability *because* it indicated an absence of an intention to create legal relations. Consideration, in such cases, becomes merely an indicator of an intention to create legal relations and the distinction between the two doctrines blurs. In such instances, the position under common law is similar to Islamic law in that consideration is not an independent doctrine or element of contract law but rather is attached to the intention to create legal relations as expressed by the *riba* principle.

As for the question, 'what distinguishes a commercial agreement from a non-commercial agreement that deems a commercial agreement eligible to elicit consideration?' The common law position can be explained by a two-fold answer: first, that mutuality exists in commercial agreements that does not in social or domestic agreements. This was stated in the case of *Simpkins v Pays*[96] where the house owner (defendant) refused to pay a share of a prize winning to the plaintiff (lodger in defendant's home) alleging that the agreement made between them was not intended to be legally binding. Again, this mutuality lies not in the form or setting of the transaction but rather the intention behind it. Sellers LJ in *Simpkins* held:

> It may well be there are many family associations where some sort of rough and ready thing is said which would not, on a proper estimate of circumstances, establish a contract which was contemplated to have legal consequences, but I do not so find here. I think that there was here a mutuality in the arrangement between the parties. It was not very formal, but certainly in effect, it was agreed.[97]

Legal commentary[98] on Seller J's reference to 'mutuality' in *Simpkins v Pays* notes that 'it [mutuality] refers to the presence of consideration rather than the presence of an intention to create legal relations'. This point is made as part of a wider argument to the effect that 'absence of consideration … provides a simpler and more realistic explanation of the special quality of domestic agreements' than does the intention to create legal relations. Second, that social and domestic agreements are not contracts precisely because they lack the ingredient of 'an intention to create legal relations'. Since only agreements with the requisite intention are valid contracts, and commercial contracts are deemed to possess this intention, commercial agreements are, as a general rule, deemed valid contracts whilst social domestic agreements are not.

What, then, if at all, is the difference between whether the parties intended to contract and/or whether they intend to create legal relations? Mance LJ explains this in the case of *Baird Textile Holdings Ltd v Marks & Spencer Plc*.[99] In fact, he seems to combine the concepts underlying *gharar* and *riba*, as we have discussed them in this book, as key components of forming a valid contract. He states:

> For a contract to come into existence, there must be both (a) and agreement on essentials with sufficient certainty to be enforceable and (b) an intention to create legal relations. Both requirements are usually judged objectively. Absence of the former may involve or be explained by the latter. But this is not always so. A sufficiently certain agreement may be reached but there may be either expressly or impliedly (in some family situations) no intention to create legal relations.
>
> An intention to create legal relations is normally presumed in the case of an express or apparent agreement satisfying the first requirement … If the parties would or might have acted as they did without any such contract, there is no necessity to imply any contract. It is merely putting the same point another way to say that no intention to make any contract will be inferred.

Note Mance LJ's order, that is, that intention to create legal relations may be presumed if certainty of terms is fulfilled, not the other way round.

Recent case law indicates that the English common law is shifting in its focus pertaining to the intention to create legal relations in a manner that places the intention to create legal relations as a prerequisite for triggering the doctrine of consideration, rather than the other way round as per the status quo. A move in this direction would align the common law with Islamic law because, as we have discussed above, it the commercial nature of a transaction (which possesses an intention to create legal relations) that legitimises the elicitation of consideration, not the other way round. This shift follows after the case of *Williams v Roffey Bros & Nicholls (Contractors) Ltd*,[100] which has made the doctrine of consideration much easier to satisfy, though not without much criticism.[101] In *Williams v Roffey*, Russell LJ stated that: 'the courts nowadays should be more ready to find [the existence of consideration] so as to reflect the intention of the parties'. *Antons Trawlings v Smith*[102] applied the reasoning in *Williams v Roffey* so as to hold that 'in on-going, arm's length commercial transactions where it is utterly fictional to describe what is being conceded as a gift, and which there ought to be a strong presumption that good commercial "consideration" underlie any seemingly detrimental modifications'. More recently, in *Chwee Kin Keong v Digilandmall.com Pte Ltd*,[103] Rajah JC took a step further in observing that: 'The time may have to come for the common law to shed the pretence of searching for consideration to uphold commercial contracts. The marrow of contractual relationships should be the parties' intention to create a legal relationship'. It must be noted that *Williams v Roffey* dealt primarily with consideration for variations of contract as opposed to consideration for contract. Thus, *Antons Trawlings* and *Chwee Kin Keong* may have gone slightly out on a limb in using *Williams v Roffey* in justifying a relaxed approach towards the requirement of consideration. Professor Coote[104] may be better justified in disagreeing with the approach in *Williams v Roffey* by opining that a better and more principled approach would be to dispense with the requirement of consideration for variations of contract, whilst recognising that a contract is still necessary. In other words, a contract requires consideration whilst the variation of an already valid contract ought not to require consideration. Ultimately, however, Coote and *Roffey* may be speaking the same language as it is not difficult to discover 'benefit' in varying a contract.

Conclusion

This chapter established that:

- The *Quran* explains *riba* as pertaining to illegitimate gain; illegitimate gain arises from any inequitable or unjust transaction.
- The *Quran* distinguishes between commercial and non-commercial transactions for purposes of applying the *riba* prohibition. This implies that the no consideration *riba* rule pertains only to non-commercial transactions.
- Accordingly, the sayings of Muhammad explain that all commercial transactions using money as a medium of exchange are free to elicit

profit/gain without triggering the vitiating element of *riba*. Barter transactions, though subject to market forces are not amenable to an objective measure of value and thus prone to inequity. Therefore, all barter transactions are subject to the requirement of equanimity in exchange.

- With specific regard to credit transactions, which includes loans, the 0% interest/gain rule applies only to non-commercial credit transactions.
- Commercial lending and finance falls within the ambit of trade/lawful endeavour for which increased return/profit may be charged. Interest may therefore be charged on commercial loans and finance transactions at the best market rate, as is the case with any other commercial transaction.
- The motivation and impetus for any non-commercial lending or exchange lies in it being an act of religious/charitable character in the cause of God.

The proposals and conclusions presented in this chapter have the potential of revolutionising Islamic finance, both economically and socially – by allowing for unprecedented growth unimpeded by pedantic restrictions of form over substance and simultaneously catering to social justice and equity. Consequently, the distinction of 'us versus them' for purposes of commercial arbitrage crumbles and the adoption and adaptation of financial structures and methods from other legal jurisdictions such as the common law (and conventional finance in general) becomes possible as long as the substance of legitimate gain through equitable transactions is adhered to.

6

THE NATURE OF DEBT AND THE LEGALITY OF ITS SALE

This chapter examines the nature of debt within Islamic law for purposes of ascertaining the legality of the sale of debt and the ensuing implications for sharia compliant securitisations. The task is complicated by the lack of clarity, even within one school of legal thought, pertaining to the definition and nature of debt and, consequently, as to the legality of the 'sale of debt' (receivables transaction). The significance of such ascertainment for sharia compliant securitisations cannot be overstated, as illustrated by the ENSEC Home Finance Pool 1 transaction – a securitisation that closed in May 2005. Whilst many thought it to be the first Middle East sharia compliant securitisation, scratching below the surface reveals the fact that it does not strictly qualify as such because of its fully cash collateralised obligations (i.e. no debt obligations were securitised). Therefore, whilst the cash collateralised obligations earned the transaction an AAA rating, it was not a securitisation in the traditional legal sense that entails the conversion of collateralised debt obligations (receivables) into tradable securities – the missing factor in the ENSEC transaction. The relevance of ENSEC's structure for purposes of this chapter lies in the fact that the transaction was structured as a fully cash-collateralised securitisation for purposes of evading the perceived sharia prohibition on the 'sale of debt' which, needless to say, severely curtails the use and development of securitisation structures in Islamic finance. The two main questions that arise in this respect are: why is the sale of debt prohibited under Islamic law; and what does the nature of debt have to do with such prohibition?

Islamic finance (in theory) drawing from Islamic law of contract and property restricts the sale of debt/receivables on two main grounds: First, debt is deemed non-proprietary on the basis of juristic likening of debt to money. Debt, on this basis, is deemed incapable of forming the subject matter of a sale beyond the relationship of debtor and creditor,[1] just as is the case with money. Even the 'sale' between debtor and creditor is in essence simply a set-off arrangement and does not qualify as a proper sale contract. Even within the most progressive Islamic finance jurisdiction, Malaysia, the sale of debts/receivables to third parties is only valid if representative of an underlying proprietary asset. Further, the Islamic jurists' likening debt to money creates the effect whereby any increased return element of the securities trigger the *riba* prohibition and all receivables, including future streams of income, are characterised as purely personal rights – eliminating the viability of secondary markets. Second, given the intangible and/or future nature of debts/receivables, even if the receivable is asset-backed, the sale of receivable securities on the secondary market is perceived to trigger the prohibition of *gharar* (speculative uncertainty) and the legal maxim[2] that prohibits the 'sale of one deferred obligation with another' (*bay' al kali bi al kali*)[3] which is linked, again, to the issue of homogeneity and *riba*.

Therefore, the two fundamental reasons why the sale of debt is prohibited by Muslim jurists[4] are:

- the non-proprietary nature of debt as a result of likening debt to money; and
- the intangible and future nature of debt that is deemed alien to traditional conceptions of property.

To resolve the nature and legality of the state of debt in Islamic law, this chapter must therefore consider the following issues:

1 What is debt? How is it defined? Is debt money? And, what are the consequences, either way, of the sale of debt?
2 Is debt a personal or proprietary right? Is debt capable of being sold only if it is proprietary? And what are the consequences for Islamic finance securitisations, either way?
3 Must the sale of debt be asset-backed? If so, why and on what basis?
4 If Muhammad, and commercial practice, allow debt rights to be freely transferable to third parties via the contract of *hawalat al dayn* (transfer of debt) and, thus, impliedly granting debt proprietary nature, why are receivables (debt rights) not allowed to be freely traded on primary and secondary capital markets?
5 If the sale of debt is prohibited on the sole basis of it being likened to money (money being non-proprietary) how do we explain the fact that gold and silver are directly likeable to money yet they are proprietary

and freely tradable in nature; and why is debt not accorded the same allowance?

Before the above questions are addressed, it is important to note that the issue of sale of debt in Islamic law is *ijtihadic*[5] in nature – it is not spelt out in the *Quran* or by Muhammad but rather it is open to independent reasoning and determination. Therefore, different jurisdictions have reached different conclusions pertaining to the application of the sale of debt. The *ijtihadic* nature of this issue is of great significance because it allows for the drawing of fresh conclusions and evolution within the objectives of the sharia, rather than having to be rigid and restrictive. This is especially so given that the general principle operative with regard to commercial affairs is that of permissibility.[6] The permissibility of the sale of debt in Islamic finance can, therefore, be based on the opinions of one or several schools of jurisprudence[7] through a selective approach as long as the general objectives of the sharia in transactions are achieved whilst addressing the current social and economic challenges faced by Muslim societies.

6.1 The concept of debt

To consider the concept and application of the sale of debt in Islam, it is useful to commence with a consideration of the concept of debt. So, what is a debt and what does it comprise?

A debt is a liquidated money demand, as opposed to a claim for damages or other unliquidated money demands, and has thus been defined as a monetary obligation owed by one person to another.[8] Debts, commonly, are also referred to as receivables. A receivable is a single or periodic payment owed by one (debtor) and payable to another (creditor). Receivables include, but are not limited to, book debts and would cover assets as diverse as rents issuing from land or personal property, freights, bank loans and a simple debt for goods sold.[9]

In the context of this book, the term 'debt' is used to represent not only an amount borrowed but also an amount owed or due to another as a result of a credit transaction or deferred payment. Credit arises, mainly, out of either of three types of commercial transactions: a loan, sale or hire.[10] Whichever the transaction, the arising *obligation to repay* the loan or for the goods or services supplied (or to be supplied) is what gives rise to a debt which then subsists until settled.[11] Once settled, the debt ceases to exist.[12] Oditah points out that it is difficult to conceive of a situation where a debt or other obligation does not arise prior to its discharge.[13] Even where money is paid over the counter at the time of sale, there must be a moment in time during which the purchaser is indebted to the vendor.[14] In most, if not all transactions, there is always a *scintilla temporis* during which one party is the creditor of the other.[15]

A critical point to make, however, is that the credit transaction, whichever kind it is, is distinct from the right to receive payment it gives rise to. In other words, a debt right is separate and distinct from the loan or sale or lease contract that creates it. The subject of enquiry for our purposes is, thus, the right to receive repayment and not the credit transactions giving rise to it. To illustrate the distinction, recall the distinction between the proprietary right of usufruct or lease and the underlying property that may be leased. An enquiry into the nature of leases and the legality of the sale of usufruct rights may be conducted independently of the underlying (varying) properties that may be leased. The same is true for our present enquiry regarding debt and the sale of debt rights. A major part of the analysis revolves around the determination whether, respectively, the debt and debt right and obligation arising are personal or proprietary in nature (section 6.4).

6.2 The relationship between debt and money under Islamic law

To resolve the status of debt effectively in Islamic law, we must resolve the relationship between debt and money. Muslim scholars persist in their likening of debt to money which, in turn, attracts to all debts the restrictive *riba* rules that they apply to restrict the exchange of homogenous items, that is, debt (money) for money. The significance of the comparison is at once apparent in view of the fact that money is not transferable because it is not proprietary under Islamic law, neither is debt. As we shall see in section 6.5.1, though debt is freely assignable to third parties under Islamic law, it is, nonetheless, denied proprietary character on the basis of the above comparison. This juristic position contradicts both the traditions of Muhammad and Islamic commercial practice that demonstrate debt's proprietary nature through its free assignability between contracting parties. For these reasons, debt's relationship to money under Islamic law must be addressed. Before I proceed to consider the relationship between debt and money, a word on drawing comparison in the Islamic *intellectual* tradition is fitting.[16] Drawing comparison has long been a means of intellectual enquiry and theoretical research employed both in philosophical aspects of cosmology as well as everyday matters of commerce and society. It is referred to as *tashbih* and the likening one thing to another is called *tamthil*. What is important, however, is that Islamic intellectualism has always operated on a qualitative (as opposed to literal) basis of drawing similarity or likeness. This is understood directly by the famous verse in the *Quran, al-Baqara*: 275 when those who question the prohibition of *riba* in transactions say, 'verily, trade is like *riba*'; the response to which was, 'And Allah made lawful trade and prohibited *riba*'. Thus, on the basis of appearance (form), trading and the *riba* transactions prohibited were similar yet, the distinction being drawn by the *Quran* was qualitative – trade and *riba* transactions differed qualitatively in that one is, in effect, equitable and efficient (or at the very least less amenable to inequity and the ensuing market inefficiency) whilst the other is inequitable. In addressing the arguments pertaining to debt's similarity to money, I shall use this qualitative yardstick to determine its veracity.

6.2.1 Is debt money?

Money, both within the context of Islam and generally, forms part of one's wealth or tangible assets, especially in its origins of gold and silver. Money, today, at the very least, serves the function of being a measure of value, as did gold – or salt – once upon a time; its two other functions are: a store of value and a medium of exchange. There is nothing peculiar about money under Islamic law, neither is there a distinct definition special to Islam. Money is money, as is commonly defined and used, except in one specific aspect – money is not itself a commodity and has little value beyond its function as a medium of exchange, a measure of value and a store of value.[17]

A debt may be distinguished from money in that though it is representative of money owed, is not itself money. It is a claim or a right one has against another for money or things owed. It may be described as a *right* one possesses *in* another's assets equivalent to the value of his claim of money or kind owed. A debt claim is thus an asset to the claimant, and in that respect similar to money, but not the *same* as money. The apparent similarity between the two is that both are assets of the owner by virtue of their monetary value. However, if measurability in monetary value is what determines the similarity between money and an item of value, then most things on this planet could be likened to money because they are valued and valuable in monetary terms, just as a debt is. Monetary valuation of all commodities for purposes of encouraging equitable and efficient market exchange is, in fact, what Muhammad implied in his saying (II) regarding the exchange of dates by Bilal.[18]

The claim by most Muslim scholars[19] that debt is equivalent to money attracts all the restrictions pertaining to *riba* (either of no increased return or demanding equivalence in quantity and quality exchanged on spot basis).[20] These rules are derived from the saying of Muhammad (I) directing the exchange of homogenous items which have, in turn, been interpreted and extended to require their application to all sale of debt transactions. One version of this tradition provides:

Gold is to be paid for by gold, silver by silver, wheat by wheat, barley by barley, dates by dates, salt by salt, like by like, payment being made hand to hand. If these types differ, then sell as you wish, if it is hand to hand.[21]

Before the different strands of arguments from the similarity (of debt and money) based on the above saying are addressed, consider that:

1 The saying does not restrict the sale (for money) of any of the items it refers to and it, therefore, cannot be used to restrict the sale of any other (non-mentioned) item in doing the same. What the saying does is to regulate the barter of such mentioned items based on equanimity only.
2 It follows from the saying, as commercial practice universally demonstrates, even gold and silver can be sold for money despite these two commodities being the two core universal metal currencies that symbolise money. If, therefore, gold and silver are proprietary in nature and freely transferable, the argument cannot stand that debt rights cannot be sold for money because of their monetary value. Further, Islamic commercial practice today seems to have embraced the trading of foreign exchange at a profit.

That said, the similarity could best be addressed by breaking it into (distinct) components of arguments establishing it, as follows:

1 At a conceptual level, debt is equivalent to money, thus a transaction of debt for money is equivalent to a transaction of money for money, attracting all the *riba* rules pertaining to the exchange of money for money (derived from Muhammad's saying on the exchange of 'gold for gold').
2 The *riba* rules pertaining to debt sales (as money) prohibit both an exchange at an increase or discount of the value of the debt as well as require any exchange to be executed on spot basis. Likewise, any indebtedness assigned to a third party should be done on the spot basis for cash of exact equivalent to the debt's worth, that is, at no gain to either side.
3 The sale of debt rights to third parties is prohibited since, debt being equivalent to money, Islam does not regard money as a proprietary commodity exchangeable beyond the contracting parties.

The first two components are linked hence are dealt with together. The last argument pertains to whether debt is proprietary or not and shall be deal with in section 6.5.

1 At a conceptual level, debt is equivalent to money, thus a transaction of debt for money is equivalent to a transaction of money for money, attracting all the *riba* rules pertaining to the exchange of money for money; and

2 The *riba* rules prohibit both an exchange at an increase or discount of the value of the debt itself as well as require any exchange to be executed on spot basis. Any indebtedness assigned to a third party should therefore be done on spot basis for cash of exact equivalent to the debt's worth.

There are two levels to this argument. First, that money and debt are equivalent in value and therefore a loan of £1,000 is worth £1,000 in cash. Second, that money and debt are conceptually equivalent and, therefore, a *right* to receive money is conceptually equivalent to money.

The first level of the argument is predicated on the limited concept of debt being loan credit, that is, arising from the loan of money by one to another. Not all debts, however, take the form of loan credit. Debts may also arise through trade credit transactions and it is a universal fact that trade credit is an obligation to pay another a specified amount in the future. As the well-known English saying goes, 'A bird in the hand is worth two in the bush', likewise, cash in hand (liquidity) is worth much more than the right to be paid the same amount in the future. This rule indicating the time value of money has long since governed credit transactions in Islam as is clearly illustrated by Muhammad in dealing with the Jews of Bani Nadhir upon asking them to leave Madina, to discount their debt rights for spot payment. Time has a monetary value and, thus, money and credit, even in the view and practice of Muhammad, are not equivalent in value. The similarity drawn is unsustainable.

Second, the argument, falsely, assumes a conceptual equivalency between debt and money. Debt and money are two distinct concepts. Money (paper currency), under Islamic law – as under all other legal systems – is used today mainly as a measure of value and a medium of exchange, within the prescribed boundaries of *riba* (inequity) and *gharar* (speculative uncertainty). Money can be used to buy whatever one wishes (provided it is *halal* (lawful)) at any price agreed upon. Debt, unlike money, is not a *measure of value* or a *medium of exchange*. The twin indicia of money forms the ratio that Muslim scholars derived from Muhammad's saying demanding reciprocity in the sale or exchange of currency metals (gold, silver) which they then extended to the exchange of all currency, by analogy. Given, therefore, that debt lacks this twin indicia, the *riba* rules do not apply to it because neither is debt money (conceptually) nor is it homogenous to money. The relied upon Hadith on *riba* provides 'where the species differ, sell as you wish' and, thus, the creditor may sell his right/s to receive payment for cash as he wishes. This answers the third component of the similarity.

6.3 The relationship between debt and money under English law
6.3.1 Defining money

The legal definition of money under English law is physical money, that is, notes issued by the Bank of England and coins distributed by the mint, when transferred as currency, not as a curio or other commodity.[22] It does not include bank money or electronic money.[23] It has also been said that:

> the quality of money is to be attributable to all chattels which, issued by the authority of the law and denominated with reference to a unit of account, are meant to serve as a universal means of exchange in the state of issue.[24]

Money is a negotiable chattel and title even to stolen money is said to pass to a bona fide purchaser of value without notice.[25] In modern times, money has become a tradable commodity in its own right and the subject of intense trading on foreign exchange markets.[26]

6.3.2 Debt

The term debt implies not only an amount borrowed but also an amount owed or due to another as a result of a credit transaction or deferred payment. In this sense, debt stands for credit (i.e. a money obligation one owes to another). Accordingly, it has been said that 'from a commercial viewpoint all credit takes one of three forms: loans, sale or lease'.[27] I refer to Goode's definition of all three terms:

> A loan is a payment of money to the debtor, or to a third party at the debtor's request, by way of financial accommodation upon terms that the sum advanced, with any stipulated interest, is to be repaid by the debtor in due course.
>
> Sales credit is price deferment. Price deferment agreements involve sales on open account, instalment sale and hire purchase agreements, revolving charge accounts ... as opposed to lease or hire at a rent.
>
> Finance leasing, that is, the leasing of equipment to a single lessee for all or most of its estimated working life, and without an option to purchase, at a rental which, instead of representing the use-value of the equipment intended to be leased ... is calculated to ensure the

return to the lessor of its capital outlay and desired return on capital
... it is thus a finance tool by which legal title remains in the lessor but
economic benefit of ownership belong to the lessee.[28]

Loans are, thus, only one facet of credit and the concept of credit accom-
modates the different treatment, at law, of debt, sale and lease transaction.
Goode notes:

> The courts have always regarded price-deferment as essentially
> different from loan, so that legislation regulating the lending of
> money has never applied to instalment sales and hire purchase,
> finance charges under sale and hire purchase agreements have been
> immune from attack under usury legislation and the two types of
> financial accommodation have been subjected to entirely different
> common law rules.[29]

From the above it is clear that Islamic law of transaction is not peculiar or
superior to the common law in the distinct rules and treatment applicable
to loan or debt transactions. The common law recognise the commercial
nature of debt transactions yet regulates them distinctly from sale or lease
transactions. Further, a clear conceptual distinction is made between debt
and money under the common law of England.[30]

6.3.3 Legal characteristics of physical money
It is frequently claimed in Islamic scholarship that Islamic finance today
differs from, and is barred from various aspects of, conventional finance due
to the fundamentally different nature and treatment of money under Islam.
The ensuing outline self-evidently renders this claim inaccurate.

Physical money has five important characteristics under English law.

1 Its value in law is not its intrinsic value (of the paper or metal that represents it) but rather the unit of account in which the note or coin is
   designated. Thus, a £1 coin is of £1 value even though the metal that
   represents it is worthless. This is effectively demonstrated with notes
   where a £20 note is of equally negligible value as a £500 note yet one is
   worth £20 and the other £500.
2 It is not bought or exchanged; it is either borrowed or received by way of
   gift or in discharge of an obligation owed to the recipient.[31] Where notes
   or coins are bought or held as curios (not money), then they are ordinary
   commodities.

3 It is fully negotiable in that someone who receives notes or coins in good faith and for value, obtains good title even if his transferor stole the money or his title was otherwise defective.[32]

4 Unless otherwise agreed, a creditor is not obliged to accept anything other than money in discharge of the debt owed to him.

5 Money is a fungible, that is, any unit is legally interchangeable with any other unit or combination of units of the same denominated value. That when one borrows money, one becomes the absolute owner of the notes and coins borrowed and is under an obligation to restore, not the notes and coins, but their equivalent value. Thus, it is said, a creditor's right to be paid is purely a personal right in that the creditor does not *own* the money representing the debt but rather is *owed* money by the debtor.[33] The creditor does, however, *own* the *right* to be paid.

The above description confirms the conceptual similarity between money under Islamic law and the common law of England. Even if a difference did exist, there is nothing divine about Islam's current position on money. The currently held position was invented by human beings, like you and me, and it can equally be changed by human beings like you and me because, unlike other legal systems, Islamic law is not controlled by any country or people but belongs to the collective agreement of the community. Better yet, one Muslim community has the right to differ from another community on such non-ritual issues. On this basis, the Islamic practice of Saudi Arabia is starkly different from that of even Dubai, let alone Malaysia, and that of India distinct from that of Indonesia.

6.3.4 *The distinction between physical money and intangible money*

It is an accepted fact in today's world that though cash remains the overall dominant medium of payment, bank money or transfers represents by far the most important method of discharging money obligations in commercial transactions.[34] The question, then, is whether physical money is equivalent to intangible money (bank credit and credit notes)?

The answer is no. A clear distinction is drawn under the English common law between physical (notes and coins) and intangible (bank) money. This is expressed clearly by Lawson and Rudden:

> A debt is an abstract thing quite distinct from the money which will be the creditors if it is paid. For if X promises to pay Y £5, what belongs to Y is not the note which may possibly be at that moment in X's pocket, but a totally distinct thing, namely the contractual right to be paid

the £5. Each of the two things, the note and the right to be paid the £5, can be objects of distinct transfers, for X can effectually and quite properly make A the owner of the note and Y can just as effectually and properly make B the owner of the right to be paid the £5.[35]

Intangible money is not the same as physical money in that it does not pass on delivery and otherwise lacks many of the legal characteristics of physical money, that is, it is not issued under state authority, it is not legal tender, it does not serve as a universal medium of exchange, and it is not negotiable. The same is said to be true of electronic money or digital cash.[36]

6.4 What is property?

The crux of the enquiry into the legality of the sale of debt revolves around the nature of debt under Islamic law, and specifically, as to whether debt rights are personal or proprietary. To determine this we must consider the concept of property and answer the questions: whether property is a right in a thing or the thing itself; what are the criteria that defines property; and what distinguishes a proprietary from a non-proprietary right? It is intended, by answering these three questions, to demonstrate that debt, in Islamic law and commercial practice, displays both the nature and criteria of property. Nonetheless, as will become clear in the discussion that follows, whether debt is personal or proprietary in nature has no impeding effect as to whether it may validly form the subject matter of a contract of sale. Non-proprietary rights have long since been capable of being sold (or leased) through contract, even before and at the time of Muhammad. Either way, therefore, debt rights being free of its misconceived similarity to money, may validly be sold as securities (at least) on the (primary) capital market under contract law. Under the common law, this is made clear in the observation of Rose LJ in *Re Bank of Credit and Commerce International (No. 8)*,[37] that 'Since a chargeback is incapable of vesting a proprietary interest, its effect is purely contractual'. Further, Lord Hoffman, on appeal at the House of Lords, in *Re BCCI (No. 8)*,[38] distinguished between proprietary interest in the chargeback and proprietary interest in the deposits (debt). Though no proprietary interest subsisted in the chargeback, this did not preclude the subsistence of proprietary interest in the deposits (debt). We return to this in greater detail below.

Next, we commence with a consideration of property under the English common law given that the evolution of debt rights, from personal to proprietary, is already well established within the English common law.

Property, generally, falls under two categories: real property (land) and personal property (personalty).[39] Both categories of property comprise of *proprietary rights*. Real property comprises all land rights (and proprietary rights attached to the land) while personal property comprises all residual proprietary rights after real property (land and items that form part of the land) have been subtracted. Not surprisingly, therefore, personalty is described as being residual in nature, a characteristic that is said to contribute to its formless nature[40] since personalty, unlike land, is capable of expansion both in respect of recognition of novel kinds of property and quantity and can be multiplied indefinitely in number.[41] It is on this basis that the English common law came to recognise debts, company shares and various forms of intellectual property rights all of which evolved from a status of mere *personal* rights in a thing to *proprietary* rights.[42]

The non-expanding nature of real property/land is widely acknowledged, as by Bernard Rudden for instance, when he says, 'In very general terms, then, all systems limit, or at least greatly restrict, the creation of real rights: "fancies" are for contract, not property'.[43] Many systems enact as a basic rule the proposition that 'no real rights can be created other than those provided for in this Code or other legislation'.[44]

The 'fancies' that Rudden speaks of are the non-proprietary rights one has in a thing that can nonetheless be transferred through contract. This is what we indicated would be the position of debt under Islamic law in the case that debt continues to be denied a proprietary nature of rights. Hence, whilst deemed personal, debt may still form the subject matter of a contract for purposes of transfer between contracting parties without the ability to transfer to or affect the rights of a third party. More importantly, Rudden's statement regarding the restricted category of property rights refers to the real property (land), not personal property rights that may change and/or expand with time and context. His meaning is a reflection of judicial statements expressing the same distinction.[45] A few instances are:

> [T]here are certain known incidents to property and its enjoyment; among others certain burthens ... recognised by the law ... but it must not therefore be supposed that interests of a novel kind can be devised.[46]
>
> It is a well-settled principle of law that new modes of holding and enjoying real property cannot be created.[47]
>
> New and unusual burdens cannot be imposed on land. It strikes our ears strangely to hear a right of services from an individual called a right of property as distinguished from contract.[48]

Therefore, the fundamental distinction between land and personalty is that land rights are fixed whereas personalty is expanding.[49] Accordingly, debt achieved recognition as one of many forms of intangible property as a result of legal evolution that saw debt shift from being a pure personal right to personal property rights. This is also true of debts under Islamic law, as we consider later in this chapter. Note, however, that even the position of the law pertaining to land is relative – the judicial pronouncements are not indicative of an absolute position of crystallised rights for as Gray and Gray explain:

> Property is socially constructed[50] ... and it is even possible, that in large historic processes of evolutionary development, some kinds of claim affecting land can actually alter their status, moving backward or forwards across this threshold of proprietary character.[51]

Hegel expressed this relativity thus, 'the march of mental development is the long and hard struggle to free a feudal content from its sensuous and immediate form'.[52]

6.4.1 Distinguishing personal from proprietary rights

It is intended, in distinguishing between proprietary and personal rights, to highlight the criteria that define property rights as opposed to personal rights. The distinction hinges on the understanding that just as *property* is divided into real (land) and personalty, *rights* are also divisible into either proprietary or personal in nature. Property rights, whether real or personal in nature, are proprietary nature and can be dealt with accordingly. Personal rights, on the other hand, are non-proprietary and cannot be dealt with except through contracts as between the contracting parties. There is, therefore, a clear distinction between personal *property* (property other than land) and personal *rights* (non-property rights *in* a thing).

Gray and Gray point out that conventional wisdom dictates that in order to enjoy a proprietary as distinct from merely personal character, (land) rights must be capable of third party impact.[53] This characterisation is of course not limited to land (real) property but is equally indicative of personal property. According to Bridge, 'the touch stone of a property right is its universality: it can be asserted against the world at large and not, for example, only against another individual such as a contracting partner'.[54] These twin indicia of property, assignability of benefit and enforceability of burden, are deeply embedded in one of the classic statement of English property law.[55]

In *National Provincial Bank Ltd v Ainsworth*, Lord Wilberforce, in the course of his judgement, identified the essential characteristics of a property right as follows:

> Before a right or an interest can be admitted into the category of property, or of a right affecting property, it must be definable, identifiable by third parties, capable in its nature of assumption by third parties, and have some degree of permanence or stability.[56]

Note that Lord Wilberforce speaks of *rights* or *interests*, not things, being *admitted* into the category of property (having previously been merely personal rights or interests). He points out a threefold criterion of property rights: identifiable by third parties, ability of assumption by third parties, and *some* degree of permanence. This threefold criteria in *Ainsworth* was applied in the recent case of *Mubarak v Mubarik*[57] as to whether the 'right or interest the wife had under the discretionary trust … as property at all'. Holman J held that her right or interest did not have any degree of permanence or stability and was not capable of assumption by third parties. Two of the three requirements set out in *Ainsworth* thus stood as unfulfilled, denying the right or interest in question, proprietary character.

English common law, not too long ago, considered debt to be a right of mere personal nature (that could not be traded in though it could be contractually assigned). Through the Courts of Chancery and the principles of equity, debt rights were granted proprietary status and thus they took the character of proprietary rights (assignability to as well as enforceability against third parties). Debt rights thus took on the character of being rights *ad rem* (against the world) as opposed to rights *in personam* (against an individual).

The common law was resistant to the notion that intangible things (aka chose in action), the best example of which is debt, could be transferred.[58] This resistance stemmed from the notion, as Muslims are currently operating under, that debts and similar things such as intellectual property (IP) rights and company shares were intangible and thus personal rights (as opposed to personal property) whereas property was mainly thought of in terms of tangibility (or permanence in form). The transfer of what was perceived as personal obligations, to third parties or the permitting of third parties to interfere in personal rights was seen as contrary to public policy. This deficiency in the law of property was left to equity to repair through enforcement in the courts of Equity and, eventually, by permitting the bringing of a debt claim by the assignor in the name of the assignee, the assignability of debt became accepted. With this acceptance emerged the recognition of debt as property just as any other tangible item, like a car or a computer.[59] The only distinction between a debt and a car for instance is that a debt comprises solely of a right to payment, and thus, once paid it ceases to exist. This, however, is where Lord Wilberforces' third criterion assumes significance because what is required is a *degree* of permanence. The degree of permanence of a debt is thus relatively shorter than that of a car but it, nonetheless, possesses a degree of permanence. It is further important to point out that, as far as assignability being a criterion of property, there stands absolutely no difference between a building and a debt because in both instances what is assigned is the *right* in the thing and *not* the *thing* itself. Therefore, the resistance in the common law towards the acceptance of debt as property stemmed not from the peculiarity of assigning intangible rights (which is what assignment entails) but from the peculiarity of recognising an intangible as property given that hitherto, property was tangible in form.

A major distinction between property and personal (non-property) rights is, therefore, that property rights can be assigned to third parties while non-property rights are purely personal rights that, though capable of passing in contract, are not amenable to third party assignment and are incapable of otherwise affecting third parties. Accordingly, debt rights, under Islamic law, are also proprietary. To illustrate the distinction between proprietary rights and personal rights, Gray and Gray explain that 'an informal dinner party invitation – being an occasion of ill-defined content and uncertain duration – is neither *transferable* to others nor apt to endure through a change of ownership of the freehold estate in the land'[60] (emphasis added).

However, Gray and Gray also point out that, contrary to what *Ainsworth*[61] indicates, proprietary quality, as is now widely acknowledged,[62] does not necessitate transferability or alienability. That, while it is often an important incident of proprietary entitlement, transferability is far from being an indispensable index of proprietary character.[63] He adds that the snare of market psychology has led to the crude belief of the property lawyer that if something is property one can buy and sell it. He notes, therefore, that the misconception that proprietary rights are those that can be bought and sold is prevalent. *Property need not be capable of sale and non-proprietary rights have always been the subject of contractual exchange between private parties.* According to Gray and Gray, it is the binding impact on third parties that is the threshold criterion of proprietary rights and, on this basis, what begins as a personal contractual relationship may evolve into a proprietary relationship. Nonetheless, the general perception and application of proprietary rights has it that a debtor's duty to pay the creditor creates a valuable property because of its exchange value (transferability). If a debt (receivable) could not be transferred (assigned) it would be no more than a contractual expectancy of the creditor's and, as such, non-proprietary.[64] The same line of thought was expressed in the judgement of the Australia High Court in the case *Dorman v Rodgers*[65] where a Dr Dorman claimed an appeal 'as of right' under S35 (3)(b) of the Judiciary Act 1903 (Cth) from a final judgement of the full Court of a State Supreme Court 'in any proceedings in which the matter in issue amounts to or is of the value of $20,000 or upwards or which involve directly or indirectly a claim, demand or question to or respecting any property or any civil right amounting to or of the value of $20,000 or upwards'. Dr Dorman relied on the second limb of the above provision in appeal against a decision to strike his name off the register of practitioners as a result of being convicted of 44 charges under the Health Insurance Act 1973 (briefly, of making dishonest claims for payment for medical services between February 1975 and 1 October 1977).[66] Gibbs CJ, in *Dorman*, relied on the judgement of the same court in *Clyne v N.S.W. Bar Association*[67] that no appeal lay as of right from an order striking the name of the appellant off the roll of barristers. The court in *Clyne* held that: 'There is no property that can be said to be involved, and no civil right capable of being valued'.[68]

Gibbs CJ observed 'that decision governs the present case, and in my opinion it was correct'. He explained that what was valuable was the person's own earning capacity, which is something '*personal*' to him (emphasis added). 'The right to practice is of course not transmittable.'

The judgement of Murphy J in *Dorman* discusses the concept of property and describes various rights falling within the category of property.[69] He observes that:

> *In legal usage property is not the land or thing, but is in the land or thing.* Throughout the history of the common law the concept of property has been used to recognise the legitimacy of claims and to secure them by bringing them within the scope of legal remedies.[70] (emphasis added)
> They might first be formulated as social claims with no legal recognition. As they became accepted by reason of social or political changes they are tentatively and then more surely recognised as property. The limits of property are the interfaces between accepted and unaccepted social claims. The great case of *Ashby v White* established that the right to vote in elections for parliament was property and its denial a deprivation, remediable by an action for damages. ...

It is not an essential characteristic of property that it be transferable. The right to vote in *Ashby v White* [1790] Eng R 55 and in *Amalgamated Society of Engineers v Smith* [1913] HCA 44 was not transferable. Numerous other property rights are non-transferable, for example licences of various kinds.[71]

Murphy J's observations resonate with Gray and Gray's observations made earlier in this section as well as those referred to in the next section. Nonetheless, he goes on to hold that Dr Dorman's 'appeal is hopeless' and that it should be dismissed. His decision appears to be based more on considerations of public policy given Dr Dorman's 44 convictions rather than on the conclusion that his right to practice was non-proprietary.

Note, however, Gray and Gray's warning against the 'vice of circuity'.[72] He thus explains that rights are not enforced against third parties because they are proprietary but that they are proprietary precisely because they are so enforceable. Hence, 'proprietary character is not the basis upon which that protection is given, but is simply a term descriptive of the effect of that protection'.

6.4.2 Property: a right or a thing?

Austin long since hinted at the answer to this question in explaining that, 'The *right* of property, is resolvable into two elements: First, the power of using indefinitely the subject of the right ... secondly, the power of excluding others'.[73] Gray and Gray explain, in other words, that 'property ... connotes, ultimately, a deep instinctive, self-affirming sense of belonging, control and domain'.[74] Accordingly, Gray and Gray explain that 'property is not a thing but a power relationship ... It is the condition of a thing "being *proper* to me"[75] ... It is a relationship of social and legal legitimacy existing between a person and a valued resource' (whether tangible or intangible).

Therefore, Gray adds, 'once property is defined as a relationship of socially approved control,[76] it becomes infinitely more accurate to say that one has property *in* a thing than to declare that *something* is one's property' (emphasis added). He emphasises that in legal usage property is not the land or thing, but is (a right) *in* the land or thing;[77] that is, property is the right we have in things and not the things we think we have.[78] They point to a 'mistaken reification of property' and explains that much of our false thinking about property stems from the residual perception that 'property' is itself a thing or a resource rather than a legally endorsed concentration of power over things and resources.[79] They cite C.B. Macpherson as the one who drew attention to the way in which, in the transition from the pre-capitalist world to the world of the exchange economy, the distinction between a right to a thing (i.e. the legal relation) and the thing itself, became blurred. That, 'the thing itself became, in common parlance, the property'.[80] It is in this light that Gray and Gray state, definitively, that at the heart of the phenomena of property lies the semantic reality that *property' is not a thing, but rather the condition of being 'proper' to a particular person* (e.g. 'that book/car/house/ is *proper* to me').[81] He explains that in archaic English, the word '*proper*' served to indicate relationships of proprietary significance[82] (emphasis added).

Accordingly, a creditor owns the *right* to payment for the debts he has claim to against other people and may deal with them (rights) the same way he would his computer or company shares.

The same is true of Islamic conceptions of property even at the time of Muhammad. First, the word property in Arabic, though often assumed to be *mal*, actually originates from the word *haqq* which means 'right' or 'what is proper' or 'appropriate' or 'proprietary'.[83] When one says in Arabic that something 'is mine' or 'my property' or 'my *right*' one says in Quranic terminology (with which we are here concerned) '*haqq-i*'. Second, as we discuss in section 6.5.1, a debt is the *right* to receive payment that subsists *in* a fund, thing or person until such payment is made. This fact is confirmed by the ability of a debtor (or creditor) to assign one's debt obligations (or rights) to another person and so extinguish his or her obligation or right towards payment, as we shall discuss in section 6.5.2.

6.5 Debt vis-à-vis property under Islamic law

A debt is agreed by the sharia scholars to be a *right* of the creditor and the *obligation* of the debtor.[84] The creditor has the right to repayment of the amount owing and the debtor has the obligation of repayment of the amount owed, between the creditor and debtor, respectively. The right or obligation is, therefore, not to the thing itself (debt or credit) but rather subsists *in* the debt as a *right or obligation to repayment* between the parties that gave rise to the credit contract. To this point, Islamic law and the common law is agreed.[85] However, sharia scholars, generally, insist that the right of the creditor and the obligation of the debtor to payment is a purely personal right, hence, only capable of transfer between the contracting parties and incapable of passing through contract to third parties. In support of such characterisation, Muslim jurists refer to the distinct terminology used: *ain* pertaining to property and *dayn* pertaining to debt. They argue, therefore, that debt cannot be property; and property cannot be debt, leaving us at an apparent deadlock as far as deeming debt rights proprietary is concerned.

6.5.1 Is Debt property?

In section 6.2.1 above we concluded that gold and silver are directly representative of money (in value and kind) yet perfectly proprietary, and, therefore, debt, too, can be proprietary whilst representative of money (in value). The question then is: are debt rights freely tradeable?[86] The answer is indicated in the tradition of Muhammad and the commercial practice of his time: that debt rights are not only transferable to third parties, they are also tradable for cash at a mark-up or discount evidenced by the tradition of Banu Nadhir in which Muhammad advised the Jewish community leaving Madina to discount their debt rights for spot cash. The same tradition also underscores the fact that debt is not homogenous to money because Muhammad allowed the exchange of debt rights for money and the rules of equanimity in Muhammad's saying on *riba* does not apply in the case of sale of debt for cash as he allowed debts to be discounted.

The Fiqh Academy of the Organisation of the Islamic Conference, under its decision number 5 of 1998, gave support to the conclusion that financial rights are freely tradable proprietary rights that may be evidenced on paper and sold on the capital market as bonds (securities) on the condition that interpersonal debts and cash form only a limited proportion thereof. In the referred to decision the Fiqh Academy ruled that:[87]

- 'Any collection of assets can be represented in a written note or bond; and
- This bond or note can be sold at any market price provided that the composition of the group of assets represented by the security consists of a majority of physical assets and financial rights with only a minority being *cash and interpersonal debts*'.[88]

Pertaining to the distinction drawn between debt rights (*dayn*) and property (*ain*), we already noted that the terminology for property is *haqq* which means one's *right*. A debt (*dayn*) is a right *haqq*: it is a right to payment, of a sum of money or money's worth, by another. In any case, the concept of property under Islamic law is elastic and has evolved at different times based on the values and objectives of the society. Thus, at one time, under Islamic law, slaves and women were socially approved as property and were regularly bought and sold (or even leased or loaned) but are now no longer deemed property. It is universally accepted that all people are sovereign individuals in their own right with the ability to own property as opposed to being owned as property. Pertinent to note, in this respect, is that there is no express statement in the *Quran* or made by Muhammad that prohibited women and slaves from being deemed property. Rather, their status as sovereign individuals is an implication drawn from Muhammad's (and eventually, society at large) treatment and manner towards them. The same can be applied to debt rights transitioning from personal to proprietary. The *Quran* and traditions of Muhammad need not contain an express statement as to their being property. It suffices that this is implied in the treatment accorded to debt rights by Muhammad and that there is no express negation of debt rights being proprietary.

The argument that debt has always been considered distinct from property, therefore, does not mean debt is not property. Islamic law terms (and treats) lease of usufruct (*ijara*) distinctly from *ain* (property). In fact, seldom, if ever, are lease rights referred to as my 'property' but rather merely as rights of proprietary nature. It is the underlying property, upon which the lease right subsists, that is deemed *ain* (property), in the traditional sense, whilst the leased usufruct being simply rights. Lease or usufruct rights in property were once also personal in nature. Eventually, social evolution led to such rights being granted proprietary status via customary practice (even before the time of Muhammad) to facilitate commercial and social welfare. Moreover, the property subject to lease rights may differ and change from time to time or society to society as long as it does not embody something the *Quran* and tradition of Muhammad expressly prohibited.

It is also possible that the distinct terminology of *ain* and *dayn* arises much like the common law distinction between real property and personal property. *Ain* was before and is usually used to denote real property as opposed to personal property (tangible or intangible). For instance, one would not term a bag of grains *ain*, even though it is definitely saleable and proprietary in nature (saleability and proprietary nature being distinct characteristics). The same applies to debt and, thus, the argument distinguishing *dayn* from *ain* does not stand.

6.5.2 Transferability of debt under Islamic law and the contextual evolution of property rights

In section 6.4 it was noted that a fundamental criterion of property rights is transferability to third parties. Transferability of rights to third parties signifies, through effect beyond contracting parties, the admissibility of a right into the category of property rights, as indicated by Lord Wilberforce in the case of *National Provincial Bank Ltd v Ainsworth*.[89] In section 6.4.2 Gray and Gray cautioned against the 'vice of circuity',[90] that rights are not enforced against third parties because they are proprietary but that they are proprietary precisely because they are so enforced. Hence, 'proprietary character is not the basis upon which that protection is given, but is simply a term descriptive of the effect of that protection'. Transferability of a right, therefore, crystallises its character, for instance, debt rights or lease rights that were once personal, as proprietary.

It is of great significance, therefore, that under Islamic law the transfer of debt to third parties (*hawalat al dayn*) is a universally accepted concept with broad commercial application. It commenced as a social, and later commercial, practice of transferring debt *obligations* to third parties, even before the time of Muhammad. Legally, *hawalat al dayn* has been defined as, 'the shifting or assignment of debt from the liability of the original debtor to the liability of another person'.[91] Essentially, it is described as the substitution of one obligor for another with the agreement (consent) of the creditor.[92] Such transfer is similar to the concept of novation of debt under the English common law since,[93] in contrast to an assignment, *hawala* envisages the transfer of the debt obligation of the debtor to a third party and such transfer requires the consent of the creditor. The requirement of the creditor's consent, however, does not negate the assignability of debt rights since the position under discussion is that of the practice in sixth- and seventh-century AD Arabia and parallels the initial position under the common law as Chitty confirms:

> Contractual rights, being things in action as opposed to things in possession were not assignable at common law without the consent of both parties. This rule seems to have been based initially on the difficulty of conceiving of the transfer of an intangible, at any rate one of such personal nature, and later on the desire to avoid maintenance, viz. officious intermeddling in litigation.[94]
>
> Everybody has a right to choose with whom he will contract … consequently, the burden of the contract cannot in principle be transferred without the consent of the other party, so as to discharge the original contractor.[95] As Sir R. Collins M.R. said in *Tolhurst v Associated Cement Manufacturers Ltd*:[96]
>
> Neither at law nor in equity could the burden of a contract be shifted off the shoulders of a contractor on those of another without the consent of the contractee.

Therefore, Chitty adds, the requirement of consent as a prerequisite of the discharge of the original contractor from his obligation means, 'as a general rule the assignee of the benefit of a contract involving mutual rights and obligations does not acquire the assignor's contractual obligations'.[97]

Muhammad expressly affirmed and encouraged the transferability of debt obligations (for purposes of legality under Islamic law) for purposes of facilitating the repayment of debt within the society generally. The sayings of Muhammad, used to establish the transferability of debt, are all a slight variation of the following narration by Abu Hurayra on what Muhammad said:

> To evade and defer (payment of a loan) on the part of a person who is rich, is tyranny. If a loan is transferred to a rich person, he should be pursued for its repayment.

From the saying/s of Muhammad, Muslims inferred both that debt obligations may be transferred, that such transfer completely discharges the transferor from liability and therefore it is the transferee that is to be pursued for the repayment of the debt obligation. To this inference the sharia scholars added two more: that the consent of all three parties (creditor, debtor and transferee) are required for the transfer and the creditor should accept the transfer as long as the transferee is solvent (this being in line with the underlying purpose of *hawala*, that is, facilitating the repayment of debt obligations).

It is important to add that the concept of *hawala*, as earlier mentioned, existed even before the birth and message of Muhammad and, thus, it cannot be classified as an 'Islamic' law or textual creation other than by incorporation. It is common knowledge that Muhammad did not create an entirely new way of life for his people nor did he stipulate each and everything they could or could not do. Rather, especially in the domain of human affairs (as opposed to faith), the principle of permissibility remains the general rule and Muhammad simply incorporated the practices he found among his people that did not conflict with the overarching principle of justice, equality and social welfare. He changed or replaced only those practices that conflicted with these principles. This process confirms both the evolutionary nature of commercial practice in the history of Islam and the evolutionary nature of debt as a social and commercial concept. In fact, the concept and negotiability of debt as we now know it to be permissible under Islamic law is not how it originally was at conception, nor as it was at the time of Muhammad. With passage of time, both before and after the sixth and seventh century ad, the concept, use and negotiability of debt evolved to facilitate both commercial practice and socio-economic welfare. Muhammad's acknowledgement and encouragement of debt transfers certifies both the imperative value of credit and a well-functioning credit repayment system in a society. Taken in this light, one easily appreciates the tradition of Banu Nadhir, in which Muhammad advised Banu Nadhir upon their emigration from Madina to discount their debts due in the future for spot payment. The discounting of debt established, as far back as seventh-century Arabia, the credit value of time as well as the value of liquidity (spot cash).

The sale of receivables and the full-fledged proprietary nature of debt is, thus, simply the continuing evolution of debt rights from what they were then to what they have now become. The discounting of debt rights and their transferability to third parties at that time marked the foundations of modern commercial and financial practices that other civilisations embraced and built upon. It's about time we picked up where we wandered off on this evolutionary trail.

6.6 Future (debt) contracts under Islamic law and practice

Contrary to claims, consequent to the similarity of debt and money, Islam recognises and provides for, in the express text of the *Quran*, future credit contracts. The exact words used are significant: '*idha tadayantum bi dayn liajallin musamma, fa'qutubuhu*' ('when you incur indebtedness for a fixed future period of time, reduce it to writing'). The manner in which indebtedness is incurred is not specified, and, therefore, this could be through any credit transactions: loan, sale or lease. The complete translation of the above verse[98] provides a detailed procedure for future credit transactions comparable to contracts by deed under section 1 of the Law of Property (Miscellaneous Provisions), Act 1989. It states:

> O ye who believe! When ye incur indebtedness with each other, in transactions involving future obligations for a fixed period of time, reduce them to writing. Let a scribe write down faithfully as between the parties: let not the scribe refuse to write as Allah has taught him. So let him write and let him who incurs the liability dictate, but let him fear his Lord, and not diminish aught of what he owes. If the party liable is mentally deficient, or weak, or unable himself to dictate, let his guardian dictate faithfully, and get two witnesses, out of your own men; and if there are not two men, then a man and two women, such as ye are content with as witnesses, so that if one of them errs, the other can remind her. The witnesses should not decline when they are called on (for evidence). Disdain not to reduce to writing (your contract) for a future period, whether it be small or big: that is more just in the sight of Allah and more upright as evidence, and least amenable to your

engaging in *riba* among yourselves. Except, if it be a transaction which ye carry out on the spot, frequently among yourselves, then there is no blame on you if ye reduce it not to writing. But take witness whenever you enter into a commercial contract; and let neither scribe nor witness suffer harm. If ye do (such harm), it would be wickedness in you. So fear Allah, and Allah teaches you, and Allah is well acquainted with all things.

If ye are on a journey, and cannot find a scribe, a pledge with possession (may serve the purpose). And if one of you deposits a thing on trust with another, let the trustee (faithfully) discharge his trust, and let him Fear his Lord conceal not evidence; for whoever conceals it – his heart is tainted with sin. And Allah knows all that ye do.

The sophistication of the provisions of the above text of the *Quran* is astounding even by modern standards. Together, the two verses provide for:

- future credit agreements,
- the requirements of writing and witnesses of the agreement,
- conditions excepting the requirement of writing (i.e. spot transactions and customary transactions),
- an alternative to the requirement of reducing the contract to writing in absence of scribes to write (i.e. a pledge with possession),
- the concept of trust and its ensuing requirement of utmost good faith.

In appreciating the term *dayn* (debt) as credit extended, one also appreciates that the *Quran* does not distinguish between loan (*qardh*), sale (*bay*) or lease (*ijara*) credit transactions, requiring only that transactions be contractual,[99] by mutual consent[100] and equitable[101] (not for *riba* and unjust enrichment). Credit is, by implication of the Quranic references, independent of the underlying transaction that gives rise to it. It is a universal fact that extending credit earns the creditor a time value for which he or she may charge a profit. This time value is expressly affirmed in Muhammad's tradition pertaining to discounting the debts of Banu Nadhir. Given, therefore, that all credit within a commercial context may be extended at a profit or discount, requiring only caution against inequity, one can equally deduce by extension that credit rights may be transferred or exchanged for profit or discount without restriction as long as everyone adhere to the principle of contractual fairness.

6.6.1 *Future (debt) contracts and* gharar

We noted earlier that one of the reasons the sale of debt to third parties is prohibited is because debt rights are intangible and future in nature which creates the perception that sale of debt transactions are risky (*gharar*) transactions. This is an indirect objection that, though not denying the proprietary nature of debt in principle, attempts to do so on the basis of *gharar*.[102] As discussed in chapter 4, *gharar* is a vitiating factor that threatens the validity of a commercial contract it taints. Two points must however be recalled

First, the fact that any contract for sale or transfer of a thing is open (or even prone) to being tainted by *gharar* does not mean that that the thing itself cannot be the subject of a contractual exchange or assignment. For instance, selling birds in the air, or carrots in the ground or products yet to come into existence are all prohibited as *gharar* contracts because the subject matter is deemed too uncertain to comprise a legally binding contract. Nonetheless, this does not mean that birds, carrots or future products cannot be the subject of contractual exchange. In fact, two of the most popular and oft-used contracts in Islamic commerce, both historically and today, involve contractual exchanges pertaining to subject matters not yet in existence: *bay al-salam* (pre-payment transactions) and *bay al Istisna'a* (commission to manufacture).[103] The fact that both these contracts are widely acknowledged to contain excessive *gharar* did not, and still does not, negate either the validity of the contracts or the transferability of the contractual subject matter. Contractual mechanisms were simply created to minimise the *gharar* whilst allowing the contracts to serve the social needs of the time, both then and now. The key point to note, thus, is that social need for a transaction or a practice greatly facilitates the permissibility of the transaction or practice in question because the benefit to society to be created through satisfaction of a social need outweighs any other consideration of perceived harm that would otherwise deem it impermissible. This is especially so in non-ritual matters with no religious prescriptions, as is the case with commercial transactions, and can be easily understood if appreciated in light of Islam's overarching concern with social justice. Thus, Muhammad is reported to have said that my people will never agree upon an error.

The fact that debt transactions, be they sale or transfer, may be speculative or uncertain does not negate the validity of the contract. The social and commercial evolution since the seventh century AD and the apparent social need for debt or receivable transactions is a major factor in facilitating the permissibility of receivable transactions. In any case, we have already established above that the patent endorsement by Muhammad of the transferability of debts grants debt rights proprietary status. This book is only putting forth an already acknowledged position by Muhammad himself.

Second, not all *gharar* is of vitiating effect; only *gharar* of excessive degree is vitiating and, even then, only if incurable in nature.[104] In other words, *gharar* is an evidential concept which acts as a vitiating factor to protect against inequity that may arise from uncertainty of contractual terms. Considering therefore that, as with any other relatively novel mode of transaction, time and prevalence of sale of debt transaction is giving rise to mechanisms that are reducing their speculative nature for purposes of contractual equity. The *gharar* element in sale of debt transactions can be regulated, should it be deemed excessive (like *bay al-salam*'s case), and the *gharar* is certainly not incurable as to deny the transaction legal effect.

Applying the above to Islamic finance securitisations would allow for the sale of securitised receivables on the capital markets for purposes of creating liquidity and generating finance as part of the evolution of commercial practices and transactions.

6.6.2 Deferred 'sale of debt' transactions

The general Islamic jurisprudential (*fiqh*) rulings regarding the sale of debt prohibit the sale of receivables on credit (deferred payment) basis because of the legal maxim[105] that prohibits the 'sale of one deferred obligation with another' (*bay' al kali bi al kali*).[106] It is likely that this maxim was derived from the Hadith pertaining to exchanges of homogenous items as we discussed and addressed in 6.2 and 6.5 above. The maxim is wider in scope of application than the Hadith on homogeneity so as to prohibit, for instance, a contract to buy 10 kg of dates at a total price of £100, both delivery of the subject matter and payment to be made at a deferred date. A current example would be a contract to purchase property with deferred delivery of vacant possession on credit. The prohibition arises because the transaction is deemed to be one of credit[107] (deferred payment) for another deferred obligation (delivery of possession or subject matter). To make the transaction lawful, one of the parties must deliver their side of the bargain, be it the subject matter or the price. In all such contracts, the amount owed is a debt until payment is made which then converts the subject matter into property and cures the contract of its nullifying character. The question, therefore, given the sale of securitised assets evidenced by a note as security (*shahadat al-dayn*) on the primary market creates an obligation to repay a borrowed amount (debt) at a later date (deferred payment), is whether this is prohibited under the above maxim? The answer is, no. Such sale of debt obligation is permitted by the Islamic jurisprudence on the basis that the sale entails the sale of property rights (securities/notes) on credit (much like usufruct can be sold for deferred payment) and therefore though it is a credit (debt) transaction, it is not a sale of one debt obligation for another as only one side of the contractual equation is comprised of debt.[108] So far so good. A complication arises with further sale of such debt obligations (the securitised asset) to third parties, that is, any subsequent sale on the secondary market. This is currently prohibited, by a majority of the juris-prudential schools, however the debt arises and regardless of whether the payment is made on the spot or on a deferred basis,[109] again, on the basis of the maxim prohibiting the sale of debt for debt. The securities (notes), once sold, are representative of an obligation to receive future payment (debt) and any subsequent sale transactions of such securities (whether on cash or credit basis) are deemed to be caught by the above maxim (prohibition). It is only the Maliki school that allows such sales of debt to third parties for spot payment and as long as the debt object is not food and does not involve prohibited *riba* of delay (*al nasia*).

Thus, we find that the *fiqh* ruling goes beyond the scope of the maxim prohibiting the sale of debt for debt (just as we noted that the maxim goes beyond the scope of Muhammad's saying) in that it even prohibits the sale of debt (securities) for cash in hand simply because such sale is to third parties. The prohibition seems to pertain more to the issue of credit sales being erro-neously thought to taint the contract with excessive *gharar* (making it a *gharar* contract) which was addressed in section 6.6.1 above. There is no reason why the same transaction attracts different legal outcomes merely based on whether the transaction is between primary contractual parties, or extends to a third party. This is especially so when one realises that it was already concluded that debt or receivables are proprietary rights and, thus, any secu-rities purchase on the secondary market is a fresh contract between the secu-rity (asset) holder and a buyer of that asset. Once the security is sold, the previous party drops out of the equation and the buyer assumes his position in almost bearer bond fashion. No implications of *gharar* or 'credit for credit' exist in the transactions even at the secondary market level. Further, the *fiqh* ruling must be contextualised to appreciate that twenty-first-century finan-cial and economic markets are far advanced in sophistication to overcome risks involved in credit transactions as opposed to seventh-century Arabia.

6.7 The common law attitude to sale of future debts

Marathon Electrical Manufacturing Corp v Mashreqbank PSC is the key case discussing the distinction between future and existing receivables and succinctly summarises the common law position and attitude towards future debts.[110] In *Marathon*, Mance J held that English law treated as existing debts not only those which had been earned by the promisee, whether or not presently payable, but also those which were unearned. In so holding, he quotes Oditah at length as follows:

> The attitude of English law to existing and future indebtedness is described by Mr Moss's junior, Dr Oditah in Legal Aspects of Receivables Financing (1st edn, 1991, pp. 1–8, 29, 135) as follows:
>
>> English Law draws an arbitrary distinction between existing and future receivables on the one hand, and future receivables and other contingent liabilities, on the other. All contractual rights are vested from the moment when the contract is made, even though they may not be presently enforceable, whether because the promisee must first perform his own part of the bargain, or because some condition independent of the will of either party (such as the elapsing of time) has to be satisfied. The result is that English law treats as existing debts not only those which have been earned by the promisee, whether or not presently payable, but also those which are unearned. The basis for the inclusion of unearned rights to payment in the category of existing receivables even where the contract is wholly executory is that they grow out of a present obligation. So it is that for a long time the courts have treated as existing or present receivables a legal right to be paid only at a future date if it depends upon an existing contract on the repudiation of which an action could be brought for an anticipatory breach. The contract is the tree, the future debts which may arise, the fruits. The unearned debts are potential and hence existing. But in so lumping earned (even though not presently payable) debts and unearned, albeit potential, debts, as existing debts, the common law has, in a somewhat extravagant fashion, destroyed the vital distinction between rights *in esse* and rights *in potentia*. Thus, a right to interest under a fixed-term loan, future rent from existing leases, sums payable under an existing construction contract, royalties payable under an existing copyright, freight payable under a signed bill of lading, and sums payable for goods or services not yet delivered or rendered, are all present receivables. Uncertainty as to the amount payable is immaterial. Similarly the fact that under some of these contracts nothing may be earned because the right is conditional on counter-

performance is not considered important . . . The hardship and inconvenience engendered by this rule is mitigated by two factors. The first is a generous interpretation of 'existing receivables'. As we have already seen, English law treats as existing, not only earned receivables whether or not presently payable, and whether or not ascertained, but also unearned receivables expected under existing contracts. Many contractual relationships are of a long-term nature, and individual contracts are usually implemented within a pre-existing framework. Whether the existence of the framework alone is sufficient to stamp the expected receivables with the badge of existing property is unclear.[111]

He concluded, that:

> Whether one is considering an assignment of the benefit of the right to receive payments under a credit or, as here, an assignment of the actual proceeds as and when collected under a credit, the facility to assign is one which has obvious commercial benefit to the beneficiary. The facts of the present case illustrate how it may assist a beneficiary to continue and to finance his business generally as well as, quite possibly, the very business the subject of the letter of credit.

It can be readily appreciated that, given the permissive approach of the common law towards existing receivables as extending to future receivables flowing from present obligations, the adoption of the common law position in Islamic finance transactions will be greatly facilitative of successfully structured securitisation transactions. This is because the common law position allows the avoidance of triggering both the vitiating factor of *gharar* (given the ensuing conceptual certainty gained from adopting the common law position on existing receivables); and maxim prohibiting sale of debt for debt because any receivable flowing from a current obligation is deemed to be an existing (as opposed to future) receivable.

6.8 The 'asset-backed' requirement under Islamic law

The most progressive jurisdiction within Islamic finance practice, Malaysia, recognises debt as proprietary only in so far as it represents an underlying asset. Further, it has also been said that for an intangible right like debt to be tradable as a security (i.e. financial asset) it must involve 'the funding of trade in, or the production of, real assets'.[112] The argument therefore implicitly calls for all such financial assets and intangible rights to be 'asset backed' and be traded for purposes of funding the production of real property. The double layer requirement insinuates the invalidity of intangible rights as assets in their own standing. The asset-backed requirement is said to be necessary so as to avoid *riba*.[113] The intended implication of this 'asset-backed' requirement is to prevent the exchange of one money obligation for another (as considered in 6.6.2 above) because in the absence of the asset backing, debts are considered money that attract the *riba* prohibition – essentially taking us back to square one. Three issues here: first, we can agree with the explanation that the asset-backed requirement is intended to prevent *riba*, however, we concluded, in chapter 5 above, that *riba* does not mean interest or increased return in commercial context; second, we concluded that the similarity between debt and money is misconceived and inapplicable; and third, we have already demonstrated that debt rights are proprietary on the basis of the tradition of Banu Nadhir, the traditions allowing their unrestricted assignment to third parties, the ruling of the Fiqh Academy of the OIC allowing the sale of financial rights as bonds at any price, and the contextual evolution of property rights as per the maxim: *whatever is known among the business community as their custom is considered to be like what is enjoined upon them*.[114]

Accordingly, 'asset-backing' should no longer be required for the sale of debts just as is the case for leases rights or foreign exchange transactions. After all, Islamic legal theory recognises intangible property rights such as intellectual property rights, which cannot be said to be dependent on the 'backing' of real assets. One's intellectual property in a book or piece of literature or idea is quite independent of the physicality of the book and is inherently of more value than the collection of papers in the book. Intellectual property rights may be sold independently from the book just as a right to payment of a sum or sums may be sold independently from the actual, tangible money one is owed.[115] It is universally accepted that Islam permits the ownership of usufruct in a physical item (e.g. house, building, car, aeroplanes, etc.) which subsists separately and independently from the physical property – evidenced not only by the distinction between ownership of the house (real property) and ownership of lease rights in the house but also by the prevalent practices of sub-leasing and the grant of licenses to property.[116] It is, in fact, the characterisation of usufruct as a saleable thing that has caused the popularity of sale and lease-back *sukuk* structures.

Therefore, just as share ownership and trading is accepted and practiced by Muslims engaged in commerce and financial investments (including within sharia-governed nations), likewise, is the case of debt trading. Each successive seller sells not the physical money owed but the right to receive payment of that amount.

6.9 Judicial support in acknowledging the proprietary nature of debt

The Chancery court, through maxims and equitable principles, helped convert personal interests into proprietary interests and extended proprietary interests held by one person to several individuals through the equitable concept of trust and beneficial ownership. This was no doubt facilitated by the desire to relieve hardship and create equitable outcomes in commercial dealings in accordance with the principles of Equity. The significance of the judiciary's role in the transition of debt rights to property role assumes even greater magnitude when we consider how difficult it was and still is to create new proprietary rights where none existed before, even under an uncodified systems like the Common law.[117] We noted several judicial comments to this effect in section 6.2.

The validity of a bank taking an effective charge over its own customer's credit balance, for instance, permitted by the courts of equity, demonstrates how a determined jurist (Lord Hoffmann) can surmount apparently insurmountable conceptual problems in order to arrive at what is perceived to be a sensible commercial result.[118] Lord Hoffman had to expand the concept of proprietary interest to embrace chargebacks.[119] In doing so, however, Lord Hoffman drew a distinction between a lien which is a right to possession and the proprietary interest the bank has in the customers' deposits (debt). His reasoning was not without critics but the importance of the judgement lies in the fact that the House of Lords was willing to reach a decision that was commercially sensible rather than compliant with policy.[120] It is this sensible approach that has always driven England to its position as a global commercial and financial centre. Neither was Lord Hoffman blind to the sense of injustice such an approach imparted on to the depositors. He observed:

> If the depositors had been third parties in economic reality as well as in law, I imagine that it would not have been thought particularly unfair that the liquidators had chosen to exercise their undoubted choice of remedies and to proceed against the primary borrowers rather than resort to the third party security which they held. But the separate personality of depositor and borrower was an essential element in the structure which the parties chose to adopt for their borrowings and it cannot be ignored now that BCCI has become insolvent'.[121]

Lord Hoffmann, thus, ended the decade-long uncertainty over the legality of chargebacks that was deemed 'conceptually impossible' by Millett J in the earlier case of *Re Charge Card Services*.[122] In doing so, the House of

Lords reversed the decision of the Court of Appeal in line with the decision in *Re Charge Card Services* that a chargeback by a bank over a customer's deposit was invalid. In delivering his judgement, Lord Hoffman observed that chargebacks over customer's deposits, in most cases, would be as good as securities over proprietary interests. This, of course, indicates that Lord Hoffman acknowledged the non-proprietary nature of deposits (bank credit) that do not extend to third parties. Nonetheless, Lord Hoffmann rejected the reasoning in *Re Charge Card Services* that such chargebacks were 'conceptually impossible' and added that there is no reason to prevent banks and their customers from creating charges over their deposits if, for reasons of their own, they want to do so. That, where there is no threat to legal consistency and no public policy objection, the courts should be very slow to declare a practice of the commercial community 'conceptually impossible'. Clearly, this was a decision that favoured commercial reality over conceptual compliance.

Lord Hoffman's approach, in principle, is aligned with Islamic commercial legal principles. The principle of permissibility deems everything permissible unless expressly prohibited and applies equally to commercial, contract and property law issues. Lord Hoffman's dictum implies the application of this principle of permissibility. He uses legal inconsistency and public policy objections as a yardstick of determining whether a commercial practice should be prohibited and in the absence of both he permitted the practice of chargebacks between primary contractual parties. In chapters 4 and 5 we mentioned repeatedly that the yardstick in Islamic law of contract and commerce is whether the transaction is equitable between the parties and often this is a question of public policy. The issue of public policy also applies directly through the question of whether the transaction serves *maslaha* (social welfare). The role of the judiciary through equity in the transformation of personal interests to proprietary interests in England offers a great example for possible emulation by Muslim jurists in attaining the same on acknowledgement the status of debt and permitting its sale.

That such flexibility is resorted to and applied by sharia scholars (albeit selectively) is clear in numerous instances including the fact that Islamic finance structures are increasingly using the special purpose vehicle (SPV) structure. Traditionally, Islamic contract law indicates that only human beings qualify as legal entities and contractual parties yet sharia scholars and commercial practice have embraced the use of SPVs as legal entities in the structuring of financial transactions with no fuss at all. Of course, it is pragmatic to have done so as the SPV structure adds much to the efficiency of the structure as well as the equity created through using a trust mechanism.

The question to highlight, however, is why the selective approval and disapproval of novel concepts? And on what criteria is such approval and disapproval done? Preferably, such approval should be strictly based on the general principle stressed throughout this book, that is, that of permissibility unless prohibited by a clear text of the *Quran* or tradition of Muhammad. The arbitrary approval of what appears to be alien or 'non-Islamic' concepts and practices will otherwise continue to disrupt efforts towards legal and social development. It also perpetuates the legal, structural and regulatory uncertainty that currently characterises Islamic finance deals.

Conclusion

It is pertinent to mention in closing that it is a fallacy to claim that the current position on debt and its status is 'Islamic'. The *Quran* takes no stand on the issue, recognising it as a contractual transaction, and, moreover, Islam is a faith that draws expression from those who practice it. The time for revelation has come to pass, yet we must work to give the eternal principles of Islam life in our daily lives by being true to their spirit without inhibiting the natural evolution of human society in all its spheres. Time is ripe for Islamic contract and legal theory to break new ground in extending Islamic principles to current commercial practice, indeed, that is the only way Islam can continue to co-exist in a diverse world of cultures and religions. It did exactly that at the time of Muhammad, how can we now claim otherwise?

7

SECURITISATION

It was suggested in chapters 2 and 3 that sharia compliant securitisation structures are promising because they offer a sophisticated yet simple solution to the liquidity in Muslim-majority economies as well as pave the way for an organised and sustainable secondary Islamic capital market.[1] Moreover, though apparently a novel concept within Islamic finance, a securitisation structure utilises traditional contractual forms and structures already familiar to Islamic law of contract. This makes it an excellent capital raising and liquidity mopping structure. This is due to securitisation being a technique that allows the packaging and marketing of (otherwise) non-marketable assets.[2] Accordingly, it is said that:

> illiquidity in the Islamic financial sector is exacerbated by the absence of an organised secondary market for Islamic investments[3] ... one means of obtaining liquidity is through the securitisation of both short term and long term Islamic financial contracts. Securitisation in turn requires the establishment of *a sharia approved liquid secondary market*[4] for these securitised instruments.[5]

That said, we proceed to define securitisation and outline the more popular type of securitisations applied in today's global economy, its benefits, drawbacks as well as some of the important, if not problematic, issues that arise in structuring securitisations.

7.1 Defining and outlining securitisation

Securitisation, in broad terms, is the conversion of (illiquid) assets into securities to be traded on the securities market so as to create liquidity and/or raise funds. It may be explained as a method of finance whereby a lender,[6] instead of lending money to a company to finance its general business, buys assets from that company which it then converts into securities and sells on the capital market. Hence, instead of the lender looking to the company's profits as a whole to repay that lending, it agrees (by virtue of the sale) to look solely at the assets that it bought and later sold as securities for repayment. Securitisation can also be defined as a means of raising finance secured on the back of identifiable and predictable cash flows derived from a particular set of assets. Almost any assets that generate a predictable income stream can be securitised. Alternatively, a 'whole business securitisation' describes a securitisation where the cash flows derive from the entire range of operating revenues generated by a whole business (or a segregated part of a larger business). These have been used by a wide variety of businesses (in the UK) to raise finance, that is, Welcome Break, Road Chef, Westminster Healthcare, London City Airport, the Tussauds Group and many pub companies. There is no formula that determines whether a business is suitable for securitisation. However, in whole business securitisations to date, the businesses in question produced stable, predictable cash flows. The key to the suitability of a business for securitisation is thus the stability of the cash flows.[7]

Securitisation is therefore a method of raising funds and creating liquidity through the sale of tradable securities that represent an asset or an interest in an asset. In theory, therefore, securitisation relies on the transfer of title to facilitate the access to financing and it is this passing of ownership instead of borrowing money (i.e. title finance) that makes securitisation a viable financial structure in Islamic law which is perceived as prohibiting the dealing in interest that arises in debt or loan financing. Islamic finance requires therefore that the sale of the asset to be genuine, and only then can one sell securities (backed by the assets) on the capital market. In conventional finance, however, the actual sale tends to be of the security (coupons) with the sale of the asset to the SPV being mostly a function of satisfying legal form rather than economic substance.[8] This raises the issue of characterisation of the transaction depending on whether a 'true sale'[9] has occurred.[10] The 'true sale' issue, is considered in greater detail in the next chapter, and is among the more important issues to be considered in enhancing the viability of securitisation in Islamic finance in light of the current 'asset-backed' requirement.[11]

7.2 Securitisation of receivables

The securitisation of receivables is the most common type of securitisation. It ensures a continuous flow of income to cover the periodic payments on the securitised assets and usually entails the purchasing of a leased asset, a mortgaged property, unsecured commercial loans or credit card payment systems which are then securitised and sold on the capital market. It therefore employs the concept of title finance to raise funds through the capital market.[12]

The structure is generally as follows:[13]

- The owner of the receivables (originator) sells the receivables to the special purpose vehicle (SPV) that is often an 'orphan' and/or owned by a charitable trustee so as not to be a subsidiary of the originator (to ensure bankruptcy remoteness as explained in section 7.7 below)
- The purchaser or SPV borrows money, which is called the 'funding loan',[14] to finance the purchase price of the receivables and repays the borrowing out of the proceeds of the subsequent sale of the receivables.
- The purchaser authorises the originator to collect the receivables on its behalf and to remit the proceeds to the SPV.
- The purchaser SPV grants security over the receivables and its other assets to the lenders to secure the funding loan.

In order to ensure the receivables are sufficient to repay the lenders on time, 'credit enhancement' may be arranged. This is where a third party gives a guarantee to the SPV, or the originator agrees to make a subordinated[15] loan to the SPV to finance part of the purchase price of the receivables (and is repayable after the funding loan is repaid). In this case, the SPV repays the originator's subordinated loan after repaying the funding loan (i.e. if there is a surplus of receivables), and this may be done at a very high rate of interest depending on how profitable the securitisation is.

Summarily, receivables securitisation is used as a method of funding various receivables including mortgage debts, leases, loans or any steady stream of receivables income whereby securities representing interests in these receivables are sold. The basic technique requires the rights over the receivables[16] to be transferred from the originator to the special purpose vehicle (SPV or Issuer). The SPV then issues bonds and incorporates into the securitisation structure certain credit enhancing features.[17]

7.3 Requirements of a securitised transaction

A securitised transaction would generally need to fulfil the following requirements.[18]

Credit: If the funding loan is to be rated highly by a rating agency, the receivables must be sufficient to cover the funding loan made to the purchaser to finance the purchasing price. Any shortfalls or mismatches must be covered by guarantees or other credit enhancement, or by finance of part of the purchase price by a subordinated loan.

Transferability: It must be possible for the originator to transfer the receivables to the buyer without excessive expense or formality. Similarly, in the case of bulk receivables, transferability must be possible without the consent of the debtors. This is due to the inertia of communication in that often the debtors are disparate and varied and needing to require consent from them all would almost paralyse the transaction.

True sale: The sale must always be treated as a complete and final transfer of the receivables from the originator to the purchaser so that the receivables are no longer the assets of the originator and, consequently, the funding loan is not the liability of the originator.

It must also be possible to set up the securitised transaction without other burdensome restrictions or expenses that may attach to it, for example, restrictions and expenses under tax laws and securities regulation.

7.4 The benefits of securitisations[19]

Capital adequacy: Capital adequacy requirements require banks to retain a specific amount of funds with the bank for amounts lent according to the risk weighting of the loans or credit extended. This may also mean that banks and other financial institutions (e.g. home loan firms, the originator) may be required to raise extra capital in order to support new loans. The cost of retaining or raising funds to support loans made is avoided if assets are sold because the sale brings in cash and creates space on the balance sheet for the banks or institutions to lend more money. The sale also reduces regulatory reserve requirements, which are essentially a portion of deposits that a bank must pay to its central bank on the deposits funding the asset.

Better returns on capital: If accounting rules permit, the originator can raise money without the loan appearing on its balance sheet or being a liability of the originator and still keep the residual profits from the sold receivables. The cash price can then be used to pay back the originator's liabilities, leaving the originator with less liabilities and hence more borrowing space. Its financial ratios (debt to equity) may consequently be improved, for instance, if a bank has assets of 500 and debt of 300 (ratio 5 : 3) and then sells 100 worth of its assets in order to pay off 100 worth of its debt, then it has assets of 400 and debt of 200 which is a much better debt to equity ratio of 1 : 2. Return on capital is thus improved because the originator has removed the asset and liability from its balance sheet but still retains the profit.

Quicker fund raising: The originator raises funds faster through securitising the securities rather than having to wait for the receivables to be repaid.

Liquidity: The originator is able to raise more money at a cheaper cost through securitisation (especially if in bulk) hence granting him greater liquidity through the sale of otherwise illiquid assets by marketing them as securities to investors. It is a cheaper means of raising money because:

- The finance is essentially 'secured' so it is cheaper and more long-term than unsecured finance.
- The strength of the investors capital is improved by the fact that the SPV enjoys credit enhancement and is insulated from the insolvency of the originator (by virtue of the sale and because the SPV is a separate legal entity).

Diversification: The originator can diversify its funding sources, especially if the securities can be sold internationally as in global and cross border securitisations. This makes securitisation particularly attractive to developed economies that have turned to emerging or Islamic economies that possess vast amounts of dormant wealth (that can be tapped into through securitisation) to raise funds. Similarly, it has enabled emerging and Islamic economies capable of attaining the requisite global financial standards to diversify their fund raising portfolio and tap into new sources of capital.

Avoids restrictions: Securitisation is essentially similar to a secured loan. Its structure, however, allows it to escape many of the restrictions that may otherwise attach to a secured loan. For example, a securitisation will normally avoid the originator's negative pledges, borrowing restrictions and cross-defaults (assuming the purchaser or SPV is outside the originator's group) because the transaction is a sale. The funding loan is made to the SPV and the actual security over the receivables is granted by the SPV. Securitisations is often the only way banks can raise 'secured' money because it is otherwise inappropriate for them to grant security over their assets (a regulatory prohibition to protect depositors).

Cost effective: For emerging and Islamic economies, the structure of securitisation presents a more cost-effective method of financing within the framework of interest-bearing loan financing being prohibited. This is because securitisation structures remain relatively cheap and straightforward compared to other financial structures.

Facilitates future growth: Securitisation facilitates growth of the specific industry in which it is used, and of the financial market and economy as a whole. This may be explained by the structures as well as the standards that must be attained by the financial sector and the economy as a whole, that is, the accounting standards, the global rating standards, a listed stock exchange, efficient and effective dispute settlement mechanisms, etc. so as to ensure the viability of the transaction and attracting investors. In Muslim-nation economies, securitisations create a precedent that may lead to better structured securitisations and in turn facilitates progress and future development of the market.[20]

Risk: The originator has the advantage of transferring the risk of non-recovery of the receivables to the issuer (and lenders of the funding loan), whilst retaining its right to profits.

Avoids lending limits: A securitisation being a sale and not a secured loan transaction enables the bank to avoid lending limits and restrictions placed on banks with regards to both how much they can lend to any one single obligor and the lack of diversification.

7.5 The drawbacks of securitisations and issues in application

Originators often transfer their best receivables so that the originator's credit may be weakened.

- It may be expensive due to the complicated structure a securitisation may acquire and the need to ensure compliance with legal and regulatory requirements.
- It can be very technical in nature owing to the regulatory and audit insistence that the originator must not be morally obliged to support the SPV. The transfer may thus tend to be more manufactured than real.
- The debtors liable on the receivables may object to the change of creditor/s from their originator to an SPV controlled in substance by unknown bondholders and often located in a tax haven country.

Moreover, jurisdictional requirements (legal or regulatory) and the structure of a securitisation raise issues that may lead to difficulties in application.[21] The more pertinent among them are:

1 *Notice to debtors*: In the case of bulk receivables, notice of transfer of the receivables to the issuer (and subsequent purchasers) will not normally be given to the debtors because of:

   - The inconvenience and expense – by virtue of requiring change of mandate from the originator's bank to the SPV bank
   - The originator's (usual) desire to maintain its relationship with its customers and debtors and, hence, continue collecting the receivables due.

In England, unlike other jurisdictions,[22] giving notice is not mandatory and does not affect the validity of the transaction. However, failure to give notice may affect the securitisation transaction in the following manner:[23]

- The SPV might lose priority if the originator resells or charges the receivables to a third party.
- The secured investors might also lose priority if the SPV resells or recharges. This, however, is prohibited by the documentation, and investors and rating agencies are usually content to rely on the originator and SPV complying with these prohibitions.
- Debtors may continue to pay the originator as opposed to the SPV. This, however, is not usually an objection as the originator wishes to continue collecting the receivables from its debtors/customers. The issue at hand is the effect it may have on bankruptcy remoteness of the SPV from the originator because though the originator must in essence hold the receivables collected in trust for the SPV, the originator's creditors not having been given notice may demand a stake in the SPV upon the originator's bankruptcy.
- Debtors without notice can continue to acquire new set offs and defences e.g. if goods supplied are defective, or the debtors have deposit accounts with the bank originator.
- In the absence of notice, the debtors and originator can vary the terms of receivables; again one relies on contract compliance by the originator.

The rating agencies are, however, prepared to assume that the originators will comply with the securitisation documentation so as not to bring about the above referred to scenarios or act fraudulently and negligently.

2 *The true sale requirement*: The 'true sale' component of securitisation is pivotal with regards to many of the issues one faces in securitisation including sources of credit enhancement, capital adequacy, balance sheet and accounting rules, re-characterisation of security interests, etc. [24] It is also considered as determinant of the sharia compatibility of a securitisation. This is because of the existing conceptual hurdle that denies receivables proprietary status, as discussed in chapter 6. Should this misconception be dissolved, less emphasis need be placed on the legal requirement of 'true sale' with greater emphasis being placed on economic substance and the equitable effect of the transaction.

The main conceptual features of a true sale include:[25]

- The seller (originator) has no liability for the asset once sold except normal warranties for defects.
- The seller does not guarantee recoverability of the asset, or have a duty to repurchase, or to provide additional cash (for purposes of credit enhancement, for example, through loans) or additional assets either directly or under a swap, and has no commercial non-legal 'moral' duty in practice to compensate for shortfalls. If the seller has a liability, then clearly this must be recognised and indicated in the balance sheet and the regulated seller must have capital against it.
- The buyer must have exclusive control and dominion over the assets. This means that the buyer (SPV) can sell it, exchange it, pledge it, does not have to resell it to the seller (except perhaps for a clean up of the final small amounts) and can itself manage and collect the receivables. It does, however, have the prerogative to delegate this duty to the seller which it normally does for practical reasons.
- The buyer must also take all the profit made from the assets after the sale without having to remit any part of it to the seller. If the seller continues to have a certain degree of control or dominion after the sale, the assets may still be seen as belonging to the seller and consequently be available to the seller's creditors upon its insolvency.
- The sale should not be revocable on the bankruptcy of the buyer, either because it was a preferential transfer or because the buyer is really part of the seller, or because the sale was not published and must not be reachable by the creditors of the buyer – if it were, then in substance the seller still has the asset.
- The asset sold must be isolated and insulated from the creditors of the originator. In other words, the assets must be bankruptcy remote from the bankruptcy of the originator. Clearly, this non-revocability is essential for the purpose of a true sale and securitisation in general.

The two main issues arising under the true sale component of securitisations are:

- Re-characterisation of a 'sale' as a security interest;
- Bankruptcy remoteness.

7.6 True sale: the re-characterisation of a 'sale' as security interest[26]

In essence, a securitisation must involve the (genuine) sale of receivables by the originator to the SPV and, therefore, not be re-characterised as a security interest for the purpose of security and bankruptcy laws. This is because if it were to be characterised as such the results would be disastrous.

1 The assets would remain on the balance sheet of the originator and the funding loan becomes a direct liability of the originator. It would thus be subject to the originator's other loan agreements, financial covenants, cross defaults and other restrictions.[27]

2 The security may require registration or perfection by filing if it is not to be void on the insolvency of the originator, infringe negative pledges of the originator, and be subject to restrictive mortgage enforcement procedures, for example, have its enforcement frozen on the insolvency of the originator, and be subject to the enforcement laws of the originator's jurisdiction as opposed to that of the SPV.[28]

Therefore, through re-characterisation, the investors lose their insulation from the originator's credit so that a default by the originator would force the investors to realise their security prematurely.

Many legal systems seek to ensure that transactions which are like security interests are subject to the legal rules relating to security interests.[29] The main characteristic of a security interest is that the debtor has the right to get back the charged collateral if the debtor repays the secured debt. It also has the right to receive the surplus proceeds if the creditor enforces and sells the collateral. Hence, the chief factors in considering whether to re-characterise a securitisation transaction as security interest include:

- The originator's rights to repurchase the receivables become in substance the mortgagor's right to get back the mortgaged property on repayment of the loan.
- The extraction of profit by the originator (e.g. by deferred purchase price or a subordinated loan) amounts to a lender accounting to the borrower for the excess of the mortgaged property over the loan. In a true sale, the purchaser keeps the residual value (profits) of the purchased property, but in a mortgage, the borrower receives back the residual value on the repayment of the loan.
- The transaction resembles a sham whereby the parties carry out the transaction in a different way than that contemplated by the documents,

for example, where the records make reference to a loan and interest as opposed to a sale.

- The continued collection of the receivables by the originator negates a true sale. In a true sale, the buyer usually manages the asset because it belongs to the buyer.

Re-characterisation is discussed more specifically in chapter 8, section 8.2.

7.7 True sale: bankruptcy remoteness

A securitisation must also be isolated and insulated from the insolvency of the originator in order to satisfy all interested parties: investors, rating agencies, accountants and regulators. The main requirements are:

- The SPV must not be consolidated, fused or merged with the originator on the originator's bankruptcy so that all its assets and liabilities are merged with those of the originator. If that happened, then the funding lenders would have to enforce their security over the receivables prematurely on the insolvency of the originator and would be subject to the bankruptcy laws applicable to the originator, for instance, freezing orders upon a bankruptcy judgement. This is because the merger or fusion would result in the asset becoming assets of the originator and the funding loan a liability of the originator.
- The documents and their implementation must ensure separateness of the SPV, for example, separate officers, no commingling of assets, separate records, observance of corporate formalities, disclosure in financial statements and the like. Bankruptcy consolidation is rare and tends to happen only if there is extreme commingling ignoring the separate legal identities of the two or if the SPV is just an agent of the originator managing the property of the originator. The originator's management of the property of the SPV, however, does not entail such consolidation and is not usually a serious risk.
- Transfers or payments by the originator to the SPV must not be capable of being set aside as a preference or transaction at an undervalue on the bankruptcy of the originator. If set aside, the creditors of the originator have a claim on the receivables – which cease to be insulated or remote. This affects mainly the sale itself and any substitutions by the originator, that is, they must not be undervalued.
- There should be no material loss of or delay in the recovery of funds collected by the originator as servicing agent, if the originator becomes

insolvent. The document usually requires frequent turnovers to the SPV, for example, every two or three days, or payments go direct to the SPV account.

Conclusion

In concluding, it is important to note that there are other issues apart from those addressed in this chapter that may arise with regards to a securitisation transaction. This is because different jurisdictions may have different formalities of form or manner of execution relating to the instrument of transfer or indeed the notice. There may also be prohibitions on the type of assets that can be transferred; some jurisdictions, for example, prohibit the transfer of obligations owned by public authorities. The receivables themselves may contain prohibitions on assignment in their terms, although such prohibitions are not enforceable in all cases. In some jurisdictions, only receivables due and owing at the time of the transfer can be validly assigned, others contemplate the sale of future receivables which are transferred as they arise. Jurisdictions also vary with regards to the amount of detail that is required to identify the receivables which are the subject of a sale. In this light, the next chapter compares a securitisation structure in Islamic finance with a common law securitisation and considers the issues that arise in structuring a securitisation deal to be compatible with both Islamic law and the common law.

8

STRUCTURING A SECURITISATION TO BE COMPATIBLE WITH BOTH THE SHARIA AND COMMON LAW

Having reviewed the basic structure and theory of securitisations, this chapter considers how, and at which stages a basic securitisation structure is affected, specifically, by the vitiating concepts of *gharar* and *riba* and *bay al dayn* or sale of debt and, generally, by other factors involved. The purpose of the structural comparison undertaken in this chapter is to demonstrate the importance of the issues discussed in chapters 3, 4, 5, and 6 and how they are practically engaged. The comparison not only points out the distinctions between the structures but also how the proposals in the above named chapters render them no longer an impediment to structuring sharia compliant securitisations.

Initially, however, let us consider why dual compatibility of sharia compliant securitisation should even be sought. Why bother? Why not simply have Islamic finance products in consonance with the sharia made available to Muslim consumers or those who choose such financial services and products? The answer, very simply, is as we mentioned in chapter 2. Securitisation is a conventional law invention and sharia compliant securitisations would mostly be structured either in the financial centres of the world or by financial institutions governed by the rules and regulation of the global financial centres. This is so as to increase their rating, profile and marketability to institutional and other investors who seek assurance from the knowledge that Islamic finance products are at par with conventional products as far as legal and regulatory standards are concerned. As such, it is obvious that they must comply with the laws and regulations of the financial jurisdiction in which they are structured, they intend to draw investors from and the sharia. This external jurisdictional law to be complied with tends to be the common law – be it Singapore, Hong Kong, Malaysia, London, Dublin or New York. Even those structured in Doha or Dubai tend to comply with the common laws and regulations governing contractual and financial transactions for purposes of marketability. This is also, partly, because the laws of England and New York are the most developed and predictable systems of law in the world thus less risky and amenable to flexible financial structures that better suit risk averse investors. Dual compatibility is thus hardly an option for Islamic financiers; it is simply a matter of commercial survival if not common sense.[1] Therefore, the need for dual compatibility in Islamic finance structures is also fuelled by the issue of enforcement and the requisite legal certainty, as we shall discuss below.

Further, we have indicated that the distinction between 'Islamic finance' and common law or other conventional modes of finance is, currently, more a matter of form or arbitrage that the industry is cashing in on.[2] Islamic finance jurisdictions and the industry as a whole, has promulgated the theory, with the exception of few vocal academics and practitioners, that the sharia frowns upon the payment of any increased returns on loans, any contractual uncertainty and any future or intangible asset sales. Islamic finance securitisations, therefore, are camouflaged in 'sharia compliant' transactions as a matter of form so as to secure the advantages of a conventional securitisation whilst appearing to avoid interest, uncertainty (*gharar*) or the sale of receivables. In essence, they are both the same and the purpose of this chapter, therefore, is to clarify the misconceptions of the current Islamic finance theory and to reconcile it with conventional finance wherever possible.

8.1 Issues involving *gharar*, *riba* and *bay al dayn*

Securitisation in its classic form involves the sale by an originator of its income-generating assets (receivables) to a special purpose vehicle (SPV) that finances the acquisition of those assets by issuing debt securities to one or more investors. The income generated by the assets is then used by the SPV to service its obligations to the holders of the securities. The SPV will normally be a company or other legal entity which has no (or only minimum) outside creditors, and whose sole functions are to acquire and hold the assets and to issue the securities.

Therefore, at the most basic level, a securitisation structure involves the Originator, the Seller, the Trust SPV, and the Note holders as, for instance, in the following sketch.

Originators → Stage I → Seller (Oxford Mortgages) → Stage II → Trust SPV → Stage III → Note holders.

Stage I entails the sale of mortgages by the originator to Oxford Mortgages. This is a primary market transaction of sale of assets (mortgage receivables).

Stage II involves the sale of receivables by Oxford Mortgages (OM) to Trust SPV (SPV). This is a secondary market sale of debt obligations since the originator and mortgagee are the original contracting parties. Once the receivables are sold to the SPV they become the property of the SPV. In principle, the true sale requirement means that the receivables are no longer the property of OM.

At *Stage III*, SPV creates and issues (sells) notes to investors so as to raise or borrow money to pay for the purchased receivables. This transaction is, again, a primary market transaction as the SPV is the originator of the notes (created and issued for the first time).

Issues: How, and at which stages specifically, is this basic securitisation structure affected by the vitiating concepts of *gharar*, *riba* and *bay al dayn* (sale of debt)? The responses that is made here to each issue is based on current Islamic finance theory and application, much of which would not be an issue if applied within the suggested framework of this book, that is, a focus on economic substance in compliance with the principles of contractual fairness and permissibility rather than a focus on legal substance based on compliance with rules formulated in ancient context.

1   Both Stage I and II must be characterised as true sales for Islamic finance purposes. This is mainly a concern at stage I despite the fact that the economic effect of stage II is a loan attained via sale of securities to investors. The importance of characterisation pertains to the theory that a loan or mortgage transaction triggers the rules of *riba* that, currently, prohibit any increase (or decrease) on money lent or borrowed. Thus, if stage I is characterised as a loan to be repaid upon sale of notes to investors, no interest/premium or discount (over original receivables value) can be received by OM from SPV. The above concerns are dealt with in detail in chapter 5 on *riba* and the issue of increased return should not, according to the discussion therein, threaten to vitiate a securitisation structure except on the ground of being inequitable to the parties involved.

2   The sale of receivables at stage I is a sale of debt rights or obligations. The validity of such sale, given debts' (current) derivative proprietary nature, depends on the assets 'backing' the mortgage receivables being deemed

sharia compliant (i.e. not bear debts, interest-bearing loans, night club, casino, cinema complex, etc.). Under current Islamic legal theory debt, unlike lease, has no independent proprietary status. Again, this is dealt with at length in chapter 6, section 6.5.

3   The sale of debt issue at stage I also engages the *riba* rules, again, since debt is currently erroneously equated to money and, therefore, the mortgage receivables can only be sold at par, for spot payment, that is, 'equal for equal, hand to hand'. Herein lies the importance of demonstrating the distinction between debt and money (dealt with in section 6.3), otherwise, any sale of receivable or securitisation is limited by this characterisation.

4   The *gharar* objection creeps into stage II through the issue of sale of debt obligations to third parties because it is said to create a risk of repayment given that the SPV is not the originator of the receivables (i.e. the contractual link between mortgagor and mortgagee has been severed and the originator of the securities (notes) has no contractual link to the mortgagee/s). However, should stage I be well documented (perhaps also indicating the consent of the mortgagees to such sale and their agreement to pay SPV instead of OM) and repayment is guaranteed or insured, then *gharar* is eliminated from the outset. Further, assuming the evidential nature of *gharar*, the concept would allow the curing of such risk if it arises. It is, therefore, also important that the degree of *gharar* be considered – only excessive/exorbitant *gharar* renders a contract defective. Minor *gharar* has always been deemed tolerable.

5   As long as the stage II transaction is well documented so as to ensure certainty of terms of contract (parties, time of periodic payments and maturity, price, etc.) then no *gharar* arises. Otherwise, any uncertainty as to the contractual terms would trigger *gharar*. Again, the vitiating effect depends on the degree of *gharar* and, if defective, the evidential nature of the concept would allow curing *ex post factum*.

6   The sale of notes to investors at stage II may be regarded as an invalid *sale of debt* since what 'backs' them is the receivables (not the mortgaged property giving rise to the stream of receivables). This goes back to the derivative proprietary nature of debt recognised only in the more progressive jurisdictions like Malaysia. Hence, the importance of establishing debt as independent proprietary rights that can be dealt in freely as is the cases with lease rights or company shares (discussed in sections 6.5 and 6.6).

7   Again, even if the sale of debt transaction is valid, it is caught by the characterisation of debt as money that triggers the *riba* rules (spot exchange and sale at par value). See 3 above.

8.2 General issues arising from dual compatibility structuring

Using the 2003 Qatar Sovereign *ijara sukuk* (outlined below), I undertake a more elaborate comparison of the facets of a lease securitisation:

- The government of Qatar sells land parcels valued at US$700 million.
- The issuer (SPV) purchases the land parcels at a deferred payment basis.
- The SPV undertakes to resell the property to the government at certain agreed terms or subject to certain redemption conditions.
- SPV issues *sukuk* instruments which the Investors (both Islamic and conventional) purchase.
- The gross proceeds received by the issuer from the issuance and sale of the certificates are used to pay the purchase price (pursuant to the purchase agreement) to the government of Qatar.
- The SPV then leases out the land parcels under a Master *Ijara* Agreement to the government of Qatar, effectively a ground lease. The lease is for seven years after which ownership reverts back to the government.
- The returns to the certificate holders are variables. The government of Qatar pays semi-annual lease rentals under the Master *Ijara* Agreement which are calculated by reference to (i) London Inter-Bank Offer Rate (LIBOR) plus a margin of 0.4 per cent per annum, (ii) the Amortisation Payment[3] (beginning in April 2006). The two amounts equal the Periodic Distribution Amounts payable on the Periodic Distribution Date coinciding with the Rental Payment Date for such rentals.[4]
- The SPV disburses semi-annual distribution payments (equal to the government's rental payments) to the certificate holders, that is, the rental payments are the return on investments.
- The investors enjoy the irrevocable undertaking by the Qatar government to buy the parcel of land.

In comparison, a conventional lease receivables securitisation structure is as follows:[5]

- The leasing company leases assets to lessees under lease agreements.
- As a result of the lease agreements, rents (receivables) are paid by lessees to the leasing company.
- The SPV advances to the leasing company the current cash value of an aggregate number of leases in exchange for a securitisation agreement (of the leases).
- The leasing company forwards repayments from the lessees to the SPV.

- The SPV issues to investors the interest bearing notes in exchange for cash to cover the securitisation agreement.
- Investors receive interest and principal payments over the life of the notes.

Before proceeding to consider the actual or potential issues that arise in structuring the above sharia complaint structure to be dual compatible, note that a fundamental difference between the two structures is that in the conventional structure, the securitisation is not 'asset backed' in the sense currently required by Islamic law and, hence, is deemed non-sharia compliant.[6] The other main difference is that, in the conventional structure, the SPV *borrows* money through the notes issue in order to purchase the leasehold estates instead of *selling* or leasing the property or assets in question as Islamic finance would require. In the Qatar structure, on the other hand, the issuer *bought* the asset on deferred payment basis, securitised it and *sold* undivided shares of it so as to raise funds to pay the purchase price then *leased* it to repay the investors.[7] The real difference, however, lies in the form or structure of the transaction such that the conventional structure is a securitisation for the purpose of funding the *purchase* of an asset as opposed to a (sharia compliant) securitisation to finance payment of an already purchased property. The distinction is subtle but obviously deemed significant. In substance, the fact that no money is borrowed does not preclude the existence of credit transactions structured as sales or leases or the fact that the asset backing is specifically manufactured as a formality to attain the same financial objective.[8] Moreover, the 'asset-backed' requirement is not necessary as discussed in chapter 6 since debt qualifies, even under Islamic law principles, as (personal) property in its own right and may be freely dealt with as one does with the share/s of a company without insisting that it be 'asset backed'.

That said, structuring the Qatar securitisation to be dual compatible raised the following issues.

8.2.1 *True sale and the risk of re-characterisation*
A major issue under sharia-compatible securitisation has been structuring one that embodies the ownership characteristic of an equity instrument as well as the priority status and the fixed income characteristics of a bond instrument. A concern within the issue is that upon winding up of the originator, there was a possibility of re-characterisation (by the courts)[9] of the transfer of interests from the originator to the SPV as a loan as opposed to a true sale.[10] The theoretical effects of such re-characterisation

is outlined in section 7.6 and issue of substance verses form is elaborated in chapter 1.

For sharia compliance, as the theory stands, a re-characterisation of the securitisation as a financing transaction, throws up the issues of increased periodic returns to investors as *riba*, the sale of debt (debt being non-proprietary) with possible vitiating effect, and/or vitiation of the transaction for uncertainty as a *gharar*-tainted transaction. Re-characterisation is a concern that arises from the fact that most Islamic finance transactions are governed by English common law. The case of *Orion Finance Ltd v Crown Financial Management Ltd*[11] demonstrates the effect re-characterisation can have on an otherwise structured transaction being deemed a security transaction.

In *Orion*, Vinelott J's considered whether the assignment was by way of charge. He concluded that it was in fact an outright assignment of book debts by way of charge and thus was void for lack of registration.[12]

In the Qatar Global *Sukuk* securitisation, for instance, it was difficult to reconcile the investment banks' requirement that the risk of the securitisation be linked to the Government of Qatar as clearly as possible with the requirement of the sharia that a true commercial transaction (sale) take place. Sharia compliance required that the fee simple title or discernable ownership move into the SPV. The leasehold payments then attach to it and the certificates represent an undivided beneficial right to the land for a seven-year term. Unlike notes in a conventional asset backed securitisation which are due whether or not the underlying lessee pays, the investors in the Qatar issue were theoretically at full property risk (though substantially mitigated by other features of the transaction).

Accordingly, it has been noted[13] that for any sharia securitisation structure to work, it is critical that the issuing vehicle have good title to the asset being securitised and, if the funding is to comply with the issuance the sharia StandardNo.17[14] on Investment *sukuk*, the *sukuk* holders must have effective title over the assets. It is vital, therefore, that the true sale requirement in *sukuk* structures be complied with over and beyond the mere balance sheet accounting and capital adequacy purposes, that is, it must be a true sale of economic, rather than legal, substance. As discussed in chapter 5, as long as the economic substance is equitable, the issue of *riba* should no longer arise as all such structured transactions are commercial in nature.

A likely solution to the concerns pertaining to the risk of re-characterising a sharia compliant securitisation as an interest earning loan structure is the use of the common law concept of 'trust'. A trust may be defined as an agreement under which one person transfers title to specific property to another (trustee) who agrees to hold or manage it for the benefit of a third person (beneficiary). The beneficiary on whose behalf the trustee holds the asset/s on trust for is the beneficial owner of the asset. The relationship between the trustee and the beneficiary is evidenced by a trust deed executed (often unilaterally) by the settler or the trustee himself.[15] These characteristics of the trust instrument squarely meet the requirements of sharia.[16] The risk of re-characterisation is thus avoided altogether when a trust or trustee element is incorporated into the structure because the trustee is deemed to hold the property on trust for the beneficial owners of the assets (*sukuk* or security holders) whilst the financier, leasor or seller maintains legal title.

8.2.2 Bankruptcy remoteness

Bankruptcy remoteness, generally, is satisfied through the true sale requirement or the trust structure and requires that, so far as is legally possible, the potential for bankruptcy or other insolvency proceeding being brought against the SPV is remote. This means that the transaction is to be structured so that the SPV is unlikely to be bankrupted which normally entail restricting the SPV purpose exclusively to its role in the transaction (often through orphan vehicles) and confirming that non-petition[17] clauses and provisions for limited recourse[18] will be legally binding in the relevant jurisdiction/s. It usually also means that the transaction is structured as such that the bankruptcy of the originator does not affect the SPV which is achieved by using the trust structure as explained in 8.2.1. The principle purpose of this requirement is therefore to make the initiation of bankruptcy or insolvency proceedings unlikely in any and all relevant jurisdictions.

8.2.3 Security interest

Security interest is the right acquired by a creditor or lender, on the property held by him as security for the amount due to him, to use the right on the property to recover the amount due to him. In a securitisation, the security interests purported to be created over the collateral constitute first priority security interests perfected in accordance with the applicable law and procedures. The concept of security interest, however, is not recognised by sharia law in a manner consistent with the common law understanding as a consequence of the prohibition on the sale of debts and interest based transactions as discussed in chapters 5 and 6. Securitisations under Islamic finance are (as we have seen) ideally structured on the basis of the investors' shared ownership in the trust asset whilst conventional securitisations take the form of a loan backed by collateral (asset) the increased returns on which are deemed interest (*riba*) and thus non-amenable to Islamic finance. The nature of the security interests, if at all created, under the *sukuk* structure therefore needs to be clarified.[19]

One way of approaching the issue of security interest in sharia securitisations is that the land parcel/s or assets sold or leased under Islamic finance are the security interests and the periodic returns are the principle plus interest. This approach attains the same ends by different means and under different labels. Alternatively, the security interest created by the SPV over the receivables, which it has purchased, could be granted in favour of a trustee who would hold it on trust for the investors (holding undivided ownership in the asset). The interposition of a security trust in this type of transaction provides a means whereby a group of assets can be retained by its current owner and yet made available as security to investors thus ensuring sharia compatibility. This is achieved by providing a proprietary link between investors and the underlying receivables through the shared/ divided ownership of the trust concept (which is comparable to the *sharikat al mulk* (shared-ownership) concept in Islam). The above approach also enables the securities or *sukuk* to be rated based on the assets without taking into account the credit risk of the originator.

8.2.4 Tax

The SPV should generally be structured so as to minimise, or ideally eliminate, any liability to tax. Tax issues are particularly important in deciding where to domicile an investment vehicle whether sharia compliant or not. Tax advice is also required to understand the taxation treatment of both the establishment and operation of an investment vehicle and in order to confirm the favourable tax treatment of a particular jurisdiction to all aspects of the business and the operation of the investment vehicle.[20] In structuring a sharia-compliant dual compatible securitisation it is vital (for purposes of legal certainty) that all tax obligations are predictable and that no withholding tax or other taxes are payable by the SPV.[21] However, since the use of SPV for financing transactions is relatively new to sharia jurisdictions, tax classifications and absolute tax obligations of an SPV remain uncertain. It is therefore important that sharia jurisdictions minimise unfavourable tax treatment for foreign investors or commercial entities generally and create certainty as to the tax treatment of both the originator and SPV.

Since tax stability is required for securitisation to flourish and to attract investors confidence. It has been suggested that the issue be addressed by a tax directive from the appropriate authority, or an opinion by reputable tax consultants.[22] In Malaysia, for example, through recent tax changes such as the elimination of real property tax on certain types of lending, transactions have removed obstacles that held back investors.[23] The Asset Securitisation Consultative Committee (ASCC),[24] in its report,[25] noted that there was no specific tax legislation that dealt with asset securitisation and thus each transaction was to be examined based on its own facts and circumstances by reference to existing tax legislation[26] and practices.[27] The report noted further that in the absence of tax incentives for the asset securitisation, the importance of tax neutrality cannot be overemphasised.[28] The report noted that where an SPV (in Malaysia) exists in the form of a limited company, its tax status remains unclear in terms of whether it should be considered an investment dealing/trading company or an investment holding company.[29] Finally, the report proposes that in order to clarify the tax treatment applicable to the SPV, the following options should be considered:

- exempt the SPV from corporate income tax;
- accord the SPV a trading status to treat it as a company involved in the purchase of discounted securities; and
- tax the SPV on a cash basis.

The absence of specific tax legislation, tax impediments can erode the economic advantages of securitisation transactions. For instance, in a two tier structure where the 'owner SPV' has to route funds to an offshore 'issuer SPV', such funds may be subject to withholding tax. Such a charge may be avoided by entering into tax treaties or establishing SPV in tax friendly countries.[30] Where tax legislation does exist, complications may, nonetheless, arise when such legislation is amended by the government[31] or is subject to other legislative/tax requirements in a way that negates the benefits of the tax legislations.[32] Such alteration may further render payment to investors unworkable leading to a default in the structure and the undesirable consequences that follow a default.

8.2.5 Uncertainty regarding choice of law and enforcements of judgements

The form of uncertainty referred to here is distinct from that of *gharar* in chapter 5 and pertains to the law governing a dispute that arises and the enforcement of judgement. The issue is pressing for the very fact that most Islamic finance jurisdictions are relatively young in their laws, or at least some aspects of their laws, which have been imported and adapted to meet local requirements whilst ensuring they do not contravene the principles of the sharia. The issue also includes the subjective nature of the courts and/or other adjudicative authorities.[33]

Therefore, whilst the sharia explicitly recognises the concept of a contract, in the event of a dispute the sharia courts are more likely to place emphasis on the actual performance of the parties under the contract and the fulfilment of the contractual obligations as opposed to the underlying intentions of a contracting party.

Sharia courts are also unlikely to consider previously decided cases as precedent applicable in the case before them. They would turn to the sources of the sharia (primary, then secondary) so as to arrive at a decision. The judges would consider national laws but their overriding mandate remains to adjudicate the dispute according to the sharia. Remedies for breach of contract are also at the discretion of the sharia court and compensation will normally be limited to the amount of any direct loss, with little or no allowance made for punitive or expectation loss.

There are at least four schools of Islamic jurisprudence each of which may interpret the precepts of the sharia differently, yet equally, in value. Hence, though a jurisdiction would normally adhere to one school of jurisprudence, it is possible for the courts to apply the precepts of another school if deemed appropriate. Malaysia, for instance, adheres to the Shafi'i school yet permits the sale of debt (permitted by the Hanafi school and prohibited by the Shafi'i school). It is also possible for different views to exist on particular issues within the same school.[34]

More importantly, Islamic finance transactions, whether structured as securitisations or otherwise, are increasingly drawn up as agreements governed by, and to be construed in accordance with English law. In certain instances, the agreement also provides that the courts of England shall have exclusive jurisdiction to hear and determine any suit, action, or proceeding, and for such purposes, the parties irrevocably submit to the jurisdiction of such courts.[35] The legal uncertainty caused by the above factors creates unease among foreign investors and renders sharia investment structures comparatively less attractive than their common law counterparts.[36]

In the case of *Shamil Bank of Bahrain v Beximco Pharmaceuticals Ltd*,[37] for instance, the English High Court held that English law would take precedence notwithstanding a choice of law provision in the contract that, 'subject to the principles of the glorious sharia, this agreement shall be governed by and construed in accordance with English law'.[38] The Court of Appeal thus affirmed the decision of Morison J and held that the judge had been correct in holding that English law was the governing law of the contracts.[39] Morison J concluded that, on the proper construction of the applicable law clause, he was not at all concerned with the principles of sharia law; the agreements were enforceable in accordance with English law despite the fact that they amounted to agreements interest and would thus be unlawful in sharia law.

If a securitisation deal is to be rated by a rating agency, for example, Fitch Ratings, it is expected that if the parties choose the laws of a given jurisdiction to govern aspects of the transaction, its choice would be recognised and upheld by: (i) the courts or adjudicative authorities of the chosen jurisdiction; (ii) the jurisdiction of the incorporation of the parties; (iii) the jurisdiction in which the assets are located.[40]

Choice of law concerns and the consequent uncertainty is not limited to sharia jurisdictions and may arise under the common law as demonstrated by the abovementioned case of *Shamil Bank* where the English courts were invited to decide whether 'sharia' as a body of jurisprudence could be incorporated into and govern agreements made under English law through the operation of a choice of law clause. The court held that provisions of the sharia were too indeterminate to be validly incorporated into a contract as the governing law. The Court of Appeal affirmed Morison J's decision[41] that:

> The doctrine of incorporation could only sensibly operate where the parties had by the terms of their contract sufficiently identified specific 'black letter' provisions of a foreign law or an international code or set of rules apt to be incorporated as terms of the relevant contract, such as a particular article or articles of the French Civil Code or the Hague Rules. By that method, English law was applied as the governing law to a contract into which the foreign rules had been incorporated. The general reference to sharia in the instant case afforded no reference to, or identification of, those aspects of sharia law which were intended to be incorporated into the contract, let alone the terms in which they were framed. The words were intended simply to reflect the Islamic principles according to which the bank held itself out as doing business, rather than a system of law intended to 'trump' the application of English law as the law to be applied in ascertaining the liability of the parties under the terms of the agreement.

Similarly, in the case of *Symphony Gems*,[42] despite the court hearing evidence from two expert witnesses on the nature of a *Murabaha* agreement, the applicable principles of Islamic law, and accepting the conclusion of one of the expert witnesses, Dr. Samaan, that the agreement did not have the essential characteristics of a *Murabaha* contract, Tomlinson J stressed that it was critical to note that the contract with which he was concerned (in the case) was governed by English law, not sharia law. He went on to decide the case according to English law. This leads to the conclusion, that even if the Tomlinson J had found that the contract was in accordance with the characteristics of a *Murabaha* agreement, English law was still the governing law and the fact that the contract charged interest would not have invalidated the financing agreement between the parties. To understand Tomlinson J's reasoning and conclusion it is helpful to set out relevant extracts of his opinion:

> It will be noted that cl 25, which I have just set out, provides that the agreement and each purchase agreement made pursuant thereto shall be governed by and shall be construed in accordance with English law, and cl 26.1 contains an irrevocable submission to the jurisdiction of this court by the purchaser, who is of course the first Defendant.
>
> There has been placed before the court some evidence concerning the nature of a Murabaha agreement. Thus I have the benefit of an expert report from Dr Yahya Al-Samaan ... and I also have an expert opinion of a Dr Martin Lau ... I do not need to go into the minutiae of the matters with which they deal. However, it is interesting to note that Dr Samaan describes the legal nature of a Murabaha contract and the prerequisite conditions for such a contract.
>
> For a contract of Murabaha to be valid, two separate procedural requirements have to be satisfied by the prospective Purchaser (the client) and the Seller (the bank). The first requirement involves mutual promises by the two parties, namely a promise by the bank to acquire and sell goods to its client, and a corresponding promise by the bank's client to purchase the goods.
>
> Dr Lau points out that two principles central to Islamic law, namely the prohibition on interest and the prohibition on uncertainty in the object of a contract, limit the scope of commercial activity in Islamic law. The Murabaha contract is intended in Islamic law to be a contract which complies strictly with the requirements of the sharia.
>
> However, it is important to note – indeed, in my judgement, it is absolutely critical to note – that the contract with which I am concerned is governed not by sharia law but by English law. Indeed, it is equally critical to note that Dr Samaan, after examining the nature and terms of the contract with which I am concerned, comes to this conclusion:
>
> 'I have therefore come to the conclusion that the Agreement in issue does not have the essential characteristics of a Murabaha contract'.

In the later case of *Shamil Bank v Beximco Pharmaceuticals*[43], the defendants on appeal, readily conceded that there could not be two governing laws in respect of the financing (*Murabaha*) agreements, and the governing law was English law, not sharia law. Charging interest is an acceptable part of financing arrangements under English law and the court, having accepted the evidence of the Bank's expert witness of Dr Martin Lau, former director of the Centre of Islamic and Middle Eastern Law at the School of Oriental and African Studies at the University of London,[44] that the concern whether the agreements were in compliance with the Murabaha agreements was of no relevance to whether the Murabaha agreements complied with Islamic law.

Further, the Court of Appeal held, having considered the case of *Symphony Gems*, observed that as far as the principles of the sharia are concerned, these were not settled principles but rather an area of considerable controversy and difficulty arising from their ancient moral and religious nature and the need to pay heed to the opinions of the various schools of jurisprudence. On this basis, the principles of the sharia would only have been successfully incorporated into the agreement so as to vitiate the contract on its interest paying character if the parties had sufficiently set out the specific principles applicable. In this case, therefore, mere reference to the principles of the sharia was insufficient, and the validity of the contract and the defendant's obligation thus fell to be decided according to English law.[45] Paragraphs 52 and 55 of the judgement are useful to set out:

52. The general reference to principles of sharia in this case affords no reference to, or identification of, those aspects of sharia law which are intended to be incorporated into the contract, let alone the terms in which they are framed. It is plainly insufficient for the defendants to contend that the basic rules of the sharia applicable in this case are not controversial. Such 'basic rules' are neither referred to nor identified. Thus the reference to the 'principles of ... sharia' stands unqualified as a reference to the body of sharia law generally. As such, they are inevitably repugnant to the choice of English law as the law of the contract and render the clause self-contradictory and therefore meaningless.

55. Finally, so far as the 'principles of ... sharia' are concerned, it was the evidence of both experts that there are indeed areas of considerable controversy and difficulty arising not only from the need to translate into propositions of modern law texts which centuries ago were set out as religious and moral codes, but because of the existence of a variety of schools of thought with which the court may have to concern itself

in any given case before reaching a conclusion upon the principle or rule in dispute. The fact that there may be general consensus upon the proscription of *riba* and the essentials of a valid Murabaha agreement does no more than indicate that, if the sharia law proviso were sufficient to incorporate the principles of sharia law into the parties' agreements, the defendants would have been likely to succeed. However, since I would hold that the proviso is plainly inadequate for that purpose, the validity of the contract and the defendants' obligations thereunder fall to be decided according to English law. It is conceded in this appeal that, if that is so, the first and second defendants are liable to the Bank.

Shamil Bank thus demonstrates that the proscription against *riba* and the essential characteristics of a Murabaha agreement did nothing more than to indicate that had the proviso incorporating the principles of the sharia been sufficient, the defendants would have been successful. In this case it was not and, as the defendants conceded, the first and second defendants were liable to the bank under the Murabaha financing agreements despite its interest paying character.

Prior to the decisions in *Shamil* and *Symphony Gems*, parties to an agreement were able to incorporate specific sharia rules into agreements they made. In the case of *Glencore International AG v Metro Trading Inc*[46] Moore-Bick J's judgement establishes that the principle of '*ghasb*' (misappropriation or usurpation) was validly incorporated into the contract and it was therefore necessary for the court, having heard expert evidence on the relevant jurisprudence, to determine how the principle should be interpreted. Therefore, whilst it appears that the governing position on choice of governing law in securitisation transactions is that expressed in *Shamil*, the issue remains uncertain and in need of clarity.

8.2.6 Asset selection

The underlying asset/s of a securitisation has to be *halal* (lawful) both in and of itself as well as pertaining to its purpose.[47] For instance, enterprises involved in alcohol or gambling, or the use of interest are therefore not deemed sharia compatible. The assets in securitised pools are invariably interest-bearing debt instruments, such as credit card receivables, mortgages, etc. and, as the theory stands, the payment or receipt of interest is prohibited as is the sale or purchase of debt obligations unless they are asset backed, interest-free and sold at par-value. A sharia compliant securitisation will thus require the underlying assets to be securitised based on lease financing, sale or shared ownership, all of which are conventionally established. However, given the conclusions reached in the chapters on *gharar*, *riba* and the sale of debt obligations, the above concerns with Islamic securitisations and the apparent distinctions between them and those under conventional finance are likely to fade. We discussed and concluded that interest is not the subject of the *riba* prohibition in commercial transactions except where the effect of such transaction is inequity, and that the sale of debt obligations at a discount was envisaged and practiced at the time of the Prophet implying its proprietary nature. Further any uncertainty (*gharar*) arising in the structure pertaining to assets would not vitiate the contract unless it was excessive or a major component of the contract and, based on *gharar*'s evidential nature, would be remediable.

8.2.7 *The use of the London inter-bank offered rate* (Libor)

A securitisation structure, whether intended for international investors or not, tends to have its rent rates pegged to LIBOR for marketability purposes. These rent returns to *sukuk* (certificate) holders are variable and may be deemed to be interest (*riba*) based. As discussed in earlier chapters this need will no longer be an issue of concern given the transaction is commercial in nature and the rates of return are equitable or market based.

The concern only persists if the current theory and position towards interest is kept. Yet, even then, it need not be cause for concern as the payments are made for the use of the asset parcel (i.e. rent) and not the money. Pricing the rent off the international exchange makes the certificate competitive with and similar to conventional floating-rate notes. This basis has not been explicitly accepted by most sharia scholars, but neither has it been rejected nor has an alternative benchmark been proposed. What has been suggested is that the sooner an alternative benchmark is developed the better it will be for the development of *sukuk* structures. Further, that returns alternatively be calculated in relation to the profitability of the projects being financed by the *sukuk* as opposed to being priced off the international exchange rates.[48]

8.2.8 *Late payment and penalty charges*

Under the Master agreement of the Qatar global *sukuk* issue, the consequence for late payments of rentals was the government's irrevocable undertaking to donate a late payment amount to be paid directly to a charity of the issuer's choice in respect of the period from and including the due date for payment to the date payment was made but excluding the date of full payment. It is possible for such payments to be considered interest payments parallel to *riba*. The arrangement has, however, been acquiesced to by a large number of sharia scholars since the beneficiary of such penalty is not the party to whom the rentals is owed and incentivises the borrower (through added transaction costs) to make timely payments. In this regard, attention must be drawn to the emphasis Islamic law places on timely payment of contractual obligations. A saying of the prophet Muhammad encourages one to pay workers their wages before their 'sweat dries'. By analogy, this translates to the emphasis to make timely payments for any other commercial obligation owed. Similarly, such payments could not be classified as *riba*, as per our earlier analysis, as banking and finance are commercial activities on which increased returns may be made as long as the effect of the payment is equitable. Alternatively, the *riba* characterisation of the late payment charge fails because the rationale behind the prohibition of *riba* as explained earlier is to avoid inequity, for instance, the exploitation of others' need of cash/finance. To impose a penalty for late payment as an inducement for timely payments is clearly not an exploitative measure.

8.2.9 *The creation of a trust within a civil law framework*
In chapter 1 we noted the similarities between the common law and Islamic law – the availability and use of the concept of 'trusts' being one such similarity. Recent historical studies have traced the roots of the common law system of trusts to the Islamic concept of *waqf*.[49] This similarity of legal reasoning and concepts has been taken as explanation of the relative success of Islamic finance in countries with a common law heritage for instance those within the Gulf Co-operation Council and Malaysia.[50] It is thus an issue of major concern pertaining to the structuring of a sharia compatible securitisation that many sharia jurisdictions do not recognise the trust (because they are civil law jurisdictions) yet the trust as noted above resolves several difficulties that arise with regards to the true sale or re-characterisation issues.[51] In the Islamic securitisation structure illustrated at the beginning of this chapter for instance, the fact that Qatar has no trust law and posed severe restrictions on foreign ownership of real property, meant that structuring the Qatar Global *sukuk ijara* transaction required creativity. The apparent difficulty was, therefore, resolved through the issuer being incorporated as an SPV under Art 68 of Qatar's Commercial Company Law which created an exemption from the general application of Qatar's company law in respect of companies whose shares are owned by the government. This exemption was helpful in the creation of a 'golden share' transaction whereby the issuer's ordinary shares were owned by the government, while the bank held the golden shares as agent for the *sukuk* holders pursuant to a share

agency declaration. Accordingly, notwithstanding Qatar's majority ownership of the issuer,[52] the share agency declaration (using the trust concept)
and the golden share regime, served to protect the interest of the *sukuk*
holders.[53] The added benefit of the structure lay also in that foreign investors
were able to participate in the *sukuk* structure despite the foreign ownership
restrictions due to the fact that the golden shares were held by the bank (on
the investors' behalf).

The issuer, in the Qatar structure, thus acted in a trustee capacity for and
on behalf of the *sukuk* holders. Since Qatari law does not recognise trusts,
the trust relationship between the *sukuk* holders and the issuer was created
under an English law trust instrument. Any choice of law and enforcement
difficulties arising therefrom was overcome principally by the abovementioned Qatari law creating: (i) an agency relationship between the issuer and
sukuk holders that gave the issuer a recognised Qatari legal relationship to
sukuk holders in any local enforcement proceedings against the Government
therefore ensuring that the interest of the *sukuk* holders in any such proceedings would be recognised by the Qatari courts;[54] and (ii) an exemption from
the application of Qatari law with regards to the *sukuk* structure.

An issue that arises from the above transaction is whether an exemption
from the application of a jurisdiction's law, as was in the case of Qatar, is
necessary in order for the trust to be applicable. The laws of any Muslim
nation – whether civil, common or other law – remain subject to the sharia
as a body of law. The concept of trust (*amanah*) and agency (*wakalah*)
has always existed and applied in contractual and financial transactions
throughout the history of Islam. The concept of trust, in fact, finds application in Islam in different forms, that is, *waqf* (charitable trusts), *amanah*
(trusteeship) and *sharikat al mulk* (shared ownership/partnership). The
main reason why the use of trust structures remains a problem within
Middle Eastern countries is because many of them belong to the civil law
legal family that does not recognise the trust. This 'disconnection' between
the legal system and compliance with the sharia is thus proving unneces-
sarily detrimental and serves only to complicate matters. This book proposes
that the trust concept be freely applicable as a sharia concept as opposed to
a borrowed concept from common law. The contract of *mudharaba* (trust
financing) clearly demonstrates the compatibility and application of the
trust in Islamic finance. Under a *mudharaba*, the financier entrusts his assets
or funds to an asset or fund manager in an agreed profit sharing arrangement. Further, Malaysia's application of the trust concept in *sukuk* structures,
albeit through the common law, demonstrates in reality the compatibility of
the trust with the sharia.

8.2.10 Interpretation of commercial laws and contracts in sharia jurisdictions

The uncertainty over the interpretation of the commercial laws and contracts drafted and signed under those commercial laws in sharia jurisdictions is another concern pertaining to dual compatibility of sharia compliant securitisations. The nascent sharia compliant securitisation market is especially hampered by the fact that not only do judicial decisions often differ from scholars' decisions but also by the fact that each jurisdiction seems to sport its own scholarly decisions on any given issue pertaining to Islamic finance transactions and structures.

The importance of addressing this issue cannot be stressed enough due to the fundamental impact it has on securitisations. To mention but a few, on the part of investors, the prevalent disagreement and disparity in opinions and judicial decisions undermines investor confidence because it negates certainty of outcome in the event of default and could possibly jeopardise investors' rights. On the part of the capital market and Islamic finance economies, it shakes the foundation of structuring a securitisation because it could possibly deny the securitisation being rated by the rating agencies. Major rating agencies, such as Fitch Ratings or Moody's, are only concerned with the credit aspects of the financial structure. They will not rate such structures merely based on their sharia compliance or otherwise.

In summary, among the main reasons why such uncertainty over interpretation and effect of contractual and commercial laws arises is that:

- Various aspects of the national legislation have been imported and adapted to meet local requirements with particular care that these laws do not contravene the principles of the sharia.
- The sharia judges presiding over a dispute consider national laws but are more concerned about ensuring that a dispute is resolved by reference to sharia law; the Courts of England are likely to ignore sharia concepts and rules where the parties have agreed to be governed by the laws of England and Wales, as discussed in section 8.2.5.
- Sharia courts are unlikely to consider previous judgements (precedents) and remedies to breaches of contract are at the discretion of the court.

It is thus important both for rating purposes and for investor confidence, which will in turn lead to growth in demand for Islamic investments, that transactional and legal certainty be enhanced.

8.2.11 *The role of the sharia committee*

The sharia committee occupies a very important position in Islamic financial institutions and in Islamic finance generally. An Islamic bank will not participate in a transaction unless the sharia committee approves the transaction as being sharia compliant and the transaction offering documentation includes a copy of their fatwa.

The actual role of a sharia committee varies from transaction to transaction and in addition to their transaction approval role, other roles include:[55]

* studying the offering memorandum, constitutional documents and major agreements controlling the relationship between the functionaries of the structure;
* giving general advice to the manager or advisor with regards to compliance with the sharia principles;
* advising on the use of instruments and techniques for efficient cash management and their compliance with the principles of the sharia;
* advising on the separation of non-sharia compliant profit of the transaction and suggesting the charitable activities to which they may be directed;
* preparing annual sharia audit and reviews concerning the securitisation activities and the issue of a report to the investors.

Sharia committees thus have the important role of not only determining what is acceptable and what is not, but also to seek to: reconcile, as far as possible, Islamic finance with conventional finance; harmonise the practice of Islamic finance as practiced in different jurisdictions: and, generally, guide the market as it progresses and develops. The scholars, who are experts in the sharia law as it relates to financial products, have admittedly adapted to a market place that has grown in sophistication and complexity. With the emphasis on adapting conventional financial structures to meet the requirements of the sharia, there has been pressure on the sharia scholars expert in the field to build a similar level of proficiency in understanding today's complex conventional structures so that they can assist in developing similarly efficient sharia-compliant alternatives. They have risen to the challenge and though there still does not exist a codification of previous opinions into one formalised set of guidelines adopted as standard practice, there is a considerable body of expertise available for consultation.

A sharia committee can, however, play an even larger role by adopting a more open and progressive attitude towards Islamic finance and commercial transactions within today's global financial markets and the need for

Muslims to develop financial products that are both sharia compliant and competitive at the global market level.[56] Sharia committees have the ability to foster greater legal certainty in the industry (with regards to compatibility and enforcement of judgements in sharia jurisdictions) through their availability for consultation on the different aspects of a deal. The scholars on the committee, being well versed with the sharia rules and jurisprudential opinions, are well placed to give general and authoritative opinions (and even advise the rating agencies), for example, on the acceptability of an outcome or ruling in that jurisdiction should a dispute arise and, hence, whether the judgement would be enforced locally. Consideration should also be given to the formation of a single sharia committee in any given Islamic finance jurisdiction (preferably established and run independent of the government) and through it, a single coherent body of rules, laws and principles applicable not only to securitisations but the industry as a whole can begin to take shape.[57]

The effect of the above would no doubt create greater certainty and clarity in the application and effect of the sharia rules in at least three ways:

- with supervision from and consultation with the sharia committee , legal judgements are less likely to be unpredictable;
- there is less likely to be more than one prevalent view or two or more conflicting views on the acceptable rules and practices in the industry; and
- through the opinions and fatwas of the sharia council, greater clarity among the sharia judges as to the effect of contractual clauses and obligations within the overall sharia framework will be fostered for the benefit of the industry, regulatory bodies and rating agencies.

The resulting certainty and cohesion will mark an important step in the development and eventual harmonisation of practices and rules for Islamic finance both at the industry level and collectively, at the global level.

Conclusion

In closing, this chapter has examined the difficulties faced in structuring a securitisation structure compatible with both the sharia and common law. Wherever possible, suggestions have been made as to how these (potential or actual) difficulties may be avoided or overcome. It is significant to note that this chapter examines the theory and practice as it now stands and, thus, may be at variance with the conclusions drawn in chapters 4, 5 and 6 that would render the distinction between 'Islamic finance' and conventional finance a non-issue except as far as the objective of the finance is concerned.

9

ISLAMIC FINANCE IN MALAYSIA

A MODEL TO EMULATE

9.1 Genesis and growth of Islamic finance in Malaysia

Malaysia embarked on a pioneering effort to develop a comprehensive Islamic Finance (IF) system more than 30 years ago and was among the earliest to recognise the potential to create a financial system compatible with Islamic principles that provides an alternative to the conventional system. The process began with the first Islamic financial institution, Lembaga Tabung Haji[1] (the Pilgrim Fund Board aka Tabung Haji), established in 1969. Tabung Haji's objective was (and remains) to mobilise savings of Muslims intending to perform the hajj (pilgrimage) with the pool of savings being invested in sharia-permissible instruments. Malaysia was not alone in her experiments with Islamic finance at the time; Egypt had their own pilot scheme that was called Mit Ghamr by its founder. However, unlike the Mit Ghamr[2] scheme that was created and sustained by an individual without political affiliations (and subsequently extinguished at the behest of the political fabric in Egypt), Tabung Haji was inspired and supported by the leadership in Malaysia for the benefit of the populace. The tangibility of its benefit to society ensured fervent support for and popularity of Islamic banking. It is thus no surprise that the Tabung Haji model has been hailed as exemplary by Muslim majority nations. More importantly, the institutionalisation of Tabung Haji as a sharia-compliant organisation paved the way for the development of a better-structured institutional framework of Islamic banking and finance in Malaysia. The Islamic Banking Act 1983 was introduced and Malaysia's first full-fledged Islamic bank was established followed by the enactment of the Takaful Act 1984 for purposes of Islamic Insurance. The system was further complemented with the inception of the Islamic inter-bank money market in 1994 followed by the availability of short- and long-term financial instruments.[3] These sharia-compliant investments and instruments have been providing Islamic banking institutions with funding and liquidity requirements, fully supported by the state-of-the-art technology and services including settlement and custodian systems, funds transfer and scripless Islamic securities and commercial papers.[4]

In the area of regulatory development, the Islamic Financial Services Board (IFSB) was established in Kuala Lumpur in the year 2002 to develop international prudential regulatory standards globally to enhance soundness and stability of Islamic financial system. Bank Negara Malaysia, Malaysia's national bank, is a founding member of IFSB together with 15 other full members that comprises central banks, monetary and supervisory authorities. Thus far, two standards have been issued: Standards for Capital Adequacy and Guiding Principles for Risk Management for Islamic financial institutions. Bank Negara Malaysia has implemented these IFSB standards for adoption by Malaysian Islamic banking institutions since 2007[5]. The regulatory development effort was further strengthened through the establishment of the International Islamic Financial Market (IIFM) in 2005. The IIFM provides the market mechanism to facilitate capital mobilisation, stimulate the creation and trading of Islamic financial instruments, enhance investment opportunities and facilitate efficient liquidity management by Islamic financial institutions. Similarly, for the orderly development of an Islamic Capital Market (ICM), the Securities Commission has initiated various measures over the past decade. Consequently, Malaysia's ICM has witnessed a proliferation of products and services ranging from equities, unit trust funds, structured products, derivatives, index, fund management and stock broking services. At present, there are 89 Islamic unit trusts, about 85 per cent of the listed stocks are sharia-compliant and 46 per cent of the corporate bond market comprises Islamic bonds. It is, thus, fair to say that Malaysia has the most comprehensive Islamic capital market in the world. Further, Malaysia possesses social, political and economic stability in a mostly democratic setting. Malaysia's stable and consistent monetary and fiscal policies coupled by the requisite experience (evinced by the country's handling of the Asian crisis in 1998) do much to promote the country's status as a leader of Islamic finance. Political and economic stability enables the government to promote the orderly development of the market especially in preparing domestic players for the challenges posed by a more liberalised market. However, beyond mere stability, it is Malaysia's willingness to embrace innovation and develop alongside conventional banking practices that has and will continue to serve the country in future developments. Malaysia's key asset, both as an Islamic finance jurisdiction and as a global leader, is the grassroots support that the country's Islamic banking enjoys due to the tangible benefits with which Islamic banking and finance continue to provide the Malaysian population.

The Malaysian Government plays an effective ongoing role as a catalyst for the development of Islamic finance. It recognises that though the role of the public sector is to provide an environment conducive to the flourishing of the private sector, it is generally the private sector that carries the baton into further development. It therefore provided a foundational structure for Islamic finance, which is now open for the private sector to capitalise and continue to build upon it so that a free market evolves from it. It is also encouraging that while the Malaysian Islamic financial market offers a comprehensive range of product and services in banking, insurance, and investments, its institutions are themselves turning into originators of a wide range of Islamic products and services. This is a marked development from when the financial institutions took on the business model of adapting conventional structures as templates for 'off-the-shelf' Islamic products largely for the retail market. It is, however, not certain whether this development also means a shift from 'form-based' Islamic finance to a more substance-based approach. Nonetheless, having built up their knowledge of the underpinning sharia principles and in line with the growth of demand in Islamic banking products, private institutions now realise the potential of sharia-compliant products as a viable driver of profitability, market differentiation and enhancer of shareholder value. The industry simply needs to continue moving up the value chain, injecting effort into the development of increasingly sophisticated structured products applicable to the needs of increasingly demanding domestic and international markets. From being a policy driven initiative, Islamic finance in Malaysia is slowly developing into a market-driven one. It is, thus, encouraging that the Malaysian government recently acknowledged that the fast-growing Islamic financial sector needs strong regulation to ensure it never faces the damage caused by the financial crisis. Malaysia's prime minister, Najib Razak, is reported to have said that it was 'imperative for the industry to draw upon the lessons learnt to ensure that we avoid any such financial instability in the future'. Malaysia's government is also reported to oversee one of the world's largest and most comprehensive Islamic financial sectors as this chapter details.[6]

An area of initiative that could be undertaken by Malaysia towards the development of Islamic finance globally is the treatment of income derived from various Islamic finance jurisdictions. Currently, individual countries rely on local conventional-based tax legislation to govern the treatment of income from Islamic finance activities. In most cases, such legislation is inadequate to deal with the intricacies of Islamic financing. This results in the possibility of Islamic finance profits being taxed differently depending on the individual country's tax legislation and how these profits are categorised. The inadequacy of local tax legislation in most countries, in dealing with such issues, causes tax-cost inefficiencies for Islamic investors. Similarly, the resulting uncertainties and inconsistencies represent a significant obstacle to the cross border movement of Islamic capital. However, this inadequacy also presents an opportunity for innovation. Labuan Offshore Financial Service Authority (LOFSA) can take the lead on studying the development of an Islamic Model Tax Convention (IMTC), similar to the Double Taxation Agreement (DTA) of the Organisation for Economic Co-operation and Development (OECD). The objective of an IMTC would be to provide a framework of clear and transparent rules for the uniform taxation of such income in the signatory countries. The framework will facilitate the flow of Islamic funds across international borders, making it possible for market players to package and price Islamic products with greater liquidity and certainty. LOFSA's experience gained from the many years of networking abroad and with its working knowledge in regards to the issues of international taxation will place it in good stead to undertake this study and more importantly, it will pave way for further development of Islamic finance through enhancing product efficacy alongside cost efficiency.

It is Malaysia's declared mission to develop a vibrant, innovative and competitive international Islamic financial services industry that is supported by high calibre human capital, world-class infrastructure and best international standards and practices. So far, Malaysia has proved its commitment to extend all that is necessary to ensure that this is accomplished. Whether the country remains so, and more importantly, whether it attains this goal is largely dependent on whether Malaysia continues to focus on the efficiency and equitable nature of the Islamic finance industry it develops at home – it is these two factors that will grant Malaysia industry leadership and continued global presence.

9.2 Malaysia's distinct structural and institutional advantages over other Islamic finance participants

In discussing the four outlined components of Malaysia's structural and institutional framework it is intended that the appraisal will serve as an example from which other Islamic finance jurisdictions, including the UK, may draw from for their better performance in the Islamic Capital Market (ICM). These are:

- a common law jurisdiction;
- a dual banking system;
- a multifaceted approach to Islamic banking; and
- the Labuan International Offshore Financial Centre (IOFC).

9.2.1 A common law jurisdiction

International trade and finance, because of its global nature, is necessarily affected by many factors that may give rise to uncertainty as to the application of contractual terms under which certain trade and financing arrangements are made. These factors range from political to environmental and global economic stability to specific laws governing the agreement. As a common law jurisdiction, therefore, Malaysia enjoys the advantage of a mature legal system that is well equipped to deal with lacunae in the law or legal structure in an established manner and provides the requisite level of certainty for purposes of equity. Therefore, whilst other Islamic finance jurisdictions have patched together bits and pieces of various legal systems according to what the political fabric preferred and/or was most aligned with their concept of Islam, Malaysia simply embraced the common law framework, replacing only those aspects of the common law that are explicitly provided for or prohibited by the primary texts of Islam. This augurs very well with the contractual and commercial principle of Islam that permits anything unless explicitly prohibited by the primary sources. Among the pertinent benefits of inheriting the common law system is, thus, the mechanism it provides for filling any lacunae in the law, that is, through precedent, judicial law making, rules of equity, customs and trade practices in addition to legislating new laws. Common law jurisdictions can also rely on, as persuasive authority, decisions of other common law jurisdictions in determining how to address a novel or unforeseen outcome or situation. Though these mechanisms find direct parallel with concepts under Islamic law – i.e. *ijtihad* (independent legal reasoning), *qiyas* (drawing analogy from past cases), *maslaha* (equity) and *urf* (customs and practices) – the distinct advantage Malaysia's common law system possesses over other Islamic finance jurisdictions is the certainty and reassurance it provides foreign investors and regulators (through the application of common law concepts and principles) whilst retaining an Islamic law framework that facilitates Islamic banking. Two clear examples of how certainty is fostered through the common law in Malaysia are: (i) the concept of binding precedent that allows Malaysia to build up a repository of judicial guidance on Islamic finance issues, and (ii) the possession of a judicial system and arbitration framework that recognises and enforces foreign judgements. Both these factors are either missing or patchy in Middle Eastern countries due to, firstly, the codified civil law system that is not underpinned by the principle of judicial precedent and, secondly, due to the fact that sharia courts in the Middle East are unlikely to enforce any foreign judgement without enquiring into the merits of the case (which it may then agree or disagree with). Therefore, although Islamic law provides a mechanism to address any lacunae in the law, the conservatism with which the law is applied, the heightened unpredictability of decisions as a consequence of individual judge's religious views or jurisdictional preferences (as is illustrated by the disparity between the fatwas issued), an absence of the concept of binding judicial precedent and the alien nature of the Islamic legal system to foreigners, have all served to spread a veneer of uncertainty in its financial products. For these reasons other Islamic finance jurisdictions tend to limit the application of Islamic law only to the certification of 'sharia compliant' – which generally means no predetermined rate of interest payable on loans, an acceptable level of risk, and assets that are *halal* (lawful) in Islam. Beyond such certification, foreign laws (mainly the common law) are adopted to structure 'global Islamic deals' so as to provide the requisite level of certainty that make the investments attractive to foreign investors. Alternatively, as witnessed in the Qatar global securitisation in 2004, the 'sharia compliant' structures may be altogether exempted from the application of local laws through royal decree/s so as to provide the requisite legal and regulatory certainty.

Another advantage of Malaysia's common law system is its principles and law of equity. Among equity's greatest inventions is the concept of *trust*. Before creation of the trust, the settlor had both legal and equitable title. After invention of the trust, legal title was vested in the trustee (or trustees), and equitable title in the beneficiary (or beneficiaries). A trust, therefore, inevitably involves the separation of legal and equitable title. The significance and importance of the law of trust to sharia compliant securitisations is that it allows for the replication of conventional financial structures in Islamic finance and facilitates the passing of beneficial title in the securitised assets or receivables of the underlying assets to the note holders whilst legal title is retained by the SPV.[7] Using the trust structure further ensures that greater credibility attaches to the sharia compliance certification since the implausible disguise of a financial transaction behind a sale à la *Exfinco*[8] becomes unnecessary. Malaysia has thus enjoyed the advantage of the ability to attain the requisite form for purposes of sharia compliance by transferring the assets in a securitisation to a trustee SPV as opposed to non-common law jurisdictions[9] that must contend themselves with 'selling' the assets to the SPV so as to attain remoteness of risk in the structures. Ironically, property laws in most Middle Eastern Islamic finance jurisdictions restrict or prohibit the foreign ownership of property which either negates the viability of the 'sale' structure or otherwise reinforces the effect of the sale as merely a matter of formality. The use of trust structures would thus simplify and facilitate securitisation deals in other Islamic finance jurisdictions both practically and for purposes of sharia compliance. And, while it is the principle of equity that balances the scales of risk and profit, the trust structure allows for flexibility and innovation in creating new financial structures to serve both individual and societal needs. In this regard, it may also be noted that, though Malaysia inherited the concept of trust as a common law concept, the trust is an established concept in Islamic law (*amanah*) that is implemented in the social sphere through *waqf* (charitable trusts) that allows for the divisibility of property that may be held under different ownership and by different legal persons.

9.2.2 *Dual banking system*

Unlike any other Islamic finance jurisdictions, Malaysia has seamlessly integrated its Islamic banking system within its pre-existing conventional banking fabric without denigration of or separation from the latter. The dual banking system is thus complementary and supplementary in nature rather than exclusionary. Islamic banks and financial institutions draw upon the expertise and technical acumen of conventional banks in setting up parallel services and products. The main difference between conventional and Islamic banking products being qualitative, with a greater emphasis on fairness and socio-economics in Islam, by ensuring the majority of the population has access to the direct benefits of their products. It is thus hardly surprising that Malaysia is a leader in the Islamic finance jurisdiction.

The fact that Malaysia chose to develop Islamic finance in tandem with the already existing conventional banking structure, as opposed to determinately wanting to differentiate one from the other, has enabled the country to draw from the conventional banking experience and framework. Islamic banking's only potential distinction from conventional banking, as has been discussed throughout this book, is nothing more than attainment of the dual objectives of equitable outcomes and efficiency of structure. Therefore, it is not *what* transaction but rather *how* the transaction is executed that legitimately distinguishes sharia compliant transactions from other transactions.

It follows that if conventional finance structures and transactions are equitable and efficient, they too qualify as 'sharia-compliant'.

9.2.3 Multifaceted approach to Islamic banking

Section 9.1 outlines Malaysia's Islamic banking industry from inception as a local selfhelp pilgrimage fund to what it has become today by detailing the institutions' services Malaysia has in place so as to put the country on the global scene of Islamic finance. The result is a comprehensive Islamic banking sector. Malaysia has an effective regulatory body in the Malaysian Securities Commission which, in overseeing the regulatory compliance of the Islamic Capital Market (ICM), supports and compliments the regulatory role of Malaysia's central bank. Bank Islam, founded in 1983 as the first Malaysian financial institution to operate on sharia-compliant principles, continues to develop innovative banking products to benefit the population. The bank's vision of being 'the global leader in Islamic banking' has caused the formation of both local and international partnerships, for instance, its partnership with the Tabung Haji scheme to continue financing prospective pilgrims for the hajj on the one hand and the Dubai Investment Group's acquisition of a 40 per cent stake in Bank Islam late in 2006 for approximately US$240 million, on the other. These strategic alliances do not stop with Islamic banks but extend to conventional banks which operate Islamic finance windows and from which Bank Islam draws valuable experience. Malaysia also possesses a thriving home-grown *takaful* (Islamic insurance) sector to provide insurance for her Islamic finance structures. Further, as section 9.2.4 will detail, the Labuan offshore centre provides an attractive alternative to the worlds existing tax-free havens that attract foreign investors and where global deals may be structured with ease. Malaysia has developed its Islamic banking industry using a kaleidoscope of institutions and perspectives catering for both the nations and foreign investors' financial needs and foreseeable eventuality, yet retaining a commitment to serving the individual and collective need of society through her spread of sharia compliant products. Similarly, Malaysia exports her own Islamic finance products through attracting foreign investor subscription to her Islamic finance structures as well as attracting foreign investors to structure deals in Labuan.

In contrast to Malaysia, other Islamic finance jurisdictions are largely dependent on foreign institutions for regulation, foreign legal provisions for the offshore structuring of transactions and legal enforcement and, at times, even for purposes of taxation. With no grassroots germination, à la Tabung Haji, no equivalents to the Securities Commission, Labuan international offshore financial centre or the comprehensive legal framework the common law provides: the main advantage these other jurisdictions retain globally is a perception of religious superiority and a surplus of funds to cushion inefficient structures – both being non-durable advantages. Certainty cannot be secured by money, nor can religious form replace substance. It has taken Malaysia more than half a century to attain what she has today and it is likely to take most other Islamic finance jurisdictions the same. No quick fix solution will suffice because, just as icing on a mud pie doesn't make a cake, foreign substitutions in place of a lacking national framework will eventually be an impediment to Islamic finance's development. The sooner effort is channelled into the development of a comprehensive legal, regulatory and financial framework, the better the prospects of growth and development will be.

9.2.4 *Labuan international offshore financial centre*

Malaysia has its own international offshore financial centre (IOFC) known as the Labuan IOFC which plays a central role in the development of the Islamic financial services sector in Malaysia.[10] It is of significance, therefore, that Labuan IOFC was the jurisdiction for the issuance of the world's first global sovereign *sukuk*: the US$600 million Malaysian Government *sukuk*. The issuance of the global sovereign *sukuk* signified a new era in international Islamic finance. Numerous institutions including those from Asia, Middle East, Europe, North America and the Indian sub-continent subscribed to the groundbreaking issue. It was the catalyst and precursor to the development of the international *sukuk* market and, as a sovereign issue that was twice oversubscribed, it placed Labuan IOFC in the annals of international Islamic finance history.

Labuan IOFC is now an integrated offshore financial centre that offers the full range of offshore financial services including banking, insurance, trust business, fund management, investment holding companies, investment management and management services activities. Labuan IOFC has become increasingly popular for advising and structuring Islamic financing. The better-known centres for setting up funds have always been traditional tax haven jurisdictions, such as the British Virgin Islands, the Cayman Islands, Luxembourg and Dublin. However, these locations may not be best suited for fund investments in the Asia region, particularly in developing economies such as China and India. Labuan provides an alternative to these traditional jurisdictions.[11] Labuan is also fast becoming a popular tax haven for Middle Eastern funds and, though a new player among the international offshore centres, it provides readily available infrastructure, facilities and expertise. The full potential of the fund management industry has yet to be realised but, so far, fund managers from Malaysia, British Virgin Islands, Canada, Hong Kong, Singapore and Switzerland have established funds in Labuan IOFC. Its key attraction lies in its strict laws and regulations that protect investors' interests, its effective privacy laws and the fact that it is constantly reviewed to meet global offshore market demands.[12] The legislation governs and facilitates the smooth establishment and operation of funds. Among other things, the legislation and rules provide that private and public funds are required to appoint trustees to maintain records and ensure investors are protected. Further, to protect the interests of investors and to comply with the Labuan offshore requirements, at least one of the administrator, custodian, or trustee and manager functions must be carried out within Labuan IOFC. With respect to fund managers, there is no licensing restriction. However, when a public fund is set up, the fund manager must be licensed in a recognised jurisdiction and Labuan Offshore Financial Service Authority (LOFSA) must approve their appointment to the fund.[13]

Among the laws and regulations that protect investors are the requirements of ongoing reporting to LOFSA. Companies and partnerships must file annual returns as well as annual audited accounts. A public fund carrying on business under the supervision of another authority must file a certificate of compliance from the governing authority with LOFSA annually. Properly structured, activities of the fund could fall within the definition of an offshore business activity and specifically as an offshore trading activity. When carrying on an offshore trading activity, the fund benefits from a low tax regime of 3 per cent or a lump sum payment of $5,300 a year. The proceeds from redemption of units (in a unit trust fund), preference shares (of fund companies) or payment of any dividends from fund companies are also exempted from withholding tax as income derived from an offshore business activity or out of exempt income; this is also the case with interest paid by a Labuan offshore company (LOC) to a non-resident person, a resident person or another offshore company. Technical or management fees paid by an LOC to a non-resident person or another offshore company are also not subject to tax and an LOC is able to access some of Malaysia's double taxation agreements with over 47 countries to minimise withholding and capital gains tax. The operational cost of a fund in Malaysia is thus lower, from an Asian perspective, than that of other offshore financial centres in the Asia Pacific region. The operational cost is estimated to be 40 per cent less than the cost in Hong Kong and Singapore. It is also undoubtedly lower than tax havens in the US and Europe. Likewise, Labuan boasts over 50 international banks through which fund administrators have the flexibility to hold multi-currency accounts as well as access to the cost-effective and fast transmission of funds.

The roles required for a typical fund set-up are set out in the diagram below. Although not legally necessary, each of the different roles can be carried out from Labuan IOFC by licensed trust companies, investment banks and fund managers. Moreover, the Labuan International Offshore Financial Exchange (LFX) also provides a venue for listing and trading funds.

9.3 Making a difference through Islamic finance

Perhaps the most important lesson learnt from the Asian financial crisis was the interdependence of financial markets. Even the most developed economies were not spared the effects of the financial turmoil, which began as a

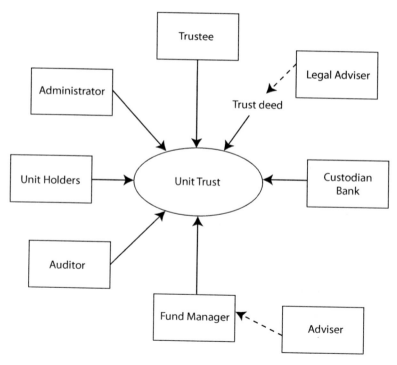

Figure 9.1 A typical unit trust set-up

result of Thailand's default on its Eurobond issue in February 1997. By May 1997, the Malaysian Ringgit (RM) was under severe pressure from currency speculators and interest rates had risen from 7 per cent to 9 per cent. It was reported that Bank Negara expended approximately RM1.2 billion of its foreign exchange reserves towards trying to stave off the attack of currency speculators.

Therefore, while a success story on the Islamic finance scene, lessons from the Asian financial crisis suggest three factors that will make a difference to Malaysia's Islamic finance industry and its socio-economic fabric in the current tumultuous global economic climate:

1 A focus on the substance of the structured transactions as a criteria of sharia compliance because, whilst in buoyant economic conditions people may subscribe to any structure labelled 'Islamic', only invest-ments and transactions that provide equitable returns will continue to attract the growing number of disillusioned customers and subscribers disappointed by the arbitrage witnessed in the Islamic finance industry. Equitable transactions, not necessarily garbed in Arabic jargon or strictly modelled after traditional structures, are more likely to serve Malaysia's population and hence be more attractive and profitable. The intention must be: *Emulate*, not imitate.

2 A focus on the development of efficient structures so as to facilitate equi-table outcomes in sharia compliant financing. Ultimately, the essence of Islamic traditional commercial structures is the attainment of equi-table and efficient outcomes – efficiency being part of the concept of equity. Equitable effect ought to be Islamic finance products' main focus and distinguishing factor if it is to continue insisting on a distinction between it and conventional financing. Again, while the Islamic capital market may appear cushioned by customers willing to pay a premium for 'Islamic' products, as the industry grows and in current tumultuous economic times, attracting customers will depend greatly on whether the products are perceived to offer equitable returns and are attained through cost-efficient transactions.

3 The continued drawing of local support for its Islamic finance industry. This can only effectively be achieved through the populations' continued enjoyment of the tangible benefits of the industry – as they did initially from the Tabung Haji scheme of finance. Malaysia rose to its current status on the Islamic finance scene partly because of its home-grown support and it would be foolhardy to neglect the Malaysian peoples' credit and financial needs in its aim for attaining global eminence. There

are numerous instances of other Islamic finance jurisdictions that began their experimentations with sharia compliant structures only to fail miserably because in their fervent efforts to compete with and discredit conventional banking, they forgot to bring the benefits of their endeavours home to the local population. In Jordan, for example, even those who supported the industry, initially, are now discrediting it for its corrupt, inefficient and exploitative nature. Those who purchase Islamic banking products do so solely because of the inculcated perception that conventional banking is sinful and wrong. If it is sinful and wrong, however, why does the Islamic finance industry put so much effort into imitating conventional finance structures and products? Egypt, the first jurisdiction in the world to experiment with Islamic banking in the mid-twentieth century through the successful Mit Ghamr scheme, is floundering on its banking and finance front not because it retains a mostly conventional banking system with a veneer of sharia-compliance but because when the government eventually took up Islamic banking, it was corrupt, inefficient and inequitable and, thus, succeeded in alienating the majority of the population who are poor and do not benefit tangibly from the industry. With the Sheikh of Al-Azhar himself calling all Islamic bankers a band of thieves, it is little wonder its potential is not fulfilled.

One may question however why Dubai, Qatar and, to a lesser extent, Saudi Arabia continue to do well in Islamic finance. The answer is twofold:

- These jurisdictions are populated with religiously orthodox yet wealthy individuals. The industry, therefore, continues to exploit the religious overtones and forms of the Islamic transactions they structure, for either local consumption (mainly government departments) or foreign investors attracted by the less risk prone investments, offering high fixed returns.
- The surplus of funds and liquidity available to the government plays a role in both the structuring and subscription of the products and cushions the inefficient and costly nature of the products through their willingness to pay a premium for 'Islamic' products.

The apparent success of Dubai and the rest of the region has been upset by the recent near default of Dubai World and the controversy surrounding the Al-Nakheel group in Dubai. These events precipitated a drop in value and capital market activity throughout the Middle East. The illusion of success created and cushioned by surplus funds and good economic times is now being tested.[14]

Conclusion

In current economic times when surplus funds no longer provides a cushion, when the scope for growth and expansion calls for subscription beyond government agencies, and when religious form loses its intrigue and appeal through the apparent lack of substance or distinction from conventional banking, it is only well-functioning legal and regulatory national institutions plus a focus on the three factors suggested above that will ensure enduring success. Without a well-functioning legal and regulatory system encompassing the requisite institutions, the structures that now exist will crumble for lack of a strong foundation. In illustration, contrast Thailand, Indonesia and the Philippines with Malaysia during the 1998 South-East Asia financial crisis. Malaysia successfully survived the 1997/8 Asian speculative capital-market crisis because of her well-regulated financial system and the efficacy of Bank Negara Malaysia (Malaysian Central Bank). Hence, Malaysia's prime minister's recent call for tighter regulation of Islamic finance in current market conditions is apt and timely. Malaysia is a leading Islamic banking jurisdiction mainly due to the continued advantages it enjoys as a result of its well-functioning legal and regulatory structure and the consequent certainty it provides investors both locally and globally.

10

THE WAY FORWARD

With Adam Smith's words, prudence is 'of all virtues that which is most useful to the individual',[1] I am reminded of the following story, the moral behind which fuelled my writing with the intention of contributing to the development and long-term sustainability of Islamic finance. The story is that of a friendly, flightless, happy-go-lucky bird – the dodo. In brief, the dodo was left behind by evolution. With no natural predators, on the Island of Mauritius, it had no need to adapt to its environment and eventually found itself defenceless against the settlers that hunted it. Eventually, it became extinct in 1681. To date, a foolish person is referred to as a 'dodo' and the story is a pragmatic example of how failure to change impedes evolution, leaves one vulnerable and leads to extinction. The same is applicable to any person, practice or sphere of life. It is applicable to the theory and practice of Islamic commerce and finance. The concept of social evolution accompanied by evolving solutions is not novel or peculiar to any civilisation, religion or community. Neither is its relevance time specific. Indeed, even as we assess the causes and outcomes of the current financial crisis, the debate of what is socially useful is acknowledged to be subject to time and context. As Lord Turner puts it, '[t]he basic proposition of securitisation is not daft. The problem was that it became over complicated'.[2] The 'complication' lies partly in the 'bogus assets' that were securitised and sold on to the market for purposes of passing on risk. This, we now know, is part of the cause of the financial crisis we now face and the reason why the regulatory arm of European Commission has gone to length to tighten regulations of securitisation transactions.

Until recently, international finance literature was rife with statistics and claims of the booming market and scope for expansion that exists for *sukuk* (Islamic bonds) and all other Islamic finance structures. Having only taken off in the past couple of decades, it is hardly surprising that the future of

Islamic finance appeared bright: novelty, of both the products and mode of investment for Muslims and non-Muslims alike, strong state support resulting in lower risk of investments and the undoubted need for liquidity and development finance in Muslim-populated jurisdictions created an appetite for Islamic finance products. The story is less glamorous today in the wake of the 2008/9 global financial crisis that has seen scores of investors leaving cities like Dubai and Doha and the Islamic finance industry slowing down considerably.[3]

Available literature and publications do not provide much detail on what Islamic finance really is beyond the hype, jargon and statistics. What makes it *substantially* different from conventional modes of finance? What is currently missing – generally or in certain jurisdictions – the presence of which would ensure the sustainability of its development both in product array and market confidence? Therein lies the key to the development of Islamic finance structures and products and this book has put forward answers, albeit non-conclusive, to these questions.

For purposes of focus and direction, this book chose a particular finance transaction that has not yet been successfully structured within the Islamic finance industry: securitisation. The intention was, thus, to facilitate the structuring of a sharia compliant securitisation by clarifying current key concepts and misconceptions within Islamic legal theory and practice. Within that framework, several pertinent issues were discussed revolving around the current meaning, application and effect of *gharar, riba* and *bay al dayn* on contractual and financial transactions as well as suggested alternatives that may be adopted towards facilitating the expression of the spirit and principles of the *Quran* and traditions of Muhammad. Further, the issues of dual compatibility structures, subjective interpretations, selective application of rules and the claim to moral superiority and religious legitimacy were discussed (and where appropriate, discredited).

The book touches briefly upon the possibility of developing a secondary Islamic capital market in chapter 6, having clarified the proprietary status of debt and intangible assets, as the next step towards growth and widening accessibility of investments in the global market. Emphasis, nonetheless, was laid on the fact that there was no necessity for an exclusive Islamic capital market, for we have seen that much of the current distinctions drawn between 'Islamic' finance and the conventional finance it closely copies, are superficial. However, should the industry insist on drawing distinctions, the only appropriate distinction, as perceived by the author, is that between finance generally and equitable finance. The label 'Islamic' finance is susceptible to confusion and preconceived notions – equity, on the other hand, is more readily discernable from inequity. In this case, a separate capital market may be cultivated to cater to those interested in equitable investments but it need not be labelled 'Islamic' and neither need it be displayed as an 'exclusive' mode of conducting finance. Principles of equitable dealings and justice belong to all cultures and civilisation – the comparability of Islamic law with common law has made this amply clear. As for the when and how it will be developed, the only sustainable means of growth and proliferation of equitable modes of finance is by commencing at the grassroots much like the Tabung Haji and Mit Ghamr schemes did in Malaysia and Egypt, respectively, or the Grameen bank project in Bangladesh. Under this model, Islamic finance products and structures as currently marketed would be free to choose and use conventional capital markets should they qualify. Unfortunately, to date, the form-driven quest for sharia arbitrage in financial investment, at the cost of economic substance, has sabotaged any such effect.

Given the fast declining scope for further growth as a result of current financial market conditions, tighter regulatory controls resulting from increased awareness about sharia arbitrage practices and the diminishing difference between conventional banking and Islamic finance, an enquiry into change in mode and scope of Islamic finance has been triggered. Inefficiencies arising from an industry built on arbitrage that resulted in an increase in transaction costs and a rise in legal and juristic fees have now been exposed by a financial crisis of global scale that has called for tighter regulatory control and monitoring. The effect of the recent global market conditions has also created an interest in synthesising conventional financial products in line with the sharia. The Islamic finance industry calls this 'innovation', the very innovation that was initially depicted as 'prohibited'.

Whilst agreeing with the shift towards harmonisation, this book emphasises that what must now be the essence of Islamic finance, if it is to be sustainable and win the hearts of the currently disenfranchised and disillusioned Muslims, is equitable outcomes through efficient processes. Further, Islamic finance cannot continue to make the profits it has enjoyed without making a meaningful difference to the financial and developmental needs of Muslims. It needs a new identity and the label 'Islamic', if it is to be retained, must be earned through the economic substance it creates. While principles of Islamic economics are entirely compatible with making profit and creating wealth, Islam stresses the requirements of equitable dealings, social justice and efficiency of outcome. How then might Islamic finance go about achieving these objectives? The most logical and simplest place to commence is what chapter 1 stresses: an emphasis on substance with the complementary use of form, for purposes of attaining such substance, in all structures and transactions.

We noted that the principles of contract and commerce in Islam, and the emphasis on substance and social justice, are neither peculiar to Islam nor distinct from the principles of conventional finance. The wake of the 2008/9 financial crisis revealed the existence of the same 'Islamic' principles within Western capitalism, as put forward by its fathers, Smith, Schumpeter and Keynes, amongst others.[4] In Edmund Phelp's words (winner of the 2006 Nobel prize in economics): 'Capitalist systems function less well without state protection of investors, lenders and companies against monopoly, deception and fraud'.[5] The shedding of a prohibition-driven and form-based Islamic finance industry may, thus, cultivate cross-jurisdictional compatibility and shed the false differences between Islamic and conventional finance. Throughout chapters 1, 4, 5, 6, 8 and 9 we have demonstrated that the common law shares much with Islamic law on all the issues considered and that the formalistic distinction drawn by Islamic finance ought to be dropped to enhance the equity and efficiency of its products. Should this be done, a long-due steer in the right direction for Islamic commercial practice will be at hand.

NOTES

1 Islamic Law and the Role of Interpretation

1 M.T. Mansuri, *Islamic law of Contracts and Business Transactions* (Adam Publishers, New Delhi, 2006), 3–4, 14–15. See also M. Hashim Kamali, *The Dignity of Man: An Islamic Perspective* (Ilmiah Publishers, Selangor, Malaysia, 2002).

2 M. Hashim Kamali, *Freedom, Equality and Justice in Islam* (Ilmiah Publishers, Selangor, Malaysia, 2002), 7.

3 H. Beale (ed.), *Chitty on Contracts*, 30th edn (Sweet & Maxwell, London, 2008), vol. I, 10.

4 Abdullah Yusuf Ali (tr.), *The Holy Quran* (King Fahd Holy *Quran* Printing Complex, Madina, by Royal Decree 12412, 1405 AH), herein after simply referred to as the *Quran*, *al-Hajj*: 78, 'It is the religion of your father Abraham who has called you *Muslim* from before and in this [revelation]'.

5 *Quran*, *al-Baqara*: 260; *al-An'am*: 74–9; *Maryam*: 41–8 and *al-Anbiyaa*: 51–8.

6 *Quran*, *al-Baqara*: 127–32 (n. 4).

7 *Quran*, *al-Baqara*: 135–41 (n. 4).

8 *Quran*, *Fussilat*: 43 (n. 1), 'Nothing is said to you (O Muhammad) except what was said to the Messengers before you'; also, *Quran*, *al-A'la*: 18–19 'Verily! This is in the former scriptures. The scriptures of Abraham and Moses'.

9 Karen Armstrong, *Islam: A short History* (Phoenix Press, London, 2001), 14–15. This Muhammad did by adopting forms of worship from the Christians and Jews living amongst the pagan Arabs at the time. The *Quran* gives examples of fasting with the Jews and on specified days (*Ashura*), praying in, initially, the same manner (including late night vigils), and in the same direction (*Qibla*) as the Jews (facing Jerusalem)

10 Karen Armstrong 4–5 (n. 4).

11 M. Hashim Kamali, *Freedom, Equality and Justice in Islam* (Ilmiah Publishers, Selangor, Malaysia, 2002), 47

12 M. Hashim Kamali, *Freedom, Equality and Justice in Islam*, xi.

13 Oditah, *Legal Aspects of Receivables Financing* (Sweet & Maxwell, London, 1991), 46, 'Common law did not, and still does not, as a general rule recognise a preset transfer of future property'. Oditah cites *Lunn v Thornton* (1845) 1 C.B. 379.

14 See chapter 4 for a detailed discussion of *gharar*.

15   El-Gamal, *Islamic Finance: Law, Economics and Practice* (Cambridge University Press, New York, 2006), 81–2. See chapter 5 and 6 for a detailed discussion.
16   El-Gamal, ibid.
17   See Oditah, Legal Aspects of Receivables Financing, 46 (n. 13).
18   Mansuri, *Islamic Law of Contracts and Business Transactions*, 205–6.
19   See sections 4.1, 4.2 and 5.1 and 5.2.
20   See conclusion to chapter 5.
21   El-Gamal, 103 (n 15).
22   M. Furmston, *Cheshire, Fifoot & Furmston's Law of Contract*, 15th edn (OUP, Oxford, 2007), 1–5. The English law of contract it has been seen, was evolved and developed within the framework of *assumpsit* as a remedy for the breach of informal agreements reached by word of mouth , and, so long as that framework endured, it was not necessary to pursue too fervently the search for principle. An *assumpsit* was an undertaking. Thus, in the case of *Skyrne v Butolf* (1367) YB 2 Ric 2 (Ames Series) 223, the plaintiff sued a doctor to whom he had come to seek a cure for the ringworm. He alleged that the doctor, undertook (*assumpsit*) in London in return for a certain sum of money previously paid into his hand, competently to cure the [plaintiff] of a certain infirmity.
23   [1929] All ER Rep 679.
24   [2007] UKHL 40, per Lord Hoffman at paras 1–12.
25   [1929] All ER Rep 679 at 683.
26   [1929] All ER Rep 679 at 683.
27   Furmston, *Cheshire, Fifoot & Furmston's Law of Contract*, 404.
28   [1892] 2 QB 484 at 490–1.
29   *Ellesmere v Wallace* [1929] 2 Ch 1 at 24, 36, 48–9.
30   Furmston, *Cheshire, Fifoot & Furmston's Law of Contract* 406.
31   Carlill v Carbolic Smoke Ball Co. [1892] 2 QB 484.
32   Ibid.at 491–2.
33   Examples include the sale of next year's apple crop, the sale of the next haul of a fisherman's net, and the sale of an undeclared dividend. See *Thacker v Hardy* (1878) 4 QBD 685, CA; *Marten v Gibbon* (1875) 33 LT 561, CA.
34   [1992] BCLC 148 at 160.
35   Roy Goode, *Commercial Law* (3rd edn, Lexis Nexis Butterworths, London, 2004), 605–8
36   Ibid.
37   [2002] EWCA Civ1138.
38   [2006] EWCA Civ 694.
39   *Re Watson* (1890) 25 QBD 27; *Polsky v S & A Services* [1951] 1 All ER 185, affirmed in [1951] All ER 106n.
40   Roy Goode, *Commercial Law*, 605–6 in reference to, and drawing from, the *Exfinco case.*
41   [2009] EWCH 340 (Ch) para 51.

2 Scope, Methodology and Objective

1   See chapter 7 on Securitisation.
2   Currently interpreted and applied as a prohibition of interest on loans.
3   Vogel and Hayes, *Islamic Law and Finance: Religion, Risk and Return* (Brill-Leiden, Boston, 2006), 68.

4 Only excessive *gharar*, as opposed to merely an imputation of *gharar*, renders a contract void. See chapter 4 at 4.2 for greater detail.

5 With the exception of Malaysia as a progressive Islamic finance jurisdiction that allows the sale of debts/future obligations to the limited extent that it is backed by real assets. A full discussion follows in chapter 6.

6 *Quran, al-Baqara*: 215 (n 1); see also Karen Armstrong, *Muhammad: A Biography of the Prophet* (Phoenix Press, London, 2001), 92.

7 El-Gamal, *Islamic Finance: Law, Economics and Practice* (Cambridge University Press, New York, 2006), 15–16.

8 El-Gamal, *Islamic Finance*, 16–17.

9 See Financial Services Authority (FSA) Report, 'Islamic Finance in the UK: Regulation and Challenges', 28 November 2007 at www.fsa.gov.uk, last accessed on 2 December 2009.

10 See chapter 4, section 4.2–4.3.

11 Karen Armstrong, *Islam: A Short History* (Phoenix Press, London, 2001), 85. It was during the Mongol reign (fifteenth century ad) that 'world hegemony' was sought, that it was agreed that the *ulama* (scholars) could no longer use their independent reasoning and thus resulted in the metaphorical 'closing of the gates of *ijtihad*'. This essentially denied people their right to apply their minds to the scriptures and/or what the scholars interpreted them as. Henceforth, all interpretations of the primary sources had to be taken and applied on the basis of past authorities to be applied without introspection or question. The scholars and political rulers of the day were concerned with the possibility of the sharia being a potentially subversive source by giving rise to multiple interpretations of Islam that had proliferated from the ninth century ad. It was claimed that the intention was to stop the abuse of *ijtihad* (independent reasoning) by people who were not theologically or legally qualified.

12 El-Gamal, *Islamic Finance*, xiii.

13 *Quran* Al-Nisa: 59 (n.1).

14 Armstrong, *Islam: A Short History*, 79.

15 El-Gamal, *Islamic Finance*, 15–17.

16 John Makdisi, Makdisi, John, 'The Islamic Origins of the Common Law', *North Carolina Law Review* 1999, 77 (5); cited in El-Gamal, *Islamic Finance*, 16 (n. 22). See also, Landes, David, *The Wealth and Poverty of Nations* (Abucus Publishing, London, 2000), 54. Landes states that Islam was Europe's teacher through contact made in Spain and, otherwise, through translated books.

3 Islamic Finance: An Introduction

1 Monzer Kahf, 'Islamic Banks: The rise of a New Power Alliance of Wealth and Sharia Scholarship', in C. Henry and R. Wilson (eds), *The Politics of Islamic Finance* (Edinburgh University Press, Edinburgh, 2004), 18–22. The Islamic Development Bank was founded in 1973 and the Dubai Islamic Bank in 1974. Note, however, that two micro-economic schemes pioneered Islamic finance long before the Islamic banks came onto the scene: the Mit Ghamr banking scheme established in Egypt in 1963 by Ahmad al-Najjar and the Tabung Haji finance scheme established in Kuala Lumpur by the Malaysian government in 1956.

2   Abdullah and Ismail, *International Financial Law Review*, September 2009 at www.iflr.com, last accessed on 2 December 2009.

3   Stichting Sachsen-Anhalt EURO100m Trust Certificates (*sukuk*) rated 'AAA' by Fitch Ratings as reported in the Germany Pre-sale Report, 9 July 2004.

4   William Wallis, 'Bankers Learn New Language to Manage Islamic Funds', *Financial Times* (London, 20 October 2004). See, more recently, speech by Clive Briault, Managing Director, Retail Markets, 'London: Centre of Islamic Finance', at the FSA Industry Forum, London, 17 October 2007; and HM Treasury paper, 'The Development of Islamic Finance in the UK: The Government's Perspective', December 2008 at www.hm-treasury.gov.uk , last accessed on 2 December 2009.

5   *Quran, al-Hadid*: 10; *al-Baqara*: 30; *al-Ahzab*: 72; *Sad*: 26.

6   *Quran, al-Maida*: 1 (n. 1); *al-Nisa*: 29.

7   Ibn Taymiyya, *Al-Fatawa al Kubra* (Dar al-Kutb al Ilmiyyah, Beirut, 1987), vol. 29, 16–18; M.T. Mansuri, *Islamic Law of Contracts and Business Transactions* (Adam Publishers, New Delhi, 2006), 3–4, 14–15.

8   Nabil Saleh, *Unlawful Gain and legitimate Profit in Islamic Law* (Cambridge University Press, Cambridge), 144.

9   Mansuri, *Islamic Law of Contracts and Business Transactions*, 5–6.

10   M. Hashim Kamali, *Freedom, Equality and Justice in Islam* (Ilmiah Publishers, Selangor, Malaysia, 2002), 35.

11   Al-Ghazali, *Ihya 'Ulum al-Din* A. 'Izz al-Din al Sirwan (ed.) (Dar al Kutb al Ilmiyyah, Beirut, 1985) sets out five objectives, clearly set out in the *Quran* and *sunna*; the protection of life, intellect, property, honour and conscience of a human being.

12   Ultimately, the objectives of the sharia are meant to lead to social welfare and ease (*maslaha*).

13   Al-Tirmidhi, *Sunan al-Tirmidhi* (Dar al Fikr, Beirut, 1980), vol.3, 141.

14   M. Hashim Kamali, *Islamic Commercial Laws: An analysis of Futures and Options* (Ilmiah Publishers, Selangor, 2002), 67. Kamali explains that it is not sufficient to presume that a contract is forbidden if it is not explicitly forbidden (in the primary sources).

15   The translation, in all cases, is insufficient to express the laden meaning of the Arabic text.

16   *Quran*, al-Baqara: 275.

17   *Quran, al-Baqara*: 278 (n.1).

18   *Quran, al-Rum*: 39.

19   The gist of the *riba* prohibition, in light of the *raison d'être* of the prohibition, is debatable whether it remains exploitative today.

20   El-Gamal, *Islamic Finance: Law Economics and Practice* (Cambridge University Press, Cambridge, Massachusetts, 2006), 51.

21   This is categorically stated in the *Quran, al-Baqara*: 275 ' … those who devour *riba* will not stand except as stands one whom the devil has driven to madness by his touch'.

22   See chapter 5 below and El-Gamal, *Islamic Finance*, 50–7.

23   *Quran*, al-Baqara: 219.

24   De Teran, Natasha, 'Derivatives Extend the Reach of Islamic Finance', *The Banker* (25 June 2005), vol. 155, 49–51.

25 This highlights the difference between Islamic finance and conventional finance being one of risk sharing as opposed to risk assumption. This, however, does not derogate from the validity of the capital guaranteeing Islamic financial products available in Islamic finance.

26 Nathif Adam and Abdulkader Thomas, *Islamic Bonds: Your Guide to Issuing, Structuring and Investing in Sukuk* (Euromoney Books, London, 2004), 28–30. See also El-Gamal, *Islamic Finance*, 144.

27 It is said that everything that is to occur or materialise in the future is uncertain.

28 Adam and Thomas, *Islamic Bonds*, 28.

29 This argument is dealt with at length in chapter 6 and effectively negated.

30 Note the difference between predetermined *proportion* of profit and predetermined *amount* of profit.

31 Adam and Thomas, *Islamic Bonds*, 67. There ought to be no objection to issuing *sukuk* representing a partial ownership interest in the assets, and with it the relevant share of income or risk of loss.

32 For a discussion and critique of such structures of finance, see generally El-Gamal, *Islamic Finance*, 42–5.

33 *Quran, al-Baqara*: 275.

34 Hashim Kamali, *Islamic Commercial Laws*, 67–8. See chapter 5 on *riba* and chapter 6 on the nature of debt for a complete discussion.

35 Rodney Wilson, 'Overview of the Sukuk Market', in Nathif Adam and Abdulkader Thomas, *Islamic Bonds*, 3.

36 Wilson, 'Overview of the Sukuk Market'. See, however, discussion in chapter 6, section 6.8 on the 'asset-backed' requirement.

37 The OIC Academy issued a fatwa concerning aspects of these bonds. See Decision 5 (D4/08/88) of the fourth session, Fiqh Academy Journal 3:2161.

38 Although there is no compulsion to comply with the rulings of the Fiqh Academy, they do carry considerable weight with most Islamic financial institutions and their sharia committees and advisers.

39 *Quran, al-Baqara*: 282.

40 Note that the Academy of Fiqh ruling alludes to the fact that non-personal debts are, to a restricted extent, part of financial assets.

41 Sharia Standards published by the Accounting & Auditing Organisation for Islamic Financial Institution (AAOIFI), www.aaoifi.com, last accessed 7 September 2008.

42 There are many classes of assets in conventional finance that are *halal* as are many of the techniques used in conventional securitisation equally valid in Islamic ones.

43 The argument is elaborated on in chapter 8 at section 8.2.

44 Muhammad Taqi Usmani, *An Introduction to Islamic Finance* (Kluwer Law International, The Hague, 2002), xiv–xvii.

45 We deal with this argument in chapter 4.

46 Business loans, consumer loans, student loans, credit card receivables, etc.

47 Adam and Thomas, *Islamic Bonds*, 77.

48 See discussion on the sale of debt in chapter 6.

49 Armstrong, *Islam: A Short History*, 85.

4 *Gharar* in Islamic Law

1   The term 'commercial' is used to distinguish commercial transactions from domestic and social agreements, as is commonly done under the common law, for purposes of legal treatment, application and effect. See, E. McKendrick, *Contract Law: Text, Cases and Materials* (2nd edn, OUP, Oxford, 2005), 309.

2   Vogel and Hayes, *Islamic Law and Finance: Religion, Risk and Return* (Brill Leiden, Boston, 2006), 87.

3   The Hadith is reported through Abu Hurayra Ibn Omar, Ibn Abbas, and Annas Ibn Malik and is contained in Muslim's *Sahih* annotated by Al-Nawawi (d. 676/1277) *Kitab al Majmu'* (Maktabat al-Irshad, Jeddah, 1992), Vol. III, 156.

4   Ibn Hanbal indicating that its most correct version is handed down on the authority of Ibn Masoud, not the Prophet himself. See Vogel and Hayes, *Islamic Law and Finance: Religion, Risk and Return* (Brill, Boston, 2006), 88.

5   Reported by Bukhari cited in Vogel and Hayes, *Islamic Law and Finance.*

6   Reported by Muslim cited in Vogel and Hayes, *Islamic Law and Finance.*

7   Reported by Bukhari, Muslim, Abu Daud, Tirmidhi.

8   Al-Dhareer, *Al-Gharar in Contracts and its Effects on Contemporary Transactions* (Islamic Development Bank's Eminent Scholars' Lecture Series, Jeddah, 1997), 9.

9   Ibid. See also M. Tahir Mansuri, *Islamic Law of Contracts and Business Transactions* (Adam Publishers, New Delhi, 2006), 93.

10 The *Quran* uses the root word *gha-rra* and its derivatives such as *ghuroor* frequently in speaking of the deception of the physical world that detracts from works of goodness and belief in eternity. The word *ghuroor*, literally meaning deception, is used, for instance, in *al-Isra*: 64; *al-Luqman*: 33; *al-Hadid*: 20, among many others.

11 Al Dhareer, *Al-Gharar in Contracts*, 10.

12 Abdel Razeq Al-Sanhouri, *Masadir al Haqq fi al-Fiqh al-Islami* (Dar Ihya' al-Turath al 'Arabi, Cairo, 1967–8), vol. III, 49. He uses 'want of knowledge (*jahl*)', instead of ignorance, as the essential element of *gharar*.

13 Kamali, *Islamic Commercial Laws: An analysis of Futures and Options* (Ilmiah publishers, Selangor, Malaysia, 2002), 85. Kamali describes *bai al maadum* (sale of non-existent object) and similarly the sale of something, the existence of which is doubtful as generally prohibited in Islam.

14 Ibn Rushd, *Bidayaat al Mujtahid wa Nihayaat al-Muqtasid* (Dar al Ma'rifa, Beirut, 1997), vol. 2, 156.

15 El-Gamal, Islamic Finance: Law, Economics and Practice (CUP, New York, 2006), 58.

16 El-Gamal, *Islamic Finance*, 60.

17 Vogel and Hayes, *Islamic Finance*, 88.

18 Vogel and Hayes, *Islamic Finance*, 89.

19 Ibid.

20 Ibn Abidin, *Hashiyyat Radd al Muhtar 'ala al-durr al-mukhtar sharh tanwir l-absar* (Mustapha Babi al-Halabi, Cairo, 1996), vol. 4, 147.

21 Sarakhsi, Abu Bakr Muhammad Ibn Ahmad, *Kitab al-Mabsut* (Dar al Ma'arif, Beirut, 1978), vol. 13, 194.

22 Ibn Al-Qayyim, *I'lam al Muwaqqai'in 'ala rabb al-'alamin*, edited by Taha 'Abd al-Ra'uf Sa'd (Dar al-Jil, Beirut, 1973), vol. 1, 357.

23 Tahir Mansuri, *Islamic Law of Contracts and Business Transactions* (Adam Publishers, New Delhi, 2006), 93–4.

24 See Al-Dhareer, *Al-Gharar in Contracts*, 14–17.

25 Ibn Juzzay, *Qawanin al Ahkam al-Shari'yyah wa Masa'il al Furu'iyya* (Dar al Ilm al-Malayin, Beirut, 1979), 282–3.

26 Quoted in El-Gamal, *Islamic Finance*, 59.

27 Mansuri, *Islamic Law of Contracts and Business Transactions*, 81.

28 The evidential/conceptual distinction is considered in greater detail in section 4.5.

29 Al-Dhareer, *Al-Gharar in Contracts*, 44.

30 Mansuri, *Islamic Law of Contracts and Business Transactions*, 81.

31 Al Zuhayli, *Al-Fiqh al-Islami wa Adillatuh* (Dar al-Fiqr, Damascus, 1997), vol. 5, 2408, as referred to in El-Gamal, *Islamic Finance*, 58.

32 *Quran, al-Maidah*: 90. See El-Gamal, *Islamic Finance*, 58.

33 Al-Dhareer, *Al-Gharar in Contracts*, 38–43.

34 Nabil Saleh, *Unlawful Gain and Legitimate Profit* (Cambridge University Press, Cambridge, 1986), 59–61.

35 Al-Dhareer, *Al-Gharar in Contracts*, 39.

36 Nabil Saleh, Unlawful Gain and Legitimate Profit, 85.

37 Ibn al-Qayyim (1292–1350 ad/691 AH–751 AH) was a famous Sunni Islamic jurist, commentator on the *Quran*, astronomer, chemist, philosopher, psychologist, scientist and theologian. Although he is commonly referred to as 'the scholar of the heart,' given his extensive works pertaining to human behaviour and ethics. Ibn al-Qayyim's scholarship focused in the sciences of Hadith and *Fiqh*.

38 Ibn al-Qayyim al Jawziyyah, *I'lam al-muwaqqa'in 'ala rabb al-'alamin* , edited by Taha 'Abd al-Ra'uf Sa'd (Dar al-Jil, Beirut, 1973), vol. I, 357–61; vol. II, 153–4.

39 'Motive' can also be read *raison d'être*.

40 Al-Dhareer, Al-Gharar in Contracts, Kamali, Islamic Commercial Laws and Saleh, Unlawful Gain and Legitimate Profit.

41 The four main schools being the Shafi, Hanbali, Maliki and Hanafi schools of Islamic jurisprudence – all named after their founders.

42 Al-Dhareer, *Al-Gharar in Contracts*, 15, 23.

43 Al-Dhareer, *Al-Gharar in Contracts*, 16, describes the *arbun* sale as one where the person buys an item and pays a certain amount of money to the seller on the understanding that if he did take the item the amount will form part of the total price but if he did not, he would forfeit the money already paid.

44 Al-Dhareer, *Al-Gharar in Contracts*, 16–17.

45 Al-Dhareer, *Al-Gharar in Contracts*, 18.

46 Al-Dhareer, *Al-Gharar in Contracts*, 23.

47 Ibid.

48 Ibn Juzay, a Maliki author gives a list of 10 cases which constitute, in his view, forbidden *gharar*. See Saleh, *Unlawful Gain and Legitimate Profit*, 64.

49 Solaiman Ben Khalaf Al Baji, *Al Montaqa: Annotations of Al-Muwatta* (Al-Saada Press, Cairo, AH 471), 287.

50 Al-Dhareer, *Al-Gharar in Contracts*, 51.

51 [1970] 2 All ER 228 per Lord Wilberforce at 248.

52 [1968] 3 All ER 785 at 793.

53   Beale (ed.), *Chitty on Contracts*, 30th edn (Sweet & Maxwell, London, 2008), vol. I, 223

54   Emphasis added. It is not a question of absolute certainty, which the courts acknowledge is impossible to attain, but sufficient certainty to create an enforceable contract.

55   Ewan McKendrick, *Contract Law: Text, Cases and Materials*, 2nd edn (OUP, Oxford, 2005), 138.

56   See *May and Butcher Ltd v King* [1934] 2 KB 17n; *Hillas v Arcos* (1932) 147 LT 503.

57   Beale, *Chitty on Contracts*, 223–4.

58   See section 4.2.

59   Beale, *Chitty on Contracts*, 240–3.

60   In *Walford v Miles* [1992] 2 AC 128 the House of Lords took the view that a duty to negotiate in good faith is unworkable in practice as it is inherently inconsistent with the interest of a negotiating party.

61   Encapsulated in the distinct approaches taken by the House of Lords in *Hillas v Arcos* (1932) 147 LT 503 and *May and Butcher Ltd v King* [1934] 2 KB 17n, respectively. See also, *Foley v Classique Coaches, Ltd* [1934] 2 KB 1, discussing the distinction between *May and Butcher* and *Hillas v Arcos*.

62   Beale, *Chitty on Contracts*.

63   McKendrick, *Contract Law*, 138.

64   *Hillas v Arcos* (1932) 147 LT 503, per Lord Wright, at 514.

65   Beale, *Chitty on Contract*, 203–22, 223–6.

66   *Walford v Miles* [1992] 2 AC 128. The court held that the duty to negotiate in good faith was unenforceable for uncertainty and inherently inconsistent with the position of a negotiating party. See Beale, *Chitty on Contracts*, 147.

67   *Welsh Development Agency v Export Finance Co. Ltd* [1992] BCLC 148. Undetermined facts do not render a contract ineffective, merely contingent on the ascertainment of those facts.

68   G. Scammell & Nephew Ltd v Ouston [1941] AC 251. See Beale, Chitty on Contract, 149.

69   McKendrick, *Contract Law*, 138.

70   [1934] 2 KB 17n.

71   In this context, a suppliant is one who petitions humbly of the king.

72   *May and Butcher v Regem* [1929] All ER Rep 679 at 680.

73   Ibid.

74   *May and Butcher v Regem* [1929] All ER Rep 679 at 682.

75   *May and Butcher Ltd v Regem* [1929] All ER Rep 679 at 682–3.

76   [1992] 1 All ER 453 at 461.

77   [1941] AC 251.

78   (1932) 147 LT 503.

79   [1941] 1 All ER 14 at 16.

80   [1941] 1 All ER 14 at 17–18.

81   *Hillas v Arcos* [1932] All ER Rep 494 at 495.

82   Ibid.

83   [1932] All ER Rep 494 at 500–1.

84   *May & Butcher* is currently almost unanimously disregarded by courts in deciding the issue of certainty of terms.

85 [1934] All ER Rep 88.
86 *Foley v Classique* [1934] All ER Rep 88 at 91–2, per Lord Scrutton.
87 Ibid.
88 Fletcher Challenge Energy Ltd v Electricity Corporation of New Zealand [2002] 2 NZLR 433.
89 [1934] 2 KB 17n.
90 Fletcher Challenge Energy Ltd v Electricity Corporation of New Zealand [2002] 2 NZLR 433.
91 Roy Goode, *Commercial Law* (3rd edn, Lexis Nexis, London, 2004), 73; See also, *Donwin Productions Ltd v EMI Films Ltd* (1984) *Times*, 9 March, Pain J. See also, *British Steele Corporation v Cleveland Bridge & Engineering Co. Ltd* [1984] 1 All ER 504.
92 See Alstom Signalling Ltd v Jarvis Facilities Ltd [2004] EWCH 1232; and also Mamidoil-Jetiol Greek Petroleum Co. SA v Okta Crude Oil Refinery (No.1) [2001] 2 Lloyd's Rep 76.
93 Roy Goode, *Commercial Law*, 83.
94 Roy Goode, *Commercial Law*, 84.
95 Beale, *Chitty On Contracts*, 124–5.
96 Beatson, J, *Anson's Law of Contract* (28th edn, OUP, New York, 2002), 61.
97 (1932) 147 LT 503 at 514.
98 *Brown v Gould* [1971] 2 All ER 1505.
99 Gillat v Sky Television Ltd [2000] 2 BCLC 103.
100 *May and Butcher v King* [1934] 2 K.B. 1. See also s 15(1) of the Supply of Goods and Services Act 1982.
101 *Foley v Classique* [1934] 2 KB 1.
102 [2006] EWHC 330 (Ch) paras 20–1.
103 See discussion in section 4.6.
104 For a contrasting approach to *May and Butcher* and consequent conclusion of the court, see *Sudbrook Trading Estate v Eggleton* [1983] 1 AC 444. See further, Jill Poole, *Text Book on Contract Law* (8th edn, OUP, Oxford, 2006), 95–6.
105 Jill Poole, *Text Book on Contract Law*, 91.
106 Roy Goode, *Commercial Law*, 87. For instance, the grant of first refusal of property as held in *Gardner v Coutts & Co.* [1967] 3 All ER 1064.
107 *Southern Foundries v Shirlaw* (1926) Ltd, [1940] AC 701. However, the courts are slow to imply a term on this ground. See Roy Goode, *Commercial Law*, 87–8.
108 For instance, implied terms to most contracts is the term that neither party will obstruct performance by the other. See *Mackay v Dick* (1881) 6 App Cas 251; *Bournemouth and Boscombe Athletic Football Club v Manchester United Football Club* (1980), Times, 22 May.
109 Such an implied term was not, however, actionable unless given as a warranty. See the famous case of *Chandelor v Lopus* (1603) Cro Jac 4. The prolonged influence of this case can be gauged from the fact that it was still being cited in 1957 in *Oscar Chess Ltd v Williams* [1957] 1 All ER 325. See also, Roy Goode, *Commercial Law*, 185.
110 Scally v Southern Health and Social Services Board [1992] 1 AC 294.
111 Young and Marten Ltd v McManus Childs Ltd [1969] 1 AC 454.
112 *Bolam v Friern Hospital Management Committee* [1957] 2 All ER 118; see The Supply of Goods and Services Act 1982, s 13.

113 See Saleh, Unlawful Gain and Legitimate Profit, 1–2.
114 *Quran, Muhammad*: 19; *al-Tauba*: 24.
115 *Quran, al-Rum*: 39.
116 Karen Armstrong, *Muhammad: A Biography of the Prophet* (Phoenix Publishers, London, 2001), 68.
117 It is mainly for this reason that 619 is known as the year of sorrow, for the Prophet is said to have grieved deeply upon losing his often only supporter, comforter and friend, Khadija. It is also thought that Khadija died because of the irreparable damaged to her health caused by the food shortages.
118 Armstrong, *Muhammad*.
119 *Quran, al-Baqara*: 275.
120 See Muhammad's saying (II) on *riba* in section 5.1.2.
121 See chapter 1 on form versus substance of Islamic finance.

5 *Riba*: Meaning, Scope and Application

1 *Quran, al-Baqara*: 275; See also, in subsection 5.1.2., the saying of Muhammad where he rebukes Bilal for engaging in an apparently lawful barter-trade transactions as being 'the very essence of *riba*'.
2 M. T. Mansuri, *Islamic Law of Contracts and Business Transactions* (Adam Publishers, New Delhi 2006), 119.
3 El-Gamal, *Islamic Finance: Law Economics and Practice* (CUP, New York, 2006), 51–3.
4 Commercial, as we shall see in section 5.1. below, is widely defined to encompass any lawful trade or transactional dealings mutually consented to with the intention to be contractually bound.
5 *Quran, al-Baqara*: 275 and 282 are two key verses establishing this. We refer to them repeatedly throughout this chapter.
6 See 5.4 below for a fuller discussion of *riba* and consideration.
7 Dowry is addressed in the following verses of the *Quran, al-Nisa*: 4, 20–1 and 24–5; *al-Maida*: 5; *al-Ahzab*: 30 and *al-Mumtahina*: 60.
8 See section 5.4 below.
9 *Quran, al-Baqara*: 275.
10 *Quran, al-Baqara*: 175 and 182.
11 Mansuri, *Islamic Law of Contracts*, 84.
12 See *al-Baqara*: 282 and Muhammad's saying (II) at sub-section 5.1.2.
13 *Quran, al-Baqara*: 278
14 Tarek El-Diwany *The Problem with Interest* (2nd ed. Kreatoc Ltd, London 2003), 184–92.
15 Also expressed through the prohibition on gambling.
16 The term 'wealth' is used in the broad sense of value, not riches.
17 *Al-Baqara*: 278.
18 Among them being Abdulrahman ibn 'Awf.
19 Homa Katouzian, 'Riba and Interest in an Islamic Political Economy' (Mediterranean Peoples Revue, no. 14, Jan.–Mar. 1981), 97–109.
20 This is extrapolated from the distinction drawn between prohibited *riba* and *bay'* (commerce) in *Quran, al-Baqara*: 275. The phrase is adopted from Nabil Saleh's *Unlawful gain and legitimate profit* (CUP, Cambridge, 1986). The

distinction implies that gain (*riba*) may also be of the lawful kind and profit may be illegitimate.

21 *Quran, Ali-Imran*: 130–2.
22 *Quran, al-Baqara*: 275.
23 Extrapolated from the *Quran's* distinction drawn in *al-Rum*: 39.
24 Roy Goode, *Commercial Law* (3rd edn, Lexis Nexis Butterworth, London, 2004), 579. See *Quran, al-Baqara*: 282.
25 *Quran, al-Baqara*: 282 and 275.
26 Amongst the four closest companions to the Prophet and the second Caliph after the Prophet's demise
27 Abdulkader Thomas (ed.) *Interest in Islamic Economics: Understanding Riba* (Routledge, London, 2006), 63.
28 The word *bay'* (sale) is a noun and thus, in Arabic, is preceded by the prefix *al* (the).
29 *Quran, al-Nisa*: 29; *Fatir*: 29.
30 *Al-Nisa*: 29.
31 *Quran, Ali-Imran*: 130
32 *Quran, al-Nisa*: 161
33 *Quran, al-Baqara*: 282, Yusuf Ali Translation. O ye who believe! When ye deal with each other, in transactions involving future obligations in a fixed period of time, reduce them to writing. Let a scribe write down faithfully as between the parties: let not the scribe refuse to write: as Allah Has taught him, so let him write. Let him who incurs the liability dictate, but let him fear His Lord Allah, and not diminish aught of what he owes. If they party liable is mentally deficient, or weak, or unable Himself to dictate, Let his guardian dictate faithfully, and get two witnesses, out of your own men, and if there are not two men, then a man and two women, such as ye choose, for witnesses, so that if one of them errs, the other can remind her. The witnesses should not refuse when they are called on (For evidence). Disdain not to reduce to writing (your contract) for a future period, whether it be small or big: it is more just in the sight of Allah, More suitable as evidence, and more convenient to prevent doubts among yourselves but if it be a transaction which ye carry out on the spot among yourselves, there is no blame on you if ye reduce it not to writing. But take witness whenever ye make a commercial contract; and let neither scribe nor witness suffer harm. If ye do (such harm), it would be wickedness in you. So fear Allah. For it is Good that teaches you. And Allah is well acquainted with all things. If ye are on a journey, and cannot find a scribe, a pledge with possession (may serve the purpose). And if one of you deposits a thing on trust with another, let the trustee (faithfully) discharge his trust, and let him Fear his Lord conceal not evidence; for whoever conceals it, – his heart is tainted with sin. And Allah knoweth all that ye do.
34 We return later to *Quran, al-Baqara*: 282, that is the only verse that mentions debt transactions (*dayn*) and future debt obligations between people yet makes no mention of *riba* at all. The entire verse is couched in terms of contractual agreement and commercial dealing. This is a clear indication that loan transactions fall within the category of 'trade', distinguished from *riba*, in *Quran* 2: 275.
35 Mansuri, *Islamic Law of Contract*, 126.

36   Reported by Muslim.

37   Dates are to be exchanged for dates of the same weight, measure, quality and on the spot. Dates cannot be exchanged for inferior or superior quality dates nor can dates be exchanged for barley, etc.

38   Reported by Muslim and Al-Nasai. See El-Gamal, *Islamic Finance*, 53.

39   A *sa* is a measure (of dates) and is akin to the expression, a bushel of wheat or barrel of oil, for instance.

40   *Quran, al-Nisa*: 29.

41   Oditah, *Legal Aspects of Receivables Financing* (Sweet & Maxwell, London, 1991), 1.

42   Mansuri, *Islamic Law of Contract*, 126.

43   It is however considered to be the worse of the two forms of *riba*.

44   Whereby interest was charged at maturity of debts from interest free loans or credit sales, and compounded at later maturity dates

45   This purported saying of Muhammad, not in any of the six chief collections, is related by the most respected scholars only on the authority of companions, not the Prophet. As a prophetic Hadith, scholars reject it as false. See Muhammad b. Ali al-Shawkani, *Nayl al awtar* (Mustafa Babi al-Halabi, Cairo, n.d.), 5: 262

46   Ibn Rushd, *Bidayat al-Mujtahid wa Nihayat al-Muqtasid* (Dar al-Ma'rifa, Beirut, 1997), vol. 3, 184.

47   See section 4.7 above.

48   El-Gamal, *Islamic Finance*, 53.

49   El-Gamal, *Islamic Finance*, 54.

50   Al-Misri, 'Hal Al-Faidah Haram bi Jami' Ashkaliha?' *Majallat Jami'at al Malik 'Abdulaziz lil-Iqtisad Al-Islami*, (2004), vol. 17, 1.

51   This conclusion has dire consequences for the prevalent sharia arbitrage conducted in the name of Islamic finance for the very products marketed as '*riba* free' may be the very essence of *riba*.

52   Mark up (or cost plus margin) sale.

53   A variation of a sale and repurchase transaction involving 3 parties.

54   El-Gamal, *Islamic Finance*, 43.

55   El-Gamal, *Islamic Finance*, 55.

56   El-Gamal, *Islamic Finance*, 53.

57   Muhammad Saleem, Islamic Banking – a $300Billion Deception (New York, 2005).

58   A.L.M. Abdul Ghafoor, *Interest, Usury, Riba and the Operational Cost of a Bank* (Percetakan Zafar Sdn Bhd, Kuala Lumpur, 2005).

59   Ibn Taymiyya, *Al-Fatawa al-Kubra* (Dar-al-Kutb al-Ilmiyyah, Beirut, 1987), vol. 29, 16.

60   Excessive to whom, by which standards and is it applicable to all sectors and jurisdiction?

61   A mechanism employed to determine the market interest rates for various borrowers based on credit worthiness and security of posted collateral.

62   The relevance of this distinction had otherwise only been mentioned once before Katouzian's paper in Syed Ahmad's 'The Concept and the Law of Riba in Modern Economic Environment' (Mimeo, 1978). Katouzian notes that Ahmad's paper focuses on the comparability of interest and merchant profit.

63 Eduardo Galeano, *Upside Down: A Primer for the Looking Glass World* (Picador, New York, 2000), 312.
64 See Muhammad's saying (II) in subsection 5.1.2 for illustration.
65 Adopted in *Currie v Misa* (1875) LR 10 Ex 153, 162.
66 (1966) 2 QB 617, Court of Appeal.
67 Ewan McKendrick, *Contract Law: Text, Cases and Materials* (2nd edn, OUP, Oxford, 2005), 161–2.
68 *White v Bluet* (1853) 23 LJ Ex 36. This (orthodox) view of consideration has, however, been challenged by several writers particularly Professor Atiya.
69 *Williams v Roffey Bros & Nicholls (Contractors) Ltd* [1991] 1 QB 1.
70 McKendrick, *Contract Law*, 165.
71 Treitel, *The Law of Contract* (12th edn, Sweet&Maxwell, London, 2008), 68.
72 McKendrick, *Contract Law*, 161–2.
73 McKendrick, *Contract Law*, 165.
74 [1960] AC 87, House of Lords.
75 *Williams v Roffey Bros & Nicholls (Contractors) Ltd* [1991] 1 QB 1.
76 [2009] All ER (D) 64 (Jan).
77 In *Antons Trawling Co Ltd v Smith* [2003] 2 NZLR 23 at para 93–4.
78 Oxford Paperback Dictionary, Thesaurus & Word Power Guide (OUP, Oxford, 2001), 11.
79 McKendrick, *Contract Law*, 164.
80 Treitel, *Law of Contract* (11th edn, Sweet & Maxwell, London, 2003), 68.
81 McKendrick, *Contract Law*, 164.
82 McKendrick, *Contract Law*, 165. See also, *Chappel & Co Ltd v The Nestle Co Ltd* [1960] AC 87, House of Lords.
83 (1875) LR 10 Ex 153, 162 in McKendrick, *Contract Law*, 163.
84 (1877) 2 App Cas 439 at 448.
85 *Quran*, al-Nisa: 29 and al-Baqara: 275. Generally, the *Quran* uses the term *aqd* for social and other obligations/contracts and the term *bay* for sale, trade or commercial transactions.
86 Beale (ed.), *Chitty on Contracts* (30th edn, Sweet &Maxwell, London 2008), vol. I, 253.
87 Beale, *Chitty on Contracts*, 240.
88 *Jones v Padavatton* [1969] 1 WLR 328; *Pettitt v Pettitt* [1970] AC 777; the presumption against an intention to form legal relations was rebutted in *Merritt v Merritt* [1970] 1 WLR 1211. See also *Gould v Gould* [1970] 1 Q.B. 275, where there was a division of opinion on the issue of contractual intention, the majority holding that there was no contractual intention where a husband on leaving his wife promised to pay her £15 per week so long as he could manage it.
89 *O'Brien v MGN Ltd* [2002] CLC 33; See also *Simpkins v Pays* [1955] 1 WLR 975 in which the presumption against an intention to form legal relations was rebutted.
90 *Esso Petroleum Ltd v Commissioners of Custom and Excise* [1976] 1 WLR 1; And see *Rose and Frank Co. V JR Crompton and Bros Ltd* [1925] AC 445 for a discussion on rebuttal of the presumption in commercial agreements.
91 [1919] 2 KB 571, Court of Appeal.
92 *Pearce v Merriman* [1904] 1 K.B. 80.
93 Beale, *Chitty on Contracts*, 241, citing *Synge v Synge* [1894] 1 Q.B. 466.

94 *White v Bluet* (1853) 23 LJ Ex 36.
95 *Balfour v Balfour* [1919] 2 KB 571, Court of Appeal.
96 [1955] 1 WLR 975.
97 Ibid. at 979.
98 J. Unger, 'Intent to create legal relations, mutuality and consideration' (1956) 19 MLR 96 at 98.
99 [2001] EWCA Civ 274.
100 [1991] 1 QB 1.
101 Mindy Chen-Wishart, 'Consideration, Practical Benefit and the Emperor's New Clothes', in *Good Faith and Fault in Contract Law*, Beatson and Friedman (eds) (Clarendonn Press, Oxford, 1995).
102 (2003) NZLR 23.
103 [2004] SEHC 71.
104 Coote, 'Consideration and Benefit in Fact and Law', *Journal of Contract Law* (1990), 3, 23.

6 The Nature of Debt and the Legality of its Sale

1 Islamic law theory has it that debts may be 'sold' back to (their) creditors usually for either par value or at a discount. See Vogel and Hayes, *Islamic Law and Finance: Religion, Risk and Return* (Brill-Lieden, Boston, 2006), 115–117, for a discussion on Islamic law position. This is comparable to debt factoring or discounting of receivables under the common law as defined by Fidelis Oditah in *Legal Aspects of Receivables Financing* (Sweet & Maxwell, London, 1991), 44.

2 The maxim is alleged to be a saying of Muhammad albeit one of weak authentication. See, Hammad, '*Bay' al-Kali' bi al-Kali' fi al-Fiqh al-Islami*' (Markaz Abhath al-Iqtisad al-Islami, Jami'at al-Malik al-Abd al-Aziz, Jeddah, 1986), cited in Vogel and Hayes, *Islamic Law and Finance*, 115.

3 Literally meaning the exchange of two things both 'delayed' or the exchange of a delayed counter value for another delayed counter value.

4 The position is not, however, entirely clear as scholars permit the sale of a debt obligation by the creditor to the debtor but prohibit any such sale to a third party. See, Vogel and Hayes, *Islamic Law and Finance*, 116–17, 186.

5 An *Ijtihadic* issue is one on which there is no clear textual injunction and hence with regards to which Muslims can exercise independent reasoning so as to reach a conclusion, opinion or ruling.

6 In commercial affairs and all matters other than faith, the principle of permissibility applies as long as no clear text or Hadith exists to the contrary and the application remains within the objectives of the sharia, which shall be elaborated later in this chapter.

7 Sano Koutoub, *The Sale of Debt as Implemented by the Islamic Financial Institutions in Malaysia* (IIUM Press, Kuala Lumpur, 2004), viii.

8 Michael Bridge, *Personal Property Law* (3rd edn, OUP, Oxford, 2002), 6.

9 Oditah, *Legal Aspects of Receivables Financing*, 19–20.

10 Roy Goode, *Commercial Law* (3rd edn, Lexis Nexis Butterworth, London, 2004), 579.

11 S. Mahmasani, *The General Theory of the Law of Obligation and Contracts under Islamic Jurisprudence* (Dar al-Ilm lil malayin, Beirut, 1972), 67; Roy Goode, *Commercial Law*, 109, 579.

12 Michael Bridge, *Personal Property Law*, 14; Under Islamic legal theory this cessation of debt's existence happens through a transformation process called *ta'yin*, that is, debt is transformed into (physical) property.

13 Oditah, *Legal Aspects of Receivables Financing*, 1.

14 *Timmins v Gibbins* (1852) 18 Q.B. 722 at 726; *Littlechild v Banks* (1845) 7 Q.B. 739.

15 Oditah, *Legal Aspects of Receivables Financing*, 1.

16 Sachiko Murata, *The Tao of Islam* (State University of New York Press, New York, 1992), 2, 28. A distinction is made between the intellectual tradition and legalistic approach of the sharia scholars. The intellectual tradition is a deep current in Islamic thought that goes back to the *Quran* and the tradition of Muhammad. What distinguishes the intellectuals from the sharia scholars is that the former ask about the *why* of things, as well as the *how*, while the latter are mainly concerned with the *what* because they are largely concerned with telling people *what* to do.

17 M.T. Mansuri, *Islamic Law of Contracts And Business Transactions* (Adam Publishers, New Delhi, 2006), 198–9.

18 See section 5.1.2.

19 Vogel and Hayes, *Islamic Law and Finance*, 114–24. See also, El-Diwany, *The Problem with Interest* (2nd edn, Kreatoc, London 2003), 83.

20 For a complete discussion, including Quranic verses and sayings of the Prophet, see chapter 5 on *riba*.

21 Sahih Muslim, Book 10, Number 3854.

22 Roy Goode, *Commercial Law*, 450. See *Moss v Hancock* [1899] 2 QB 111.

23 Goode, *Commercial Law*, 453.

24 Charles Proctor, *Mann on the Legal Aspects of Money* (6th edn, OUP, Oxford, 2005), 8.

25 Goode, *Commercial Law*, 452.

26 Bridge, *Personal Property Law*, 9.

27 Goode, *Commercial Law*, 579.

28 Roy Goode, *Consumer Credit* (A.W. Sijthoff, Leyden/Boston, 1978), vol. 3, ch. 40.

29 Goode, *Commercial Law*, 578.

30 Lawson and Rudden, *The Law of Property* (Clarendon Law Series, 2nd edn, Clarendon Press, Oxford, 1982), 27. See section 6.3.4.

31 Goode, *Commercial Law*, 451; see also Roy Goode, *Payment Obligations in Commercial and Financial Transactions* (Sweet & Maxwell, 1983), ch. 4.

32 *Miller v Race* (1758) 1 Burr 452.

33 Goode, *Commercial Law*, 451.

34 Goode, *Commercial Law*, 452.

35 Lawson and Rudden, *The Law of Property*, 27.

36 Now defined by statute in the Financial Services and Markets Act 2000 (Regulated Activities) Order 2001 (SI 2001/544).

37 [1996] 2 All ER 121 at 133–4.

38 [1997] 4 All ER 568 at 576.

39 Bridge, *Personal Property Law*, 1.

40 Bridge, *Personal Property Law*, 1.

41 Ibid.

42   Bridge, *Personal Property Law*, 5.
43   Bernard Rudden, 'Economic Theory v. Property Law' in Eekelaar & Bell (eds), *Oxford Essays in Jurisprudence* (Clarendon Press, Oxford, 1987), 243.
44   Rudden, 'Economic Theory v. Property Law', cites the Japanese CC 185; the Ethiopian CC 1204; the Louisiana CC 476–8 and the Thai CC 1298, among others.
45   Rudden, 'Economic Theory v. Property Law', 244.
46   Bougham LC in *Keppel v Bailey* (1834) My & K 517, 535.
47   Wilde B. in *Stockport Wwks v Potter* (1864) 3 H&C 300, 314.
48   O.W. Holmes, *The Common Law* (Cambridge, MA, 1967), 301, 316.
49   Rudden, 'Economic Theory v. Property Law', 246.
50   Gray and Gray, *Elements of Land Law* (OUP, Oxford, 2005), 107.
51   Gray and Gray, *Elements of Land Law*, 126.
52   Rudden, 'Economic Theory v. Property Law', 250.
53   Gray and Gray, *Elements of Land Law*, 127.
54   Bridge, *Personal Property Law*, 12.
55   See *Burton v London & Quadrant Housing Trust* [1998] QB at 845E, per Millett LJ.
56   *National Provincial Bank Ltd v Ainsworth* [1965] AC 1175 at 1248.
57   [2007] EWCH 220 (220) at para 72.
58   Bridge, *Personal Property Law*, 145.
59   Ibid.
60   Gray and Gray, *Elements of Land Law*, 127–8.
61   *National Provincial Bank Ltd v Ainsworth* [1965] AC 1175 at 1248.
62   *Dorman v Rodgers* (1982) 148 CLR 365 at 374 per Murphy J; *Delgamuukw v British Columbia* (1997) 153 DLR (4th) 193 at [113] per Lamer CJC.
63   *Dorman v Rodgers* (ibid.). See also K.J. Gray, 'Property, Divorce and retirement pension rights', in *Cambridge-Tilburg Law Lectures 1982* (Kluwer, 1986), 41–51.
64   Bridge, *Personal Property Law*, 7.
65   *Dorman v Rodgers* (1982) 148 CLR 365 at 368–70.
66   *Dorman v Rodgers* (1982) 148 CLR 365 at 371.
67   (1960) 104 CLR 186.
68   (1960) 104 CLR 186 at 205.
69   *Dorman v Rodgers* (1982) 148 CLR 365 at 371–2.
70   Reference is made to *Hoare & Co. v McAlpine* (1923) 1 Ch 167 at 175; and to Wallace and Grbich, 'A Judge's Guide to Legal Change in Property', *University of New South Wales Law Journal* (1979) vol. 3, 175.
71   *Dorman v Rodgers* (1982) 148 CLR 365 at 374–7.
72   Gray and Gray, *Elements of Land Law*, 128–9.
73   Rudden, 'Economic Theory v. Property Law', 249.
74   Gray and Gray, *Elements of Land Law*, 143.
75   Ibid., 102.
76   K. Gray, 'Property in Thin Air' [1991] CLJ 252 at 303–4.
77   *Dorman v Rodgers* (1982) 148 CLR 365 at 372 per Murphy J.
78   Gray and Gray, *Elements of Land Law*, 105. See also Jeremy Bentham, *An Introduction to the Principles of Morals and Legislation*, W. Harrison (ed.) (OUP, Oxford, 1948), 337.

79 Gray and Gray, *Elements of Land Law*, 102 quoting Hernando de Soto, *The Mystery of Capital: Why capitalism Triumphs in the West and fails Everywhere Else* (Bantam Press 2000), 42–3, that 'property is not the [asset] itself but an economic concept *about* the [asset], embodied in a legal representation'. See also, *Yanner v Eaton* (1999) 201 CLR 351 at [18]. Also, *Kanak v Minister for Land and Water Conservation* (NSW) (2000) 180 ALR 489 at [31].

80 C.B. MacPherson, 'Capitalism and the Changing Concept of Property', in E. Kamenka and R.S. Neale (ed.), *Feudalism, Capitalism and Beyond* (Canberra 1975), 111.

81 Gray and Gray, *Elements of Land Law*, 102.

82 *Oxford English Dictionary* (Clarendon 1933), vol. VIII, 1496.

83 William C. Chittick, *The Self Disclosure of God: Principles of Ibn Arabi's Cosmology* (State University of New York Press, Albany, 1998), xxiv.

84 Sano Koutoub, *The Sale of Debt as Implemented by the Islamic Financial Institutions in Malaysia* (IIUM Press, Kuala Lumpur, 2004), 64.

85 See section 6.1.

86 See section 6.4 generally and, specifically, views by Rudden, 'Economic Theory v. Property Law', 250, and Gray and Gray, *Elements of Land Law*, 128–9.

87 Decision 5 (D4/08/88), Fourth Session, *Fiqh* Academy Journal 3:2161.

88 Emphasis is mine.

89 [1965] AC 1175 at 1248.

90 Gray and Gray, *Elements of Land Law*, 128–9.

91 Zayla'i, *Tabyin al Haqa'iq*, vol. 4, 1717 as cited in Tahir Mansuri, *Islamic Law of Contract and Business Transactions* (Adam Publishers, New Delhi, 2006), 301.

92 Mansuri, *Islamic Law of Contracts And Business Transactions*, 301.

93 Beale, *Chitty on Contracts*, 1367. Chitty describes novation as taking place 'where two contracting parties agree that a third, who also agrees, shall stand in the relation of either of them to the other. There is a new contract and it is therefore essential that the consent of all parties shall be obtained: in this necessity for consent lies the most important difference between novation and assignment'. Chitty cites the cases of *Rasbora Ltd v J.C.L. Marine Ltd* [1977] 1 Lloyd's Rep. 645; *The Blankenstein* [1985] 1 W.L.R. 435; *The Aktion* [1987] 1 Lloyd's Rep. 283, 310–11.

94 Beale, *Chitty on Contracts*, 1327.

95 Ibid., 1362.

96 [1902] 2 .B. 660, 668 CA.

97 Beale, *Chitty on Contracts*, 1362.

98 *Al-Baqara*: 282–3.

99 *Quran, al-Baqara*: 282.

100 *Quran, al-Nisa*: 29.

101 *Quran: al-Baqara*: 275, pertaining to *riba*. See chapter 5, section 5.2.

102 Speculative uncertainty. For complete discussion and background see chapter 4.

103 El-Gamal, *Islamic Finance: Law, Economics and Practice* (Cambridge University Press, New York, 2006), 81, 90.

104 See section 4.4. and 4.5.

105 See section 6.2.

106 Literally meaning the exchange of two things both 'delayed' or the exchange of a delayed counter-value for another delayed counter value.

107 Beale, *Chitty on Contracts*, 983, defines a credit sale as an absolute contract of sale of goods in pursuance of an agreement under which payment of the whole or part of the purchase price is deferred.

108 Ibn Taymiyya in his book *Al Fatawa* vol. 3: 474 argues that the Hadith prohibiting the sale of two items at deferred delivery is the one universally accepted by scholars and not the version prohibiting the sale of debt with debt.

109 Vogel and Hayes, *Islamic Law and Finance*, 117.

110 [1997] 2 BCLC 460.

111 [1997] 2 BCLC 460 at 465–7.

112 Taqi Usmani, *An Introduction to Islamic Finance* (Kluwer Law International, The Hague, 2002), xiv–xvii.

113 El-Gamal, *Islamic Finance*, 14.

114 Koutoub, *The Sale of Debt*, 64.

115 Lawson and Rudden, *The Law of Property*, 27.

116 Art 125 of Majallat Al-Ahkam Al-Adliyya.

117 Rudden, 'Economic Theory v. Property Law', 244.

118 In *Re Bank of Credit and Commerce International SA* (No. 8) (1997) 4 All ER 568.

119 'It [the asserted charge] would be a proprietary interest in the sense that … it would be binding upon assignees or a liquidator or trustee in bankruptcy', [1997] 2 BCLC 577.

120 Lord Hoffman's judgement is in contrast to Millett J's earlier decision in, *Re Charge Card Services* [1989] Ch 497, that such a charge, taken by a bank over its own customer's deposits, was conceptually impossible. See Goode, *Commercial Law*, 610.

121 *Re Bank of Credit and Commerce International SA* (No. 8) aka BCCI (No. 8) [1997] 4 All ER 568 at 574.

122 [1986] 3 All ER 289.

7 Securitisation

1 A primary Islamic capital market of sorts exists but not a secondary market as Muslim scholars maintain a ban on trading in financial assets. For greater detail, see chapter 6.

2 Typically receivables, such as home mortgage loans or credit cards receivables or leasing receivables. See Roy Goode, *Commercial Law* (3rd edn, Sweet & Maxwell, London, 2004), 147.

3 Vogel and Hayes, *Islamic Law and Finance: Religion, Risk and Return* (Brill-Lienden, Boston, 2006), 198.

4 Emphasis is theirs.

5 Vogel and Hayes, *Islamic Law and Finance*, 238.

6 In most cases a bank, investment institution, financier or company (i.e. an entity).

7 Mitchells and Butlers 'What is a Securitisation', www.mitchellsandbutlers.com/index.asp?pageid=456 accessed on 7 January 2009.

8 See chapter 1 for more detail.

9 The sale of asset by the originator to the SPV is required to be a true or clean sale that fully transfers ownership to the SPV for purposes of accounting rules and capital adequacy requirements among others.

10 If the asset was not 'truly sold' then it still belongs to the originator which in turn means that the SPV has merely borrowed it. The securities sold, therefore, represent the 'loan' taken by the SPV from the originator, not a sold asset. The loan character of the structure invokes the *riba* prohibition and renders any increase made on the transaction, prohibited.

11 That restricts the raising of finance to means such as sale, leasing, profit-sharing agreements but not through a money lending mechanism that involves interest or usury as conventional finance allows.

12 Philip Wood, *Project Finance, Securitisations, Subordinated Debt* (Sweet & Maxwell, London, 2007), 111. A sophisticated form of factoring or discounting receivables without recourse in order to raise money – instead of pledging the receivables.

13 Wood, *Project Finance, Securitisations, Subordinated Debt*, 111–12.

14 Also known as a bridging loan, that is, funds obtained from the originator or from the proceeds of sale of the notes or bonds to the investors.

15 The term subordination means that it is payable after the funding loan has been repaid.

16 Periodic payments owed arising out of a debt owed as a result of a contact of loan, mortgage, hire or sale on deferred payment.

17 See Goode, *Commercial Law*, 147–8, for explanation and illustration of a simple securitisation by sale of receivables.

18 Wood, *Project Finance, Securitisations, Subordinated Debt*, 114.

19 Philip Wood, Global Comparative Financial Law notes, BCL class of 2004/2005, University of Oxford.

20 The government of Qatar for example in the Qatar Global *sukuk* securitisation had as one of its objectives to support the development of its Islamic securities market.

21 Scott Hall, *International Finance: Law and Regulation* (Sweet & Maxwell, 2004), 338.

22 Belgium, France, Italy, Japan and Korea, all of which are 'mandatory notice' countries.

23 Philip Wood, *Project Finance, Securitisations, Subordinated Debt*, 134–5.

24 For Islamic finance, true sale compliance is vital because while conventional ABS typically assign right, *sukuk* must assign beneficial rights (via trust or an SPV) so as to be sharia compliant.

25 Wood, *Project Finance, Securitisations, Subordinated Debt*, 114.

26 Wood, *Project Finance, Securitisations, Subordinated Debt*, 156–7.

27 Roy Goode, *Legal Problems of Credit and Security* (4th edn, Sweet & Maxwell, London, 2008), 251.

28 *Orion Finance Ltd v Crown Financial Management Ltd* [1994] 2 BCLC 607 is a clear and relevant illustration of the effects of such re-characterisation.

29 Jan H. Dalhuisen, *Dalhuisen on International Commercial, Financial and Trade Law* (Hart Publishing, Oxford, 2000), 775–8.

8 Structuring a Securitisation to be Compatible with both the Sharia and Common Law

1   C.M. Henry, 'Financial Performances of Islamic versus Conventional Banks' in Henry and Wilson (eds), *The Politics of Islamic Finance* (Edinburgh University Press, Edinburgh, 2004), 104–25.

2   El-Gamal, *Islamic Finance: Law, Economics and Practice* (CUP, New York, 2006), 20–5; Henry, 'Financial Performances of Islamic versus Conventional Banks'.

3   One tenth of the initial principal amount of the certificates.

4   This provision attracts criticism but it should be noted that LIBOR is only used as a bench mark and the returns themselves do not represent interest payments, but rather rental rates relating to a real underlying asset – the leased parcels of land. See Rodney Wilson, 'Islamic bond: Your Guide to Issuing, Structuring and Investing in Sukuk', in Adam and Thomas (eds) *Overview of the Sukuk Market* (London: Euromoney, 2004).

5   For a simple securitisation by way of sale of receivables, see Roy Goode, *Commercial Law* (3rd edn, Sweet & Maxwell, London, 2004), 147–8.

6   See section 6.8.

7   See Michael Duncan, Bimai Desai and Julie Rieger, 'Islamic Bankers Take Role on International Projects' *International Financial Law Review*, May [2004] 52. A bond issue is different from *sukuk* in that a bond issue involves the issue of debt instruments whereas the *sukuk* involves the issue of certificates containing an entitlement to an interest in the asset.

8   For a general discussion and critique on the 'form-based' orientation of Islamic finance, see El-Gamal *Islamic Finance: Law Economics and Practice*.

9   Depending on the jurisdiction, courts will study either the legal or economic, substance of the transaction. In Malaysia for instance, as in the UK, the courts will study the legal substance of the transaction as in cases involving the retention of title clauses, the objective of the transaction and the right to repurchase the property being irrelevant. Only the method (of dealing with the title/ownership in the assets) employed is scrutinised in determining whether the transaction is registerable as a charge.

10 Where certain characteristics of the transaction suggest that the transaction is more in the nature of financing rather than a sale, the SPV may risk the transfer or sale being re-characterised as one of security or financing.

11 [1994] 2 BCLC 607.

12 In *Orion*, the transaction was structured as a hire purchase that involved an assignment of the receivables (future book debts).

13 Trevor Norman, 'Securitisation Structures within an Islamic Framework' (July 2005, ISR Legal Guide), 22.

14 Issued by the sharia board of the Accounting and Auditing Organisation for Islamic Financial Institutions (AAOIFI) in May 2005.

15 Simon Gardner, *An Introduction to the Law of Trusts* (2nd edn, Oxford University Press, Oxford, 2003), 2.

16 See section 8.2.9.

17 Not to petition for the foreclosure of the SPV so as to cause the premature maturity of the securities.

18 The originator is insulated from the losses of the issuer or SPV.

19 Fitch Rating's Emerging Markets Special Report 'Securitisation and Sharia Law', March 2005, 55. www.fitchratings.com, accessed 7 September 2006.

20 A. Abdel-Khaleq, 'Offering Islamic Funds in the US and Europe', *International Financial Law Review*, May [2004] 55 at www.iflr.com, last accessed on 10 March 2007.

21 In Malaysia, the Securities Commission (SC) established the Asset Securitisation Consultative Committee (ASCC) set up in March 2000 that has as its function to advise the SC on the steps needed to develop asset securitisation in the country. One of the issues it advises the SC on is tax and accounting impediments to securitisation.

22 Fitch Report, 'Securitisation and Sharia Law'.

23 Nik Ramlah, 'How Malaysia Plans to Dominate Islamic Markets', *International Financial Law Review* [2004] 61 at www.iflr.com, last accessed 10 March 2007.

24 Established by the Securities Commission (SC) in March 2000, one of the objectives of which was to advise the SC on how to develop asset securitisation in the country.

25 Malaysia Security Commission Report, 'Asset Securitisation in Malaysia: The way forward for the Malaysian Market's Asset Securitisation Consultative Committee (ASCC) November 2002, Appendix four.

26 It should be noted however that Malaysia enacted specific modifications to its tax code to allow for Islamic instruments to have peer status with conventional instruments, leveling the playing field for basic transactions as well as capital market activities. See, Walid Hegazy, 'Islamic Finance in Malaysia: A Tax Perspective', Paper presented at the proceedings of the 3rd Harvard University Forum on Islamic Finance (Middle Eastern Studies, Harvard University, Cambridge, MA, 1999), 215–24.

27 Malaysia Security Commission Report, 'Asset Securitisation in Malaysia'.

28 Without tax neutrality securitisation may lead to additional tax burdens for originators and if so, the originators' desire to enter into a securitisation may be considerably eroded.

29 Malaysia Security Commission Report, 'Asset Securitisation in Malaysia', 24–5.

30 Ireland, UK or Labuan, Malaysia.

31 Either due to cash shortages or due to the lack of appreciation of the substance of the concepts therein.

32 Morocco, for instance, passed a securitisation legislation in August 1999. The legislation provides that FPCT (SPV) is exempt from: (i) registration tax relating to its acquisition of assets, the issue or transfer of shares and bonds, amendment of its management regulations and any other acts relating to the functioning of the FPCT; (ii) business license tax; and (iii) corporation tax. The FPCT does, however, remain subject to certain provisions of corporate tax laws (declaratory obligations, accounting obligations, justification of expenses, book keeping, tax relating to investments proceeds, withholding). See report by Gide Loyrette Nouel, 'Emerging Markets Securitisation: Morocco' (25 November 2005), 23, www.gide.com, accessed 7 September 2006.

33 These legal issues were considered by Fitch Ratings in structuring the Caravan Securitisation of the Hanco-Rent-a-car fleet securitisation.

34 As seen in the discussion on the sale of debt, the scholars in Malaysia have adopted the minority view and by using the concept of *bay'al-'ina* and *bay' al dayn* were able to permit the issuance of *bay' bi-thaman 'ajil* bonds. Both these contracts have been prohibited by scholars in the Middle East. It is also common that the views of contemporary scholars will differ from their more conventional counterparts or predecessors.

35   Clause 25 and 26 of the agreement described on its face as a '*Murabaha financing agreement*' as per Tomlinson J in *Islamic Investment Company of the Gulf (Bahamas) v Symphony Gems IV & Others* [2002] QB Division (Com Ct).
36   It is no wonder therefore that Malaysia's Islamic finance took off much faster than in the Middle East given the greater certainty by virtue of Malaysia being governed by common law (and the existence of specific banking legislation).
37   [2004] 2 All ER (D) 280.
38   Ibid.
39   Decision of Morison J [2003] 2 All ER (Comm) 849 affirmed.
40   See the report published by Fitch Rating in conjunction with Gide Loyrette Nouel titled 'Securitisation and Sharia Law'. It is telling that the article does not distinguish, in its requirements, between conventional and *sukuk*-based securitisation structures.
41   [2003] 2 All ER (Comm) 849.
42   *Islamic Investment Company of the Gulf (Bahamas) v Symphony Gems IV & Others* [2002] QB Division (Com Ct) (unreported) heard by Tomlinson J. For a summary report see [2002] All ER (D) 171 (Feb).
43   [2004] EWCA Civ 19.
44   Ibid. at para 31.
45   [2004] EWCA Civ 19 at para 45.
46   [2001] 1 All ER (Comm) 103.
47   See section 3.2.7.
48   Adam and Thomas, Islamic *Bonds: Your Guide to Issuing, Structuring and Investing in Sukuk* (Euromoney Books, London, 2004), 13.
49   El-Gamal, *Islamic Finance: Law, Economics and Practice*, 16.
50   Ibid.
51   See section 7.6.
52   That would have negated a true sale (i.e. one cannot sell to one's self) and hence runs the risk of being characterised as a loan to one's self (subsidiary company).
53   Rahail Ali, 'Sukuk Legal and Structuring Considerations', posted at www.ajif.com, accessed 21 March 2006. Mr. Ali is a partner at the International law firm Denton Wilde Sapte, based in their Dubai Office.
54   This was a smart way of getting round both problems (creation of trust and choice of law and enforcement) because even if the alternative of having an off-shore SPV in a jurisdiction amenable to the trust had been used, the problem of choice of law and enforcement persists.
55   Malaysia Securities Commission's Report on Asset Securitisation in Malaysia: 'The way Forward for the Malaysian Market', prepared by the Asset Securitisation Consultative Committee (ASCC) (November 2002), 22.
56   Malaysia is clearly a case in point that has become, by virtue of its progressive attitude towards its Islamic Capital Market (ICM), a leader to emulate in Islamic finance.
57   Kevin Brown, 'Islamic financial sector needs firm regulation, says Malaysia' (Singapore, 4 November 2009) www.ft.com, accessed 23 November 2009.

9 Islamic Finance in Malaysia: A Model to Emulate

1   The result of a working paper entitled '*Rancangan Membaiki Ekonomi Bakal-Bakal Haji*' presented by Royal Professor Ungku Aziz in 1959 to improve the economy of intending pilgrims.

2   Samer Soliman, 'The Rise and Decline of the Islamic Banking Model in Egypt', in Henry and Wilson, *The Politics of Islamic Finance* (Edinburgh University Press, Edinburgh, 2004), 267–8. Founded by Ahmad Najjar in 1963 as the first Islamic bank in Egypt, and the world. He based his bank on the German saving banks model, having earned his PhD in Germany in the field of social economics. Najjar, however, never made reference to Islam in its founding process due to fear that if he did it would be rejected 'in an era when hostility to the Islamic tendency was at its peak'.

3   This allows for interbank trading of Islamic financial instruments such as *mudharaba* (profit sharing) interbank investments (MIIs). The MII program allowed for Islamic banks in need of funds to obtain them from other Islamic banks by issuing profit-sharing certificates for a fixed investment period, from overnight to one year. The profit-sharing ratio is determined in advance, and the principal is repaid at the end of the loan period.

4   Dato', Dr. Awang Adek bin Husin deputy minister of finance 'The role of Malaysia in the internationalisation of Islamic finance', Labuan International Islamic Finance Lecture Series 1, 15 September 2006.

5   Dr. Zeti Akhtar Aziz, Governor of the Central Bank of Malaysia, 'Recent developments in Islamic finance in Malaysia', Keynote address at the Islamic Finance Issuers and Investors Forum 2006, Kuala Lumpur, 14 August 2006.

6   Kevin Brown in Singapore, 'Islamic financial sector needs firm regulation, says Malaysia', *Financial Times*, 4 November 2009 at www.ft.com.

7   Suleiman Abdi Dualeh 'Islamic Securitisation: Practical Aspects', World Conference on Islamic Banking, Geneva, 8–9 July 1998.

8   *Welsh Development Agency v Export Finance Co. Ltd* [1992] BCLC 148. See section 8.2.

9   Qatar in the Qatar's global *sukuk* in 2004.

10 www.lofsa.gov.my, last accessed on 3 October 2007.

11 Stuart Gray 'Labuan' www.investorsoffshore.com/html/specials December 2004.

12 www.lofsa.gov.my/lofsa5/legislation last accessed 3 October 2007.

13 Datuk Ali Abdul Kadir, Chairman, Securities Commission, Malaysia, 'Wealth Creation and Asset Protection: The Complementary Roles of Offshore and Onshore Capital Markets', keynote address by YBhg at the Labuan Lecture Series, 2002.

14 Robin Wigglesworth, 'Creditors mobilise over Dubai debt plan', and 'Dubai World', The *Financial Times*, 2 December 2009, 1 and 18, respectively.

10 The Way Forward

1   Kishore Mahbubani, 'Lessons for the West from Asian Capitalism' in 'Future of Capitalism', *Financial Times*, 12 May 2009, 45.

2   Michael Skapinker, 'What is "socially useful" is subject to fashion', *Financial Times*, 8 September 2009, 13.

3   Simeon Kerr, 'Dubai Stuns Debt Market', *Financial Times*, 23 November 2009, 1, 18; See also, 'Future of Capitalism', *Financial Times*, 12 May 2009, 45.
4   Paul Kennedy, 'Read the big four to know capitalism's fate', in 'Future of Capitalism', *Financial Times*, 12 May 2009, 19.
5   Edmund Phelps, 'Uncertainty bedevils the best system' in 'Future of Capitalism', *Financial Times*, 12 May 2009, 46.

BIBLIOGRAPHY

Books

Abdul Ghafoor, A.L.M., *Interest, Usury, Riba and the Operational Cost of a Bank* (Percetakan Zafar Sdn Bhd, Kuala Lumpur 2005).

Adam, N. and Thomas, A., *Islamic Bonds: Your Guide to Issuing, Structuring and Investing in Sukuk* (Euromoney Books, London 2004).

Al Baji, S.K., *Al Montaqa: Annotations of Al-Muwatta* (Al-Saada Press, Cairo AH 471).

Al-Dhareer, M.S., *Al-Gharar in Contracts and its Effects on Contemporary Transactions*, (Islamic Development Bank's Eminent Scholars' Lecture Series, Jeddah 1997).

Al-Ghazali, M., *Ihya 'Ulum al-Din* by A. 'Izz al-Din al Sirwan (ed) (Dar al Kutb al Ilmiyyah, Beirut 1985).

Ali, A.Y., (tr) *The Holy Quran* (King Fahd Holy *Quran* Printing Complex, Madina, by Royal Decree 12412, 1405 AH).

Al-Sanhouri, A., *Masadir al Haqq fi al-Fiqh al-Islami* (Dar Ihya' al-Turath al 'Arabi, Cairo 1967–1968) vol III.

Al-Shawkani, *Nayl al awtar* (Mustafa Babi al-Halabi, Cairo n.d.).

Al-Tirmidhi, *Sunan al-Tirmidhi* vol. 3 (Dar al Fikr, Beirut 1980).

Al Zuhayli, W., *Al-Fiqh al-Islami wa Adillatuh* (Dar al-Fiqr, Damascus 1997) vol. 5, 2408 as referred to in M. El-Gamal, *Islamic Finance: Law, Economics and Politics* (CUP, Cambridge 2006).

Armstrong, K., *Islam: A Short History* (Phoenix Press, London 2001).

Armstrong, K., *Muhammad: A Biography of the Prophet* (Phoenix Publishers, London 2001).

Beale, H. (ed), *Chitty on Contracts*, 30th edn, vol. I (Sweet & Maxwell, London 2008).

Beatson, J., *Anson's Law of Contract*, 28th edn (OUP, New York 2002).

Bentham, J., *An Introduction to the Principles of Morals and Legislation*, W. Harrison (ed.) (OUP, Oxford, 1948).

Bridge, M., *Personal Property Law*, 3rd edn (OUP, Oxford 2002).

Chen-Wishart, M., 'Consideration, Practical Benefit and the Emperor's New

Clothes', in J. Beatson and D. Friedman (eds), *Good Faith and Fault in Contract Law* (Clarendon Press, Oxford 1995).

Chittick, W.C., *The Self Disclosure of God: Principles of Ibn al 'Arabi's Cosmology* (State University of New York Press, Albany 1998).

Dalhuisen, J.H., *Dalhuisen on International Commercial, Financial and Trade Law,* (Hart Publishing, Oxford 2000).

El-Diwany, T., *The Problem with Interest*, 2nd edn (Kreatoc Ltd, London 2003).

El-Gamal, M., *Islamic Finance: Law, Economics and Practice* (Cambridge University Press, New York 2006).

Furmston, M., *Cheshire, Fifoot & Furmston's Law of Contract*, 15th edn (OUP, Oxford 2007) 1–5.

Galeano, E., *Upside Down: A Primer for the Looking Glass World* (Picador, New York 2000).

Gardner, S., *An Introduction to the Law of Trusts*, 2nd edn (Oxford University Press, Oxford 2003).

Goode, R., *Consumer Credit* (A.W. Sijthoff, Leyden/Boston, 1978), vol. 3, ch. 40.

Goode, R., *Payment Obligations in Commercial and Financial Transactions* (Sweet & Maxwell, 1983), ch. 4.

Goode, R., *Commercial Law*, 3rd edn (Lexis Nexis Butterworths, London 2004).

Goode, R., *Legal Problems of Credit and Security*, 4th edn (Sweet & Maxwell, London 2008).

Gray, K. and Gray, S., *Elements of Land Law* (OUP, Oxford 2005).

Hall, S., *International Finance: Law and Regulation*, (Sweet & Maxwell, International 2004).

Hammad, '*Bay' al-Kali' bi al-Kali' fi al-Fiqh al-Islami*' (Markaz Abhath al-Iqtisad al-Islami, Jami'at al-Malik al-Abd al-Aziz, Jeddah 1986) cited in Vogel and Hayes, *Islamic Law and Finance: Religion, Risk and Return* (Brill-Lieden, Boston 2006).

Henry, C.M., 'Financial Performances of Islamic versus Conventional Banks' in C. Henry and R. Wilson (eds), *The Politics of Islamic Finance* (Edinburgh University Press, Edinburgh 2004).

Holmes, O.W., *The Common Law* (Cambridge, MA, 1967).

Ibn Abidin, *Hashiyyat, Radd al Muhtar 'ala al-durr al-mukhtar sharh tanwir l-absar* (Mustapha Babi al-Halabi, Cairo 1996) vol. 4.

Ibn al-Qayyim, M., *I'lam al-muwaqqa'in 'ala rabb al-'alamin*, edited by Taha 'Abd al-Ra'uf Sa'd (Dar al-Jil, Beirut 1973)vols I and II.

Ibn Juzzay, *Qawanin al Ahkam al-Shari'yyah wa Masa'il al Furu'iyya* (Dar al Ilm al-Malayin, Beirut 1979).

Ibn Rushd, M., *Bidayaat al Mujtahid wa Nihayaat al-Muqtasid* (Dar al Ma'rifa, Beirut 1997) vols 2 and 3.

Ibn Taymiyya, A., *Al-Fatawa al Kubra* (Dar al-Kutb al Ilmiyyah, Beirut 1987) vol. 29.

Kamali, M.H., *Freedom, Equality and Justice in Islam* (Ilmiah Publishers, Selangor Malaysia 2002) .

Kamali, M.H., *Islamic Commercial Laws: An Analysis of Futures and Options* (Ilmiah Publishers, Selangor 2002).

Kamali, M.H., *The Dignity of man: An Islamic Perspective* (Ilmiah Publishers, Selangor Malaysia 2002).

Koutoub, S., *The Sale of Debt as Implemented by the Islamic Financial Institutions in Malaysia* (IIUM Press, Kuala Lumpur 2004).

Lawson, F. and Rudden, B., *The Law of Property*, 2nd edn (Clarendon Law Series, Clarendon Press, Oxford 1982).

Macpherson, C.B., 'Capitalism and the Changing Concept of Property', in E. Kamenka and R.S. Neale (eds), *Feudalism, Capitalism and Beyond* (Canberra 1975).

Mahmasani, M., *The General Theory of the Law of Obligation and Contracts under Islamic Jurisprudence* (Dar al-Ilm lil malayin, Beirut 1972).

Mansuri, M.T., *Islamic law of Contracts and Business Transactions* (Adam Publishers, New Delhi 2006).

McKendrick, E., *Contract Law: Text, Cases and Materials*, 2nd edn (OUP, Oxford 2005).

Murata, S., *The Tao of Islam* (State University of New York Press, New York 1992).

Muslim, *Sahih*, *Book 10*, Number 3854.

Oditah, F., *Legal Aspects of Receivables Financing* (Sweet & Maxwell, London 1991).

Oxford Paperback Dictionary, Thesaurus & Word Power Guide (OUP, Oxford 2001).

Poole, J., *Text Book on Contract Law*, 8th edn (OUP, Oxford 2006)

Proctor, C., *Mann on the Legal Aspect of Money*, 6th edn (OUP, Oxford, 2005)

Rudden, B., 'Economic Theory v. Property Law' in Eekelaar and Bell (eds), *Oxford Essays in Jurisprudence* (Clarendon Press, Oxford 1987) 243.

Saleem, M., *Islamic Banking – a $300Billion Deception* (New York 2005).

Saleh, N., *Unlawful Gain and legitimate Profit in Islamic Law* (Cambridge University Press, Cambridge).

Sarakhsi, A.M., *Kitab al-Mabsut* (Dar al Ma'arif, Beirut 1978) vol. 13.

Soliman, S., 'The Rise and Decline of the Islamic Banking Model in Egypt' in Henry and Wilson, *The Politics of Islamic Finance* (Edinburgh University Press, Edinburgh 2004) 267–268.

Thomas, A., (ed.) *Interest in Islamic Economics: Understanding Riba* (Routledge, London 2006).

Treitel, G., *The Law of Contract*, 12th edn (Sweet & Maxwell, London 2008).

Usmani, M.T., *An Introduction to Islamic Finance* (Kluwer Law International, The Hague 2002).

Vogel, F. and Hayes, S., *Islamic Law and Finance: Religion, Risk and Return* (Brill-Leiden, Boston 2006).

Wilson, R., 'Overview of the Sukuk Market', in Nathif Adam and Abdulkader Thomas, *Islamic Bonds: Your Guide to Issuing, Structuring and Investing in Sukuk* (Euromoney Books, London 2004).

Wood, P., *Project Finance, Securitisations, Subordinated Debt* (Sweet & Maxwell, London 2007).

Articles and Reports

Abdi, Dualeh, 'Islamic Securitisation: Practical Aspects', World Conference on Islamic Banking (Geneva 8–9 July 1998).

Abdul, Kadir (Datuk), Chairman, Securities Commission, Malaysia, 'Wealth Creation and Asset Protection The Complementary Roles of Offshore and Onshore Capital Markets', keynote Address by YBhg at the Labuan Lecture Series 2002.

Ahmad, S., 'The Concept and the Law of Riba in Modern Economic Environment' (Mimeo, 1978).

Al-Misri, 'Hal Al-Faidah Haram bi Jami' Ashkaliha?' Majallat Jami'at al Malik 'Abdulaziz lil-Iqtisad Al-Islami, 2004, vol. 17, 1.

Awang, Adek bin Husin (Dato' Dr.), 'The role of Malaysia in the internationalisation of Islamic finance' Labuan international Islamic finance lecture series 1, 15 September 2006.

Aziz, Z.A. (Dr.), Governor of the Central Bank of Malaysia, 'Recent developments in Islamic finance in Malaysia', Keynote address at the Islamic Finance Issuers and Investors Forum 2006, Kuala Lumpur, 14 August 2006.

Coote, B., 'Consideration and Benefit in Fact and Law', *Journal of Contract Law* (1990) 3, 23.

De Teran, Natasha, 'Derivatives Extend the Reach of Islamic Finance', *The Banker*, (25 June 2005) Vol. 155, 49–51.

Duncan, M., Desai, B. and Rieger, J., 'Islamic Bankers Take Role on International Projects', *International Financial Law Review*, May [2004] 52.

Fitch Rating, 'Securitisation and Sharia Law' Report published by Fitch Rating in conjunction with Gide Loyrette Nouel.

Financial Times, 'Future of Capitalism', May 12 2009, 45.

Gide Loyrette Nouel, 'Emerging Markets Securitisation: Morocco', report (25 November 2005) 23, www.gide.com, accessed 7 September 2006.

Gray, K.J., 'Property, Divorce and Retirement Pension Rights', in *Cambridge-Tilburg Law Lectures 1982* (Kluwer, 1986). 41–51.

Gray, K., 'Property in Thin Air' *CLJ* 252 (1991) at 303–304.

Hegazy, 'Islamic Finance in Malaysia: A Tax Perspective', Paper presented at the proceedings of the 3rd Harvard University Forum on Islamic Finance (Middle Eastern Studies, Harvard University, Cambridge, MA, 1999) 215–24.

Kahf, M., 'Islamic Banks: The rise of a New Power Alliance of Wealth and Sharia Scholarship', in C. Henry and R. Wilson (eds), *The Politics of Islamic Finance* (Edinburgh University Press, Edinburgh 2004) 18–22.

Katouzian, 'Riba and Interest in an Islamic Political Economy' (Mediterranean Peoples Revue, no. 14, January–March 1981) 97–109.

Kennedy, Paul, 'Read the big four to know capitalism's fate', in 'Future of Capitalism', *Financial Times*, 12 May 2009, 19.

Mahbubani, 'Lessons for the West from Asian Capitalism' in Future of Capitalism, *Financial Times*, 12 May 2009, 45.

Malaysia Securities Commission's 'Report on Asset Securitisation in Malaysia: The way Forward for Malaysian Market' prepared by the Asset Securitisation Consultative Committee (ASCC) (November 2002) 22.

Norman, T., 'Securitisation Structures within an Islamic Framework' (July 2005 ISR Legal Guide) 22.

Phelps, 'Uncertainty bedevils the best system' in 'Future of Capitalism', *Financial Times*, 12 May 2009, 46.

Rahail, A., 'Sukuk Legal and Structuring Considerations', posted at www.ajif.com accessed 21 March 2006.

Skapinker, 'What is "socially useful" is subject to fashion', *Financial Times*, 8 September 2009, 13.

Stichting Sachsen-Anhalt, EURO100m Trust Certificates (Sukuk) rated 'AAA' by Fitch Ratings as reported in the Germany Pre-sale Report, 9 July 2004.

Unger, J., 'Intent to Create Legal Relations, Mutuality and Consideration' (1956) 19 MLR 96.

Ungku, Aziz, Royal Professor, 'Rancangan Membaiki Ekonomi Bakal-Bakal Haji' presented by Malaysia, 1959.

Wallace and Grbich, 'A Judge's Guide to Legal Change in Property', *University of New South Wales Law Journal* (1979) vol. 3, 175.

Wallis, W., 'Bankers Learn New Language to Manage Islamic Funds' *Financial Times* (London, 20 October 2004).

Wigglesworth, R., 'Creditors Mobilise over Dubai Debt Plan', *Financial Times*, 2 December 2009, 1.

Wigglesworth, R., 'Dubai World', *Financial Times*, 2 December 2009, 18.

Internet Sources

Abdel-Khaleq, A., 'Offering Islamic Funds in the US and Europe', *International Financial Law Review*, May [2004] 55, on www.iflr.com, last accessed on 10 March 2007.

Abdullah and Ismail, *International Financial Law Review*, September 2009 at www.iflr.com last accessed on 2 December 2009.

Briault, Clive, 'London: Centre of Islamic Finance', at the FSA Industry Forum, London, 17 October 2007.

Brown, K., 'Islamic Financial Sector Needs Firm Regulation, says Malaysia', *Financial Times* (4 November 2009), on www.ft.com, last accessed on 23 November 2009.

Financial Services Authority (FSA) Report, 'Islamic Finance in the UK: Regulation and Challenges', 28 November 2007 at www.fsa.gov.uk, last accessed on 02 December 2009.

Fitch Rating's Emerging Markets Special Report, 'Securitisation and Sharia Law' March 2005, 55. www.fitchratings.com accessed 7 September 2006.

Gray, S., 'Labuan', www.investorsoffshore.com/html/specials, December 2004.

HM Treasury paper, The Development of Islamic Finance in the UK: The Government's Perspective, December 2008, at www.hm-treasury.gov.uk, last accessed last on 2 December 2009.

Labuan Offshore Financial Services Authority, website at: www.lofsa.gov.my/lofsa5/ legislation, last accessed 3 October 2007.

Mitchells and Butlers, 'What is a Securitisation', www.mitchellsandbutlers.com/ index. asp?pageid=456 accessed on 7 January 2009.

Ramlah, N., 'How Malaysia Plans to Dominate Islamic Markets', *International Financial Law Review* (2004) 61 at www.iflr.com, last accessed 10 March 2007.

Sharia Standards published by the Accounting & Auditing Organisation for Islamic Financial Institution (AAOIFI), www.aaoifi.com, last accessed 7 September 2008.

INDEX